ALEXANDER WILLIAM C.

LETTERS

ON

EGYPT, EDOM,

AND

THE HOLY LAND

Volume 1

Elibron Classics
www.elibron.com

W W Ramsay del.ᵗ

R. Martin & Co lith. 26, Long Acre

CITADEL OF CAIRO.

LETTERS

ON

EGYPT, EDOM,

AND

THE HOLY LAND.

BY

LORD LINDSAY.

IN TWO VOLUMES.

VOL. I.

LONDON:

HENRY COLBURN, PUBLISHER,

GREAT MARLBOROUGH STREET.

1838.

LONDON:
P. SHOBERL, JUN., 51, RUPERT STREET, HAYMARKET.

PREFACE.

I HOPE that those who do me the honour of pe-
rusing these Letters will not take them for more
than they are worth, — a simple, and, I trust,
faithful record of impressions as they arose, and
incidents as they occurred, such as I conceived
would be read with interest *at home*. In preparing
them for the press, I have divested them of much
that could possess no general interest. If certain
allusions to members of my family circle have been
allowed to stand, it is only because they arose so
naturally out of the circumstances, that they serve

to illustrate them, or that, in one or two instances, I could not find it in my heart to cut them out.

I may be permitted to allude to the subject of many reflections in these volumes — the literal accomplishment of prophecy, as displayed in the actual condition of Egypt, Edom, and Syria. Others have borne their testimony; it is but adding a stone to the cairn, yet I cannot, and ought not, to withhold mine.

I embrace with pleasure this opportunity of expressing my sincere acknowledgments for the uniform courtesy and kindness I experienced during my recent tour. To —— Tibaldi, Esq. of Alexandria, and his amiable lady; — to Colonel Campbell, Her Majesty's Consul - General in Egypt, — to M. Piozin, Vice-Consul, — to Dr. Walne, John Hannay, Esq., and the Rev. Theophilus Lieder, at Cairo; — to the Reverend the American Missionaries, and —— Moore, Esq. at Jerusalem;—and to Nathanael Moore, Esq. British Consul at Beyrout, (whose courtesies I regret having been prevented from personally acknowledging),—my peculiar thanks are due. On my

obligations to Mr. Farren, Consul General in
Syria, I will not dwell in this place.

I cannot conclude without adverting to the
lamented decease of my friend and near relation,
Mr. William Wardlaw Ramsay, the companion
of the greater part of my tour.

If excellent abilities and sound judgment, ex-
panding and maturing every day;—if singular
genius for music and drawing, and a general love
for the fine arts, balanced by an enlightened taste
for science and natural philosophy;—if sweetness
of temper, a warm, kind heart, and sincere but
unostentatious religious principle—be qualities to
render a character attractive and estimable, and
to enhance the sorrow of surviving friends for the
loss of one who, if spared by an all-wise Providence, would have been a blessing to his family,
and an ornament to society—such a character,
such qualities, were Mr. Ramsay's.

I have extracted from his private journal, and
appended to the present work in the shape of notes,
many passages which, I think, will be read with

interest by every one into whose hands these volumes may fall.

Haigh, Feb. 1838.

———

Since writing the above, I have been favoured, by the kindness of Mr. Farren, with a most interesting communication on the present state and prospects of Syria. If I have myself refrained from adding to the few general observations which forced themselves upon me, while resident in that unhappy country, it has been only in consequence of the strong conviction that, while the casual visitor has the right, and, at certain periods, almost incurs the obligation, of recording *what he sees*, the springs of evil, the sources from which the tides of misery flow, are remote and inaccessible to him without the assistance of a guide, conversant with all the tortuous and gloomy avenues that lead to them. To Mr. Farren, therefore, as to one whom many years' residence in the country, and many years' study, under peculiar advantages, of the character and prejudices of the natives, pointed out as the man of all others most able to give me the information I desired—I applied; and the letter, which closes the text of these volumes, was his answer to my request.

To invite the attention of the Public to a document emanating from such authority, and at such a moment—when Mohammed Ali is said to be on the point of openly renouncing his allegiance to the Porte, and England, it is said, actually hesitates which party to espouse! would be superfluous.

21, Berkeley Square.
    10th July, 1838.

ILLUSTRATIONS.

CONTENTS

OF

THE FIRST VOLUME.

LETTER I.

LETTER II.

LETTER III.

LETTER IV.

EDOM AND THE HOLY LAND.

LETTER VII.

ERRATA.

VOLUME I.

Page 148, line 14, after *together*, insert a comma.
Page 158, line 12, for *processes*, read *processions*.
Page 187, line 2, for *Nicholus*, read *Nicholaus*.
Page 219, line 3, after *forgotten*, insert a comma.
Page 277, last line but one, between *Egyptians* and *all*, insert a dash.
Page 315, line 12, dele dash after *looking*.
Page 373, line 19 (from the bottom), read " *lacrymas hic maesta profudi*," &c.
Page 373, line 8 (from the bottom), for *paying*, read *paging*.
Page 386, line 5, for *converture*, read *couverture*.
Page 404, line 14 (from the bottom), for 1341, read 1346.

VOLUME II.

Page 118, line 11, read " strength he had heard so highly vaunted," &c.
Page 170, line 5 (from the bottom,) for *Grecian*, read *Syrian*.
Page 171, line 14, dele " of which . . . . . standing," and read *adjoin* for *adjoined*.
Page 173, line 7, dele *the*.
Page 360, transpose lines 25 and 26.

LETTERS ON EGYPT.

"All were but Babel vanities! Time sadly overcometh all things, and is now dominant, and sitteth on a Sphinx, and looketh upon Memphis and old Thebes, while his sister, Oblivion, reclineth demi-somnous on a Pyramid, gloriously triumphing, making puzzles of Titanian erections, and turning old glories into dreams. History sinketh beneath her cloud. The traveller, as he paceth amazedly through those deserts, asketh of her, Who builded them? and she mumbleth something, but what it is he heareth not.

"Egypt itself is now become the land of obliviousness and doteth. Her ancient civility is gone, and her glory hath vanished as a phantasma. Her youthful days are over, and her face hath become wrinkled and tetrick. She poreth not upon the heavens; Astronomy is dead unto her, and Knowledge maketh other cycles. Canopus is afar off, Memnon resoundeth not to the Sun, and Nilus heareth strange voices. Her monuments are but hieroglyphically sempiternal. Osiris and Anubis, her averruncous deities, have departed, while Orus yet remains, dimly shadowing the principle of vicissitude and the effluxion of things, but receiveth little oblation."

Sir Thomas Browne.

LETTERS ON EGYPT.

LETTER I.

Cadiz—Gibraltar—The Cork Wood—Carteia.

TO LIEUTENANT COLONEL LINDSAY.

Gibraltar, November 10, 1836.

How I longed for you, yesterday, dear James, at Cadiz, and here, too, at Gibraltar, happy should I have been this morning to have had your company during the glorious scramble I have had over every ridge of the old Rock ! But of Cadiz first—I thought as we sailed away yestreen, (a delicious autumnal evening), I had

never seen a lovelier sight, her long serrated
ridge of white buildings sharply defined against
a glowing sunset sky—Rota glittering, like a
town of King Salem's sprung up from Ocean,
at the further extremity of the bay, tipping its
horn, as it were, with a diamond crown—the
lateen sails scudding around us like gigantic
nautiluses, stooping over the green waters like
the beautiful sea-birds that were sporting in
every direction — oh! it was lovely, very
lovely !

We had but four hours allowed us to visit
Cadiz ; I threw my shyness to the winds, and
used my eyes, stared into every nook and
corner, and at every one, man and woman, we
met. But you cannot have forgotten the scene,
though long familiarity with its details may
have effaced the remembrance of your first
general impressions ; to me it was all " fresh
and fresh, new and new," like the Indian
beauty in the song—a living, breathing, moving

tableau, a waking dream rather, for whether
I was in or out of the body I can scarce tell,
now that I reflect on the vision, so many ideas
familiar to my fancy were then presented to
my eyes in the warmest glow of reality; all,
too, intensely Spanish — the long black cloaks
of the sleepy hidalgos, long as their names,
threadbare many of them as the mantle of
chivalry their ancestors wore so gracefully —
the Moorish faces, conical hats, and sashes of
the lower, and, as they seemed to me, far
nobler order—the cigarillos, common to all—
the fans, mantillas, the black eyes, beautiful
feet, and graceful gliding gait of the Señoritas
—but oh ! what frights the old women are !
and then the painted balconies above, that give
such a character to the straight narrow stradas,
flowers in most of them, but, alas ! the " fairer
flowers," Eve's daughters, were few or none
visible upon them — and the dazzling white
ness of the houses, every thing, too, as clean

as if the Gaditanos were Dutchmen,—it was
like a scene of enchantment ; to say nothing of
the exquisite delight of being on Spanish
ground, and hearing the language of Calderon
and Cervantes on every lip that passed me.

I saw but two or three priests, not idly
sauntering about as in the palmy days of
Rome, but walking, it seemed to me, with an
object,—slowly, however, as if their ponderous
shells of hats were too heavy for them, and
crestfallen ; in this respect your Spanish recol-
lections must vary from existing circumstances :
the convents, too, were all shut up, and the
bells over the gates looked as if conscious of
having tolled their last. We knocked loud and
long at one of the conventual buildings, in
hopes of seeing some pictures once shown
there ; but no porter hurried to the gate, the
street was silent, only one boy to be seen in it,
and he could not tell us who had the keys.

The cathedral, however, is still building, a

most superb edifice of the richest Corinthian architecture, but overloaded in many places, I thought, with ornament; the choir, however, is truly beautiful, all marble; indeed the whole temple is so, and exquisitely finished. Yet I do not like the Corinthian; the " airy pillar" and the " decent matron grace " of the Ionic are far lovelier, far purer, far holier; the Doric and Ionic remind one of Adam and Eve as they walked in naked innocence, and in all their original brightness, through the bowers of Paradise; but the spirit of the Corinthian is meretricious, too like that of the Laises and Co. of old Corinth herself: this is fanciful, perhaps, but oh! there is a deep poetry, a hidden melody, in architecture, "frozen music," as it has been called, but it thaws now and then, when the fancy warms, and discourses most eloquently to her ear and eye.

How beautiful, by the way, are Schlegel's criticisms on the Gothic architecture! Did

A—— tell you I have him with me? Shakspeare has been my chief reading since I left
old England ; this she will be glad to hear. I
have read over again several of his plays, but
exquisitely beautiful as they are whenever he
is *himself*, the pure Poet, I cannot away with
his clowns and vile puns, *grossiéretés*, and
double entendres, bad enough even among men,
but which he allows even his heroines to hear,
ay, and understand, ay, and reply to. But
Desdemona is perfect throughout ; I was trying
her the other evening, as I lay in my cabin, by
the severest ordeal, St. Paul's exquisite de-
lineation of Charity, or, as it should be translated, Love ; Shakspeare must have had it in
his thoughts ; it fits her in every point, especially in her unsuspicious purity, " thinking no
evil ;" observe her wonder in what manner her
husband could think her false, and oh ! what a
contrast between her mind and Emilia's, at the
end of the fourth act, and, again, between her

and Juliet, the poetical passionate Juliet; I remember no one simile or metaphor that Desdemona utters, and Juliet's fancy is rich as the
orange-groves of Mola di Gaeta, and sparkling
as the waves that ripple to their feet, but she is
"of the earth, earthy," in comparison with
the pure azure heaven of Desdemona's mind,
which one can gaze up into as into infinite
space, unarrested by a cloud, unless of tears and
sorrow!   How beautiful, though, and how
natural is the moonlight scene between Juliet
and Romeo!   When I think on it, I almost
fear I have judged her harshly—and yet, no.

It has just struck twelve; I am sitting with
my window open, a brilliant starlight night,
the air balm; I could almost expect a visit
from the Diable Boiteux, and should not be
sorry to have the houses of Gibraltar unroofed
for my inspection—and this reminds me of one
of the things that most interested me at Cadiz
— a visit to the terraced roof of M. Campan's

house, a kind old French merchant, our fellow-passenger, who entertained our party most hospitably. It was the best possible commentary on many a passage not only in Spanish but Eastern romance; with a short rope-ladder one might travel over half the town. The house itself seemed but just finished, yet, in character, was quite Moorish; a court in the centre — balconied galleries opening upon it at each story — mats, &c. &c., every thing calculated to promote coolness.

I kept a sharp look-out for traces of the Moors, and they are very visible. I thought of riding across country to Gibraltar, but was advised to give up the idea : the country, they said, was uninteresting, (I should have seen manners, however) and, what decided me, my time here would have been much curtailed; I came on therefore by sea, and this morning, about nine, we anchored under the Rock of Gibraltar.

I am glad that I saw Cadiz, a thoroughly
Spanish town, before coming to this mongrel
neutral ground, intensely interesting though it
be. Bedreddin Hassan, awaking at the gate of
Damascus, entered an unknown, but still an
Eastern city; the contrast to him was nothing
to what it was to me, stepping off the quay of
Cadiz, surrounded by wild Cadesians with their
Calabrian-like hats, swarthy as their Phœnician
ancestors, to be set down among English
uniforms, sentries, and all the pomp and circumstance of British soldiery, guards changing,
officers riding past, and all speaking English.
But nothing of this incongruity offended our
eyes as we approached the Rock—Europe and
Africa,

" A palace and a prison on each hand,"

of Nature's architecture, or such rather by the
God of Nature's decree; the morning was
gloomy, a lowering mist hung heavily over the
Rock in front of us, and I could almost have

fancied we were arriving at the Table Mountain instead of the Northern pillar of Hercules. Mount Atlas was but dimly seen in the distance, but a purer light gleamed over Algesiras, as if the rays of chivalry still lingered over the death scene of the " good Lord James of Douglas ; " as the day advanced, the clouds disappeared, and when I gazed around me a few hours afterwards from the Peak of Tarif, a sunny haze was the only resemblance the scene bore to our northern atmosphere.

I need not tell you of the excavations, galleries, St. George's Hall, the blasted watchtower, &c. I scrambled over the whole mountain, taking a most intelligent artilleryman as my guide, a countryman, as I ascertained by the first word he spoke—his sergeant is a Lindsay from Dunse. I feared we should not see the monkeys, but there they were in numbers, apparently on excellent terms with the goats, their only companions on the height.

How beautiful the palmetto is! and oh! how A—— would have enjoyed our return through a perfect garden; strange tropical-looking plants, the fantastic prickly pear, and the aloe, hedging the pathway, and her old Italian acquaintances, the fig, almond, orange and lemon, and the grateful plane tree—ay, and the Scotch fir, growing luxuriantly, (and the richest vines, too), on the lower zone of the mountain. We descended by the Mediterranean steps, as they are called, cut in the precipitous face of the rock, and winding round towards Europa Point; the broad Mediterranean—with those picturesque lateen sails that look as if, at the approach of a storm, they would furl themselves up and sink to the bottom—expanded in front of us, glowing in the waning sun,

—A leaf of gold
Of Nature's Book, by Nature's God unrolled.

I have just been leaning out of the window listening to a serenade! all below me dark as

Erebus, the raven down of night, and all silent save the " lively guitar," and the deep voice of the caballero mingling in harmony and swelling richly on the night-air. And when the last note died away, I could just hear the closing strain of another, far, far off, dying into silence like the echo of the " song of the olden time," I had just been listening to. Music such as this might have been lingering on the ear of Melancholy, when Albert Durer surprised, fell in love with, and immortalized her.

Very pleasant food all this for midnight musing, yet daylight too has its attractions, and I then look down on a motley and ever-shifting scene, all nations seeming to meet here as at Venice, though Gibraltar, to be sure, is any thing but " enchanted ground;" the Moor, with his white turban, burnoosh, and trowsers; the Jew, with his black skull-cap, beard, and Israelitish face, the " index of his pedigree" the wide world over—I saw one stalk past this morning with the very air of a Maccabee, his haughty mien, and the scorn throned on his erect brow, (or I wronged him), alike contrasting with the humble subdued gait of his brethren, and the holiday attire and light springy step of the Andalusian peasant,—the contrast of a " gay Gordon," to a " Black Douglas"—no disparagement, surely, in a comparison with the Wallace of Judea; then comes the mule or donkey-driver, haranguing his beast as he trudges behind it, side by side, oh atrocity! with an English red coat! Here, at least, " motley is the only wear." And now, dear James, *buenas noches,* and God be with you! I will not wish you the misery of living a thousand years. More to-morrow.

To-day, November the 11th, we have had a delightful gallop, Missirie and I, into Andalusia, past La Roque, to the Cork-wood, about ten miles from Gibraltar; the scenery is quite

beautiful—the day, at first rainy, cleared up ere
we had ridden half a dozen miles, and the afternoon was lovely. From a ruined Moorish
tower in the centre of the wood, we enjoyed a
most beautiful prospect over the long vale we
had passed through, wooded with cork-trees,
olives, vines, oranges, lemons, and one noble
palm-tree near a convent, a steep range of
mountains closing the vista at one end, the
Rock at the other, rising over the waves like
some vast Preadamite sea-monster.

Returning, we rode here and there, this way
and that, in search of the old town of Carteia,
supposed to have been the first founded by the
Phœnicians after passing the pillars of Hercules.
After a long search we found it ; the theatre is
clearly traceable, scooped out in the side of the
hill, looking towards Gibraltar ; the back-
ground of the scene must have been noble
indeed, the Mediterranean rushing between the
two Continents.

I am more and more pleased with Missirie, he is the most attentive creature possible, good-humoured, observant, and intelligent; I had much conversation with him this morning during our ride; he is really an agreeable companion, having read not a little by fits and starts, and having seen so many countries. He had studied for two years at Odessa, when the Greek Revolution broke out, and then joined the patriots. We are on the best terms, and I am sure we shall continue to be so. His facility in acquiring languages seems extraordinary. English he speaks with singular correctness. ([1])

Saturday, November 12.

I had no idea this letter would go so soon, but a steamer, I have just heard, sails for England in a day or two, and, as I have not time to epistolise my mother at length, and she will be anxious to hear all my adventures,

I have presumed to direct this letter to her,
begging her to read and forward it to its right-
ful owner. We have a heavenly day, "blue
above and blue below," for our departure. By
the bye, they have an admirable garrison
library here; the catalogue is well drawn up
on the plan of that of the Royal Institution by
Harris. I think I should like to spend a month
or two here; nowhere, I suppose, could one
enjoy at once such a climate and such a library.

Adieu.

LETTER II.

Voyage to Malta—San Giovanni—Ruins and Catacombs
of Alexandria.

TO THE COUNTESS OF BALCARRAS.

Malta.

WE left Gibraltar, my dear Mother, on
Saturday afternoon, the 12th, and have had
charming weather, and a delightful voyage to
Malta. Sunday and Monday we were coasting Spain and Barbary, and admiring the
mountain ridges that frown from either shore,
awakening memories how interesting! of Juba
and the Romans, on the one hand— of the
Xarifas and Fatimas, the Zegris and Abencer-
rages, of poor Boabdil, and of Gonsalvo de
Cordova, on the other !

About eight on Monday night we touched at
Algiers — thrilling name !   The crescent moon
was gleaming over it, but not very clear; the
crescent is pale, pale all over the East now.
We landed a young Dane there, the son of the
Danish Consul at Tangiers, and one of the
Royal Guard of Denmark; he was going to
join the French expedition against Constantina,
and I really felt sorry when he left us on such
a perilous adventure.   I found him full of information, and very intelligent, particularly on
the subject of Northern Antiquities; he sang
me several of his Danish songs as we walked
the deck.

Still coasting the Barbary mountains — so
runs the log-book; pass Bona, old Hippo Re-
gius, dear to the memory as the home of St.
Augustine—but during the night, alas !—Bi-
zerta—the Cani rocks—Porto Farina, Cato's
Utica, and Cape Carthage, behind which lies
the site of Dido's palace, Cyprian's garden —

where the soldiers seized him, generous, noble-
minded Cyprian! Then across the Bay of
Tunis, with a beautiful view of the mountains
hemming it in to the south ; before weathering
Cape Bon, pass the vast and lofty island-
rock of Zembra, reminding one, when directly
north of it, of the volcanic isle of Sabrina. Bid
adieu to the Barbary coast, and for awhile
nothing but the sea-circle for our horizon ;
presently Gozo in sight — rough rocky hills,
but the lights and shadows beautiful — skim
past it through the waves on which Tele-
machus floated, if Gozo *be* the Isle of Calypso,
which I don't believe it was—and lo, Malta,
with her deep harbours, picturesque tiers of
houses, impregnable batteries, and English
shipping ! How changed—

But I had little time, or, in truth, inclination,
at that moment, to think of days by-gone, for
scarcely had we anchored in the quarantine
harbour, when dear William came alongside to

greet me; he had secured me rooms in Be-
verley's Hotel, and we adjourned thither without delay; he is remarkably well, and we look
forward with great pleasure to the prosecution
of our tour together.

Oh! the rapture of a first visit to San Giovanni! those gorgeous and chivalric tombs of
the Grand Masters and the Knights of St.
John! I shall not be content now till I see
Rhodes, invested with more *familiar* interest
to a clansman of Radulphus de Lindesay, Lord
David of the Byres, and Sir Walter,

> " Lord of Sainct Johne, and Knicht of Torphicane,
> By sea and land ane vailzeant Capitane,"

as Davie Lindsay calls him.

I visited the armoury in the old palace —
neither worth seeing; spacious galleries and
chambers, but nothing after Venice. The
library too, full of the fat old folios of the
seventeenth century. They seem a curious set,
these Maltese: their language is most disso-

nant, a mere jargon of Arabic, but all speak broken English; their national airs, however, are beautiful, especially one, beginning, " Sel-loom tal harir," &c. which you will find in my MS. collection of national music; I have not heard it here, nor indeed anything in the way of minstrelsy, except " Rule Britannia," which they have been chanting most uproariously in honour of their new governor, Sir Henry Bou-verie.

Before re-embarking, I paid another visit to St. John's, by far the most interesting spot at Malta—for this is not the Melita where St. Paul was wrecked. One, the last survivor, I believe, of the old knights, a countryman too of Bayard and Duguesclin, was pointed out to me — a poor decrepit, feeble old man — alas ! alas !

Alexandria, November 30.

We arrived here last Friday, to wit, November the 25th; the day was lovely, the sea of a

delicate light green, the sky exquisitely clear,
of a rosy transparent hue, smiling our welcome
to the city of Cleopatra, as we sailed into the
harbour — then a glorious oriental sunset.
There is little or no twilight in these latitudes,
and it was quite dusk by the time we reached
our inn, riding on donkeys, the general conveyance in this country.

Ah! that was a happy evening! A month's
cramp in the cabin of a steam-boat exchanged
for freedom and terra-firma, and that terra-
firma Egypt, still the land of mystery, still a
land of beauty !

> " 'Tis here that the feathery palm trees rise,
>   And the date grows ripe under sunny skies—"

and never will palm trees rustle more melo-
diously, never will the moon and stars twinkle
through their transparent foliage with more
loveliness, never shall I enjoy the stillness and
repose of an Eastern night with more thrilling
pleasure, more thorough enjoyment, than I did

that evening, walking in the pretty little garden behind Mrs. Hume's hotel, or resting in
an arbour of trelliswork, under a branching
vine, meditating on the past and present, and
anticipating the future, in which, unless it be
the mirage, I see many a hundred miles of
Father Nile, many a lengthening vista of temples and colonnades, outstretched before me;
Nature and Art beckoning me on, and offering
me the fruits of knowledge as the reward of
my wanderings. There is nothing, indeed,
new to discover, but are not Vesuvius and
Naples *new* to the eye that has never hailed
them before?

We have been riding about ever since our
arrival—over ruins, and nothing more. A town,
half Turkish, half Frank, turbans and hats
seeming equally at home in it; mounds beyond
mounds of debris stretching away to the south,
east, and west of it; whole lines of ancient
streets traceable by the wells recurring every

six or seven yards, by which the contiguous
houses, long since crumbled away, drew water
from the vast cisterns with which the whole
city was undermined; wretched hovels clustered here and there in the suburbs, and
towering groves of date trees " scattered at
wide intervals" over the cheerless solitude —
such is the present aspect of Alexandria.
The Desert has done for her what Vesuvius
did for Pompeii — buried her so completely,
that all we see above the present surface has
been brought to light by excavation; not quite
all indeed — Pompey's Pillar and Cleopatra's
needle, both misnomers, are still erect, solitary
monuments of the flight of time, of the youth
and the decrepitude of Egypt; for the needle
stood at Heliopolis, the On of Scripture, three
thousand years ago,([2]) and the shaft of Pompey's Pillar adorned the temple of Serapis and
the library of the Ptolemies till it was removed
to its present site, and furnished with a capital

and base, in honour of Diocletian, whose name
Mr. Hamilton was the first to decypher, the
whole inscription, long supposed to be entirely
lost, having been recovered, letter by letter, by
the united acumen of a few wise men of Britain. It is only distinguishable in the strong
light of the mid-day sun.([3])

One ruin only, just excavated, and a nondescript, will I trouble you with, inasmuch as
mine, too probably, may be the only record of
its discovery, for these Turks discover only to
destroy. Four or five granite columns are
still standing on their pedestals of white marble ; the rest have been removed ; and a few
Corinthian capitals, also of white marble, are
lying a short distance off, soon probably to be
reduced to lime, and applied to as vile purposes, comparatively, as that to which Hamlet's fancy traced the dust of the royal founder
of Alexandria himself. Behind these pillars
rises a solid wall of masonry, supported by

three arches, on the reverse of which we found
vestiges of curious Greek paintings, the colours
very vivid, and the subject, it would appear,
taken from Homer, the only figure that remained uninjured by the pickaxe being super-
scribed

$$O \Delta Y C$$
$$C \in Y C$$

We observed, with surprise, three or four
coats of stucco, laid one over the other, all
painted, and the lowest the best. It was
merely through the chance encounter of an
Italian monk, that we were led, through a
labyrinth of narrow lanes and groves of date
trees, to this interesting spot.

In Lucas's time, about 120 years ago, a superb piazza was traceable in the middle of the
ancient town, ornamented with lofty granite
columns, and surrounded, to all appearance,
by the principal palaces of the city, with a
beautiful fountain in the centre. We saw no

traces of it: in his day the remains were almost entirely covered with the sand.([4])

As for the far-famed library, its site can only be conjectured; the first library was attached to the palace of the Ptolemies, and was accidentally consumed when Julius Cæsar was obliged to burn his ships in the harbour, to which it was contiguous. We visited yesterday some recent excavations, which have laid bare the remains of a vast edifice, pronounced by antiquaries (I know not on what authority) to be those of the *second* library ; but nothing is certain here—not even the date of the catacombs, or whom they were worked by ; some contending they belonged to Alexandria, others, to the insignificant town of Racotis, that existed here before Alexandria was founded ; ([5]) this can hardly be. Of their Greek *origin* there can be no doubt, the architecture being uniformly Doric.

These catacombs are at some distance west

of the city, and highly interesting. We explored them with torches, creeping in many
places on our hands and knees. Entering from
the north, three chambers, running westwards,
lead you to a large circular room to the south
of the third, with a noble dome of beautiful
proportions, and opening, towards the south,
east, and west, into three small recesses, apparently for sarcophagi.

Over the door-way we found traces of the
orb, or globe with wings, that Dr. Clarke mentions, but it has been broken off since his time.
We saw the same emblem, however, (which reminded me of Isaiah's address to Ethiopia,
ch. 18, v. 1.) over both doors of the vestibule,
that we had entered, and that we proceeded by,
still westwards; the plan of the catacombs
seems modelled on this emblem, for the wings
are clearly arranged in reference to the central
and circular shrine. After exploring several
other chambers in the same direction, all

strewed with bones, we retraced our steps to the central chamber, and the rest of the party went out, while Captain Lacon (an intelligent officer who had joined our party) and I remained behind to examine what we had already seen more carefully.

The grand entrance clearly opened from the shore, and we wished, if possible, to discover it; creeping up the sloping wall, or rather bank, as it ought to be called, óf the second chamber from the present entrance, we found it was only the corner of an immense hall, supported by square pillars, that stretched away towards the shore, filled up by a long continuous mound of earth, accumulated so close to the roof, that it was impossible to proceed except by crawling on one's breast like a worm. On we crept, however, with two or three of our Arab guides, and the result of a long and painful peregrination in this uncomfortable attitude was that, following the walls, we fairly traced the three sides of the hall, and discovered what probably was the grand entrance, opposite, as nearly as we could guess, to the circular chamber.

The sea, probably, at the time of the great earthquake, when fifty thousand Alexandrians perished, and the islet was washed away to which Mark Anthony retired to enact Timon of Athens after the wreck of his fortunes, seems to have washed sand and soil into the catacombs, and, after filling as we now beheld them, to have finally choked up the entrance, so that it is undiscoverable from the shore. I do not think we have made any new discovery, for the French are said, in one of my guide-books, to have made a complete plan of these extraordinary excavations, but I am glad we made them out so satisfactorily to ourselves. Oh! that they were all cleared out, that one could enter from the shore, traverse that noble hall, and enter the shrine, just as the votaries did of old, two thousand years ago!

So much for this " City of the Dead !" living Alexandria is equally interesting, though strangely different; turbaned Turks, wild Arabs, Copts, Armenians, Jews—every nation seems to have its representatives here; and the strings of camels towering along, the women gliding about in their long veils, with holes only for the eyes to peep out at—graceful in their carriage, some carrying their children at their sides, others astride on their shoulders — are objects thoroughly Oriental. The Arabs, especially, drest just like the Ishmaelites and Midianites of old, carry one's imagination further yet back even than the catacombs — far, far into antiquity — to the days of Joseph and the Patriarchs.

But it is no use attempting to sketch so varied and shifting a scene; though already it be somewhat familiar to me, my ideas are still all in a whirl. One is really bewildered too with the crowd of associations, ancient and

modern, this place teems with, independent of
visible objects ;—Alexander the Great, who intended to make it the seat of his empire, and
the emporium of the world, which indeed it
became under the Ptolemies, as the link between
India and the West—the museum, the library,
the revival of Greek literature and philosophy
under the enlightened successors of Alexander
—the version of the Old Testament by the
seventy-two interpreters, if we may believe the
old legend, though its falsity cannot affect the
historical fact that the Law and the Prophets
were translated into Greek nearly three centuries before our Saviour's birth, and while
those wonderful prophecies of Daniel about the
kings of the North and the South, the Ptolemies and Seleucidæ, were actually fulfilling(⁶)
—Cæsar, Cleopatra, Anthony, and Shakspeare's
play—Mark and his ministry, the school of
Clement and Origen, Athanasius, the noble
patriarch, and his chequered fortunes during a

lifetime devoted to the defence of God's truth against Arius—Amrou and the Saracens —and lastly, after twelve hundred years of silence and decay, Abercrombie, gallant Abercrombie, his Highland hearts around him, the cry of victory in his ear,

> "Looking *meekly* to heaven from his death-bed of fame!"

What varied scenes—what opposite characters —what warring influences of good and evil!

And under whose banner, Orosman's or Ahriman's, must I rank Mohammed Ali himself, whose ships, proud as their mother Alexandria may well be of their magnificence, are, like his army, a very curse to the country?*

* We visited the Admiral's ship, a three-decker, on the 28th of November. " I had heard much," says Mr. Ramsay, in his private Journal, " of these vessels, and was prepared for their magnificence, and even for more than I found. The *show* certainly was very fine on the upper, the main, and the lower decks, every thing being very spacious, clean, polished, and in order; the breadth of beam, and the total freedom from all (I should imagine

But I must conclude. We start, I hope and believe, to-morrow morning, provided we get a boat, but the Pasha has impressed all he could lay his hands on, for the conveyance of his son's Harem, and we may have to wait.

Adieu, my dear Mother.

PS.—Dec. 1. Think of our scampering off this morning, on jack-asses (instinctively), on hearing that the Harem was about to embark for Cairo ! We had about three miles to ride,

even *necessary*) incumbrance, gave her a noble appearance ; but one missed a great deal ; there was no accommodation for officers — all are down in the cock-pit, and thus the whole range of the decks is thrown open from poop to stern in both decks. The officers seemed to be very poorly off, and, as this was not a *show* part of the ship, it stood no comparison with the rest. The men not dining, like us, at tables, the lower deck was free from that incumbrance, like the main deck. There was not the finish which characterises every thing in our ships, or the air of aptness and congruity which ought to pervade it. The crew are 1100, but a useless set ; every gun requires a marine to stand over the men with a musket, and eight small cannon are planted abaft to command the ship in case of a mutiny, I suppose."

and when we got near it there was nothing to be seen of the ladies, nor could we approach the carriages (English, and four-in-hand) they rode in. We watched them from a distance, and after seeing two or three children handed out, followed by a veiled lady, whom William pronounced to be dreadfully thick-ankled, we turned round and retraced our steps at a gentle trot, and have been laughed at for our wild-goose chase ever since. We were not, however, the only English who joined in it, and were the first to retreat — that is some comfort.

LETTER III.

Voyage to Cairo—Sais—Introduction to the Pasha—
  Tombs of the Mamaluke Sultans — Cairo at sunset —
  Bazars — Courtesy to Franks — Garden of Roda—Old
  Cairo—Cemetery of the Mamaluke Beys — School at
  Boulac—Printing-press — Egyptian Christians — Jews
  —Magicians, Jugglers, &c.

December 17, 1836.

HERE, my dear Mother, in Grand Cairo, we
have been settled for more than a week, delighted with all we have seen, and fully prepared to enjoy ourselves during the remainder
of our trip. We reached Cairo from Alexandria on the sixth day, the wind having been
contrary during the first two or three of the
voyage; we sailed on the Mahmoudieh canal
to Atfi, in the course of a night, and there
embarked on the Nile in one of the cangias,

or boats of the country, which hold two con-
veniently enough. Missirie and Abdallah, a
handsome Kordofani—black as ebony—whom
we have engaged as Arab interpreter and aid-
de-camp extraordinary, occupied a tent in
front of the cabin, and, altogether, we got on
very comfortably.

The only place of interest on the western
branch of the Nile is Sa-el-Hagiar, the site of
the ancient Sais, from whence the worship of
Nith, or Minerva, was carried to Athens by
Cecrops and his Egyptian colony, sixteen centuries before the Christian era. There she
stood, the idol of Egyptian worship, veiled
with her mysterious peplus, carried for ages
afterwards, though in ignorance of its mystic
meaning, in the sacred processions of Athens,
and uttering those thrilling words of wisdom,
that text for human vanity to meditate on—" I
am all that is, all that hath been, and all that
will be ; and my veil no mortal hath ever yet

uplifted!'' What know we even now of Nature's mysteries? Are we wiser than Job? I
trow not.

Long before arriving at Cairo we saw the
Pyramids towering in the distance like mountains cut down into their present shape; we
have not yet visited them; Monday next
will, I hope, dawn on our departure for that
purpose. Caviglia, the famous Italian, who
rivals Belzoni in enterprise and success,
breakfasted with us this morning; he is
certainly a very extraordinary man; there is
an account of his researches in an article of
the Quarterly, furnished some years ago by
Mr. Salt, very interesting, and well worth
your perusal.

But I have had other visitors of no less
celebrity — Linant, the French artist, who accompanied Laborde to Petra, and who discovered the ruined capital of Meroe; Gobat too,
the Abyssinian missionary—Mr. Lieder, the

resident missionary at Cairo, introduced him
to me—a tall majestic figure, benevolent countenance, long beard, and in the Turkish dress;
I had a long and interesting conversation with
him.

We have received the kindest attentions
from every one. Colonel Campbell, our Consul-General, has procured us every thing we
could desire in the way of passports, firmans,
&c. He introduced us to the Pasha a few
evenings ago; as it is now Ramadan (the
Turkish Lent, during which they fast all day
and feast all night) he receives after sunset.
We visited the old spider in his den, the
citadel, where he ensnared and murdered the
Mamalukes. Ascending a broad marble passage on an inclined plane (the substitute for a
staircase), and traversing a lofty antechamber
crowded with attendants, we found ourselves in
the presence-chamber, a noble saloon, richly
ornamented, but without an article of furniture

except a broad divan, or sofa, extending round
the three sides of the room, in one corner of
which squatted His Highness Mohammed Ali.
Six wax-candles, ten feet high, stood in a row
in the centre of the hall, yet gave but little
light.(⁷)

About half an hour's conversation ensued
between Colonel Campbell and the Pasha,
chiefly statistical, and interesting as shewing
his singular and intimate knowledge, extending
to the minutest details, of every thing going on
in his dominions.*   He does, in fact, every

* " We walked straight into the Divan Chamber without being announced, or any ceremony whatever. The
renowned Mohammed Ali was squatting in one corner of
the room, smoking a most superb pipe, clustered with
whole handfuls of diamonds; we all, after bowing, sat
down on each side of him. Coffee was brought to each in
the small cups like egg-cups, in beautiful filagree stands,
universally used in the East; a pipe is never given but to
a peer. He sent for his interpreter, and Colonel Campbell sustained the conversation for three quarters of an
hour nearly. The Pasha spoke most practically and
statistically of all his manufactures and undertakings,

thing himself; he has made a great deal of Egypt, considered as his private property, but at the expence of the people, who are fewer in number, and those few far more miserable than they were before his time.

And how could it be otherwise ?*　He " has

entered into all the details of ship-building, and the merits of particular woods, told us of some extraordinary instance of his *lenient rule* in the case of a village which he had pardoned its contributions, informed us he had exported 425,000 quintals of cotton last year, and so on.

" He did not address any of his guests, but I observed his sharp cunning eye fixing itself on every one. The light was not strong enough to remark minutely, but I can agree with former travellers as to the vivid expression of his eye, and, for the rest, under a huge tarboosh and immense white beard and mustachioes, it is absurd to talk of, or to have any clear idea of the expression of his face ; but an expression I have read somewhere, ' his cold heartless laugh,' came suddenly into my head when I heard him laugh : it sounded hard, cold, and pleasureless, and enough to make any one freeze whose head was at his mercy."—*Mr. Ramsay's Journal.*

* The following observations on the present state of Egypt are extracted from Mr. Ramsay's Journal; I have substituted them for my own, which were nearly to the same effect, though shorter and less interesting.

drained the country of all the working men.
He presses them as sailors, soldiers, workmen,
&c., and nobody can be sure of his own secu-
rity for a day. His system appears to be
infamous, and the change which has taken
place in the general appearance of the country
within a few years is said to be extraordinary.
Every where the land is falling out of cultivation, villages are deserted, houses falling to
ruin, and the people disappearing.

" He taxes all the means of industry and of
its improvement, and then taxes the product.
Irrigation is the great means of cultivation and
fertility ; he therefore charges fifteen dollars'
tax upon every Persian wheel; and, as the
people can find a way of avoiding it by manual
labour, raising the water in a very curious way
by the pole and bucket, he lays a tax of seven
dollars and a half even on that simple con-
trivance.

" He then, in the character of universal

land-proprietor in his dominions, orders what crop shall be sown, herein consulting his own interest solely, in direct opposition to that of his people. He settles the price of the crop, at which the cultivator is obliged to sell it to him, for he can sell it to no one else; and, if he wishes to keep any himself, he is obliged to buy it back from government at the new rate which the Pasha has fixed for its sale, of course, many per cents dearer than when he bought it. Numberless are his little tricks for saving money; e. g. when he has to receive money, it has always to be paid in advance; taxes, particularly, he collects always just before the plague breaks out, so that, though the people die, he has their money; in paying the troops and others, it is vice versâ; he pays after date, and gains also upon the deaths.

" We have heard much at home of the reforming enlightened spirit of Mohammed Ali, but what is it founded on? it looks more like a great and sudden blaze before the whole is extinguished and falls into total darkness ; and whether this is to happen at his death or before, seems the only question : it seems not to be far distant. Last year he had no money (and he pushed hard for it), to pay his troops and dependents, and this year he will have no more than he had last.

" He has *forced* the riches of the country prematurely, and to an extent they could not bear, at the same time removing the means of their reproduction, and thus he has procured the present means of prosecuting the really wonderful, and what, in other circumstances, would have been the useful and beneficial improvements and institutions, which we have heard so much of, and which certainly strike a traveller much.

" It is to the unprincipled roguery and ignorance of his European advisers and officials that most of this waste and expence is to

be charged. His counsellors consist of all the
needy emigrants from France and Italy, who
are scouted or in bad odour at home, and who
have the assurance to pretend to be that they
are not here, where detection is difficult, and
where success is their fortune for life. Ideas
of the most extravagant kind, such as that of
damming up the Nile, and others on which he
has thrown away many hundred thousands of
pounds, have been put into his head by these
speculating adventurers, who fill their own
pockets by it, and thus prey upon the country.

" A man, who has received the education of a
scribe or clerk, comes out, talks of cotton-
growing, and soon rises to the head of the
cotton department; another, who has thought
of, nothing but trade or manufacturing, is put
into the engineering office; and thus every
thing is mismanaged. The English are no
longer employed in his service, he has found
them too hard to deal with, too honourable and

straightforward, not supple and promising enough. Mr. Hill is the only one here who understands engineering, and is now dismissed from his service. A steam-engine has been sent out; three years have passed, and its undertaker cannot put it up, though constantly at work. Mr. Hill has offered to do it in a week, but his offer is not allowed to reach the Pasha's ear." But enough of this — the prospect is very cheerless.

Mr. Hill, by the way, is our landlord, and a very clever, ingenious, obliging man he is. With English hotels at Alexandria and Cairo, and floating palaces at command for navigating the Nile, what is there to prevent our English ladies and their beaux from wintering at Thebes, as they have done hitherto at Paris and Rome? An hotel in the city of Sesostris would in that case prove a most profitable speculation.

One word more, however, about Mohammed Ali : — few in England seem to be aware how vast his dominions really are; nominally the Pasha of Egypt, he is supreme in Nubia, Dongola, Sennaar, to the borders of Abyssinia; the Hedjaz, the Peninsula of Mount Sinai, Palestine and Syria, and Asia Minor south of Mount Taurus, pay him tribute and obey him; and even the desert-dwellers as far as Palmyra stand in awe and respect him. But it is not mere extent of dominion that gives an abiding niche in the temple of history; he sits on the throne of Zenobia, but who will remember his name a hundred years hence?

So here we are at Cairo, the City of Victory — daughter of the Fatimites and the bride of Saladin — the Tyre of Saracen commerce, and of the Thousand and one Nights at that later era when Arab chivalry had burnt out, and the children of Antar had ceased to be gentlemen. Viewed from any of the neighbouring eminences, she is still Grand Cairo, but the narrowness of the streets, a perfect labyrinth of alleys, and the general air of decay, forbid one's application of the epithet to the interior of the city.*([8]) Saladin sleeps at Damascus, and his house survived him but a few brief generations; a race of slaves succeeded them, Circassian slaves, raised successively from bondage to the throne of this "basest of kingdoms," for two hundred and thirty years previous to 1517, when Selim, the Grand Turk, conquered it. Their cemetery is one of the most interesting sights at Cairo.

Crossing a mile or so of the Desert, you come in sight of a city of tombs and mosques,

* "In the streets where there are no shops the buildings are still closer; in fact, the second stories are almost always quite joined; the little projecting windows of the houses opposite fit into each other, and the sky is only at glimpses visible from below. They give one more the idea of private passages in a house, till you are undeceived by meeting people on horseback, and by their interminable extent and labyrinthic properties. Many are not much above a yard wide, seldom more than six or eight feet. They have the merit of coolness at least."—*Mr. Ramsay's Journal.*

—the most splendid domes, pillars of the most exquisite Saracenic architecture, and minarets the lightest and airiest imaginable, rising from the desert, like an oriental Venice, to greet you ; I never saw any thing more lovely than this City of the Dead—the evening sun shining brightly and cheerfully down its silent avenues. On a nearer approach you find with sorrow that they are already crumbling with decay, the muezzin has long ceased his summons to prayer, and a few miserable Arabs are the only human tenants of their lofty courts and chambers.

After riding through the wide extent of the tombs, we climbed up to the top of the sandhills which separate the lonely sepulchral plain from the city of Cairo. Oh ! it was a scene for Mirza to dream of — an hour for years to look back upon ! the sun setting behind the Pyramids — the Nile, that once flowed blood, winding between the two deserts that are ever

striving to rob him of the rich verdure that
edges his channel — Cairo, with her thousand
minarets, rising over the thin curling smoke—
and the busy hum of men, that denotes how
densely peopled she still is, murmuring from
below,—and then to turn round and look down
on the hollow and silent valley of the dead
sultans, already lost to the sun's rays, still and
lifeless, except a string of camels winding
among the tombs — 'twas a strange contrast!
The sun sank, sank, sank, and at last disappeared, while we still stood there watching the
Pyramids piercing the glowing sky, and listening for the Muezzin ; at last, a cannon from
the citadel announced, the sun's total disappearance, and then first one, then every minaret " found a tongue," answering each
other in the self-same words, " God is great !
There is no God but God, and Mahomet is his
prophet !"

The crescent moon brightened over us as

the night fell, and, pondering on the past and
the present, we rode slowly homewards through
the motley crowds with which this strange city
is peopled, all eagerly preparing for their
evening meal..

We are now tolerably familiar with oriental
objects; but the first three or four walks we
took through the bazars were like a visit to
another world, familiar to the imagination, but
passing strange when first realised by the
eyes; portly duennas, veiled from head to foot,
waddling along, followed by their slaves —
harems taking the air on donkey-back, es-
corted by their black eunuchs, the most con-
summate puppies in Cairo — Arabs on their
dromedaries—richly-drest Bedouin Sheikhs on
their prancing steeds — Turks with their long
pipes and ataghans—water-carriers, buffaloes,
half-naked Santons,(⁹) or religious fanatics,
singing and rocking backwards and forwards
—criers perambulating the bazars with objects

of curiosity to dispose of — the small shops on
either side the street, their owners sitting
cross-legged and smoking — every thing reminded us of the Arabian Nights and Haroun
Al-Raschid.

In one respect, however, a great and happy
change has taken place ; the insults Christians
were formerly subject to are now unknown.
Whatever be one's opinion of the Pasha's domestic policy, travellers owe him much, for
throughout his dominions (in Egypt and
Syria at least) they may travel in the Frank
dress with perfect safety. What would old
Sandys or Lithgow have said, had any one
prophesied in their days that two Britons
would, in 1836, walk openly through Cairo,
preceded by a native servant clearing the road
before them by gentle hints indiscriminately
administered to donkeys and Moslemin, to get
out of the Giaour's way ?([10])

The Turks are perfect gentlemen, and never

stare — a marvel and a mystery to me, for we must cut uncouth figures in our tight European garments. But we have made up our minds in no case and nowhere to discard our national dress as if we were ashamed of it, though I think we well may be.

There is nothing, I fear, likely to be permanent of the few real improvements the Pasha has introduced here. His trees only are likely to survive him ; he has planted two hundred thousand olives in the neighbourhood of Cairo, and expects that, in a few years, they will pay him yearly a dollar per tree. We rode through this plantation a few days ago, and were delighted with it, but far more so with the gardens Ibrahim Pasha, Mohmamed Ali's stepson, has planted in the island of Roda, which you reach after traversing the olive-grounds. They are managed by two Scotchmen, at least of Scottish descent, and do them great credit.

I longed for you and dear A——; it is indeed a lovely spot; one walk, with borders of
myrtle, particularly charmed me, leading, between rows of orange-trees in full bearing, to
a fountain surrounded by cypress and lignum-
vitæ trees.　Rosemary edges the walks like
box in England, and roses bloom in profusion;
gorgeous butterflies, " winged flowers," as
some one prettily calls them, were flitting
about in every direction, and some strange
plant or other, the banana, prickly pear, the
beautiful acacia speciosa, or the date-tree, with
its graceful head-gear, constantly reminded us
of the East.

Little canals for irrigation are conducted all
over the garden, some of them of hewn stone,
others merely dug in the earth, and the water is
transferred from one into the other by opening
or damming it with the foot, as in Moses'
time.　The under-gardeners, in their gay oriental dress, were in perfect keeping with the

flowery landscape, but they were Greeks, alas !
sighing for their own dear isle of Scio !

Mr. Traill, who had the kindness to accompany us all through the garden, showed us
several foreign plants he is attempting to natu-
ralize — the india-rubber tree, the sago palm,
and one diminutive oakling—I wish it may
answer; it will do his heart good to look at
it—

" Sae far frae hame in, a strange countrie !" ([11])

On this island of Roda stands the Nilometer,
a graduated octagon pillar, on which the rise
of the river is marked during the inundation ;
we visited it, but it is scarcely worth seeing.
I believe one cannot depend on the government
reports of the rise of the Nile : His Highness
reports the height he chuses it to be, and if he

* " Mr. Traill showed us a sarcophagus, which he had
converted into a prison of state ; instead of the bastinado,
he put any refractory workman into it, and slued the
heavy top round over him, keeping him there sometimes
for two or three days. Its effects, he assured me, were
wonderful."—*Mr. Ramsay's Journal.*

is in want of money, the inundation is sure to be the right height.

Recrossing to Old Cairo, we proceeded over mounds of debris (the ruins of the Egyptian Babylon) to the Coptic Convent, and thence to the tombs of the Mameluke Beys, far inferior in point of grandeur to those of the Sultans, but still many of them very elegant, and the tout-ensemble a most impressive sight. Here, a curious situation for *him* to have selected, Mohammed Ali has erected a grand tomb for himself and his family, of coarse workmanship, but it contains several halls, with lofty domes, and the monuments are already very numerous; all bear inscriptions in letters of gold, and the floors are richly carpeted.

Re-entering Cairo, we remarked an aloe planted over the door of a new house, a custom, I am told, constantly observed here; what can be its origin?

Two or three days ago we visited the college

or school Mohammed Ali has founded at Boulac ;* give him his due ; this is an improvement he deserves much credit for ; there are separate rooms for each of the six classes, all airy, and opening on broad spacious galleries. Being Ramadan, the boys were enjoying their holi-

* " At Boulac saw the Polytechnic School, formerly Ismael Pasha's Palace, a splendid establishment. The boys are neatly enough dressed, and, except the tarboosh and slippers, might pass for Europeans. They appeared, some of them that we saw, very quick and intelligent, and I am told that their examination surpasses most such in England in outward show, but it is all head-knowledge. They apply to Algebra and abstruse mathematics. Their benches, slates, &c., were quite European. The printing-press we also saw, and were much pleased. They print a paper every week, and we saw several books in hand; the Arabian Nights is just finished; the impressions are, some of them, beautiful. One venerable old savant, with spectacle on nose, appeared to be inspecting, and deeply immersed in, some old chronicle: such an individual is much more striking and characteristic-looking in the handsome old Turkish dress he wore, with a reverend beard, than any dapper old European, in a snuffy brown coat, out at the elbows, and glorying in unbrushed classic dust."—*Mr. Ramsay's Journal.*

days, but in one of the rooms I found an
" awkward squad " of voluntary " saps," gathered round a board, on which the tutor was
working a sum in Arabic numerals. One or
two of the lads were pointed out to me as
being very clever, but, in general, the difficulty
with the Arabs is to fix their attention. They
are a lively good-humoured people, and, with
kindness, you may get them to do any thing
they are up to.

We visited the Pasha's printing establishment, also at Boulac, the same day; the workmen seemed very active and well acquainted
with their business. We saw several works in
progress, the press-work, paper, &c., neater
than the ordinary run of books printed in Ger-
many or Italy — the types are English; they
lithograph also. I shall send home a specimen
or two of Egyptian typography, the Arabian
Nights, for instance. There is at present a
quarrel, something like that between the sto-

mach and the members, between the printing-
office and the magazine, and, till it is settled,
which cannot be till after Ramadan, no books
can be purchased.

Perhaps the most useful work the Pasha has
published is an Atlas in Arabic, copied from
one the missionaries have executed at Malta.
It is forbidden to print the Koran, or even to
sell it to a Christian; I have procured, however, through the kind mediation of my friend,
Mr. Lieder, a most beautiful manuscript (once
a vizier's) of that holy volume, richly illu-
minated with gold and colours in the Arabesque
style of our old missals, a style, indeed, im-
ported from the East by Rome, and which,
though condemned by the classic taste of
Vitruvius, Raphael thought not unworthy
of revival.

Missionary exertions throughout the Levant
are chiefly directed to the conversion of the native Christians as a step to that of the Mos-

lems. This they attempt to effect by schools for
the young, and the circulation of the Scriptures
in the native dialects among those of more advanced years. Mr. Lieder is the amiable and
zealous promoter of the good cause in Egypt,
now, as in every age, emphatically a house of
bondage ; spiritual darkness, foreshadowed,
one might almost think, by the three days'
gloom of Moses, broods over the land ; the
Christians seem to differ little from the heathen ; indeed their character is, generally speaking, so bad as materially to impede the progress of the truth among the Mahometans.

There are many Arab Christians besides the
Copts and Armenians, *all* of whom rank nominally as such ; the Copts, a sort of mongrels, in
whose veins runs the blood of every nation
that has trodden down Egypt, are by far the
cleverest of the modern Egyptians, and the
business of the country is, for the most part,
in their hands ;— Boghaz Bey, the Pasha's

right-hand man, is an Armenian, but I do not
believe there are many of his sleek and comely,
honest, plodding countrymen here ;—the Jews
are numerous — the same in appearance and
character as elsewhere—scorned alike by Turk
and Christian ;

"Tribes of the wandering foot and weary breast,
When will ye flee away, and be at rest!"

You will easily gather from what I have
said, that I fear there is no hope for Egypt—at
least, at present. There *is* a gleam in the sky,
as if the light of civilization were about to rise,
but, like the false dawn in India, it will fade
away, and deeper darkness will succeed. Yet
the true dawn will come at last, and brighten
into perfect day, and then, and not till then,
will Egypt, Christian Egypt, rise from the
dust, and resume her seat among the nations.

Do you remember the strange story Miss
H—— told us of the Egyptian magician? I
have had him twice here, — that is to say, the

gentlemen at the inn had him the first time,
and, as I was not satisfied with his performance, and he hardly got fair play among us, I
had him a second time to myself, wishing to
give him a fair trial. I am not yet satisfied;
he succeeded in the first person we called for,
but failed egregiously in the others.

The first night we all assembled in the Salle
à manger of the Hotel, and, the wizard being
introduced, we seated him on the divan, furnished him with a pipe, and then proceeded
to question him as to his power, &c. He said
he was from Algiers (query of Sycorax's family, Caliban's mother ?), and that he belonged
to a tribe or caste who are ruled by sheikhs or
chiefs, and call themselves servants of Solomon.
We asked him whether he worked by Allah or
by Satan; he gave me a Scotch answer the
first day, "Does not Satan come from Allah ?"
but the following evening affirmed it was by
Allah.

I asked him whether he understood the words he used, which are not Arabic; at least one of my friends here, who speaks the language, could make nothing of them — he said Yes,—and, in answer to my further inquiries, repeated thirteen words or names, which, he said, were all a man needed the knowledge of to obtain the same power with himself;—you must learn them by heart (he is willing to teach any one " for a consideration"), then for seven days make a fire seven times every day, throw incense on it, and walk round the fire seven times, pronouncing seven times the thirteen names, — then go to sleep, and you will awake with the faculty required. A complicated receipt this !

The magician, meanwhile, was writing several lines in Arabic, which he afterwards tore into seven pieces, each containing a distich. A boy having been procured (for a child only can receive the power of magical vision), he drew a double-lined square, with strange marks in the angles, on his hand, put some ink on the palm, and bade him look into it and tell us what he saw.

A chafing-dish having now been brought in, the wizard, his beads in his hand, began mumbling prayers or invocations, the same words, I believe, over and over again, at first in a loud voice, then gradually sinking till they were quite inaudible (like a top falling asleep), though his lips continued moving apace. From time to time he placed incense and one of the torn scraps of paper on the fire, frequently interrupting his incantation to ask the boy whether he saw any thing, to which he as frequently replied in the negative; at last he said, " I saw something flit by quickly," but nothing more came, and the wizard said we must procure another boy, which we did.

The same ceremonies having been repeated, a man made his appearance, and, at the word of command, began sweeping; then he bade the boy call for seven flags in succession, all of which made their appearance, and, last of all, the Sultan, whom he described as seated on his divan drinking coffee. " Now," said the magician, " the charm is complete, and you may call for any one you like."

The first person we summoned was the Rev. —— ——, a mutual friend of William's and mine, and the first person who told him of these magicians; he was described, upon the whole, accurately, but this was the only successful summons; the spirits either would not come, or appeared by proxy, to the sad discomposure of our Arab Glendower, who, it is but fair to state, attributed the failure to its being Ramadan.

I tried him with Daniel Lambert, who, I was informed, was a thin man, and with Miss Biffin, who made her appearance with arms and legs. He has been equally unsuccessful with

a party of Americans—this is odd enough when
one considers how strongly Mr. Salt, Lord
Prudhoe, and Major Felix, who subjected him
to long and repeated examinations, were impressed with the belief of his supernatural
powers.

One thing is unquestionable—that the children *do* see a crowd of objects, following each
other, and, at the commencement of the incantation, the very same objects, — as vivid and
distinct as if they looked out of the window at
noonday.   How is this to be accounted for?
Collusion is out of the question.

We have seen the Jugglers; they shew
great dexterity in sticking daggers into their
eyes, necks, hearts, &c., running long bodkins
up their noses, sheathing swords in their sto-
machs, the skin lapping quite over them (indeed their skins seem to hang quite loose on
their bodies) ; and, lastly, applying burning
torches to their naked breasts; upon the

whole, a disagreeable exhibition, not worth seeing.

The Psylli, or serpent-charmers, were not to be found when we sent for them ; many believe in their pretensions; my friend, Mr. Lieder, told me they charmed a poisonous snake out of his house, which he himself had seen the day before, but failed to kill, besides two others which they *might* have introduced. They never pronounce God's name Allah, but Pullah.

Both Psylli and Magicians seem to have been known among the Jews; " the deaf adder that shutteth her ears" is proverbial, and " the stone of imagination, that is, certain smooth images, in which, by art magic, pictures and little faces were represented, declaring hidden things and stolen goods," mentioned by Jeremy Taylor, on the authority, I suppose, of some Rabbinical comment on Leviticus, was evidently kindred sorcery to that practised in Egypt at the present day.

Our boat is ready, and to-morrow, December 21, we start for Upper Egypt. We returned from the Pyramids to-day. — I have written A—— an account of our visit, which I enclose to you ; read and forward it.

Adieu.

LETTER IV.

Visit to the Pyramids — Pyramid of Cheops — Evening with Caviglia—Pyramids of Cephrenes and Mycerinus — Arab traditions respecting the Pyramids — The Sphinx, a talisman — Heliopolis — The Pyramids probably built by the Pali, or Shepherd-Kings of Egypt, afterwards the Philistines, in the time of Abraham.

TO MRS. JAMES LINDSAY.

Top of Cheops' Pyramid, Dec. 19, 1836.

DID you ever expect, my dear A——, to receive a letter from the top of the Great Pyramid? Here I am, and William at my side, a burning sun above us, and four half-naked Arabs chattering around us, greatly marvelling, doubtless, at the magical propensities of the English. It is a fatiguing business climbing up, but, once here, all is repaid! Such a view! the desert on one side, stretching away into Libya—waves beyond waves, as

far as the eye can reach; the vale of Egypt on
the other, green as if Hope had chosen it as
her peculiar home, with a thousand little canals
traversing it in every direction, left by the retiring Nile, for the inundation has scarcely yet
subsided.

Caviglia is working here, and we are now his
guests. He has palisadoed off a little citadel
for himself, the chambers consisting of tombs
excavated in the rock on which the Pyramids
are built. After our descent, he is going to
cicerone us through this monument of pride,
science, or superstition — who knows which ?
It was building while Abraham was in Egypt ;
Joseph and his brethren must have seen the
sun set behind it every day they sojourned in
Egypt; it must have been the last object
Moses and the departing Israelites lost sight
of as they quitted the land of bondage ; Pythagoras, Herodotus, Alexander, the Caliphs—it
has been the goal of nations ! lost nations have

pilgrimised to its foot, and looked up, as their common ancestors did before them, in awe and humility — and now, two strangers, from the " ultima Thule" of the ancients, Britain, severed from the whole world by a watery line, which they considered it impious to transgress, stand here on the summit, and, looking round, see a desert where once the " cloud-capt towers, the gorgeous palaces," the temples and tombs of Memphis arose in their calm beauty, and Wisdom dwelt among the groves of palm and acacia—solitary now and deserted except by the wandering Arab and his camel.

Midnight : Caviglia's Tomb.

After dining with Caviglia, dear A——, to continue my yarn, we started by moonlight for the Pyramid, in company with the Genius Loci, and duly provided with candles for exploration. I must premise that Caviglia, whose extraordinary discoveries you are doubtless well acquainted with, has just been set to work again by Colonel Vyse, Mr. Sloane, and Colonel Campbell, our Consul-General at Cairo. He is at present attempting to make further discoveries in the Great Pyramid, and, as soon as he gets a firman from the Pasha, intends to attack the others.

The shape of this Pyramid has been compared to " four equilateral triangles, on a square basis, mutually inclining towards each other till they meet in a point."* " Lincoln's-Inn fields, the area of which corresponds to its base, wholly filled up with an edifice higher by a third than St. Paul's, may give some idea of its dimensions."†

The entrance is on the northern face of the Pyramid, on the sixteenth step, though you can ride up to it, such immense mounds of fallen stones have accumulated at the base.   A

---

* Greaves, Pyramidographia.
† Conder, Modern Traveller—Egypt.

long, low passage, most beautifully cut and polished, runs downwards, above 260 feet, at an angle of 27 degrees, to a large hall, sixty feet long, directly under the centre of the Pyramid, cut out of the rock, and never, it would appear, finished. This was discovered by Caviglia ; the passage, before his time, was supposed to end about half-way down,([12]) being blocked up with stones at the point where another passage meets it, running upwards at the same angle of 27, and by which you might mount in a direct line to the grand gallery, and from that to the king's chamber, where stands the sarcophagus, nearly in the centre of the pile, were it not for three or four blocks of granite that have been slid down from above, in order to stop it up.

By climbing through a passage, forced, it is supposed, by the Caliph Mamoun, you wind round these blocks of granite into the passage, so that, with the exception of ten or twelve

E 2

feet, you do in fact follow the original line of
ascent ; we *de*scended by it. Close to the
opening of this passage on the grand gallery,
is the mouth of a well, about 200 feet deep, by
which we ascended from the neighbourhood of
the great lower hall. Two or three persons
had descended it before Caviglia's time, but he
cleared it out to the full depth that his prede-
cessors had reached, and, believing it went
still deeper, hearing a hollow sound as he
stamped on the bottom, he attempted to ex-
cavate there, but was obliged to desist on account of the excessive heat, which neither he
nor the Arabs could stand.

Think what his delight must have been,
when, in the course of clearing the passage
which, I mentioned to you, leads directly from
the entrance to the great lower hall, smelling
a strong scent of sulphur, and remembering he
had burnt some in the well to purify the air,
he dug in that direction, and found a passage

leading right into the bottom of the well, where the ropes, pick-axes, &c., &c., were lying that he had left there in despair, on abandoning the idea of further excavation in that direction as hopeless.

Up this well, as I said, we climbed, holding a rope, and fixing our feet in holes cut in the stone; the upper part of the ascent was very difficult, and bats in numbers came tumbling down on us; but at last we landed safely in the grand gallery, a noble nondescript of an apartment, very lofty, narrowing towards the roof, and most beautifully chiselled; it ends, towards the south, in a staircase, if I may so term an inclined plane, with notches cut in the surface for the feet to hold by; the ascent is perilous, the stone being as polished and slippery as glass; before ascending, how- ever, we proceeded by another beautifully worked passage, cut directly under the stair- case, to a handsome room, called the queen's

chamber. Returning to the gallery, we
mounted the inclined plane to the king's
chamber, directly over the queen's. The passage leading to it was defended by a portcullis
now destroyed, but you see the grooves it fell
into. His majesty's chamber is a noble apartment, cased with enormous slabs of granite,
twenty feet high ; nine similar ones (seven
large and two half-sized) form the ceiling. ([13])

At the west end stands the sarcophagus,
which rings, when struck, like a bell. From
the north and south sides, respectively, of this
room, branch two small oblong-square passages, like air-holes, cut through the granite
slabs, and slanting upwards, the first for
eighty feet in a zigzag direction, the other for
one hundred and twenty.

It is Caviglia's present object to discover
whither these lead. Being unable to pierce
the granite, he has begun cutting sideways into
the limestone at the point where the granite

casing of the chamber ends, has reached the
northern passage at the point where it is continued through the limestone, and is cutting a
large one below it, so that the former runs like
a groove in the roof of the latter, and he has
only to follow it as a guide, and cut away till
he reaches the denouement. — " Now," says
Caviglia, " I will shew you how I hope to find
out where the southern passage leads to."

Returning to the landing-place at the top of
the grand staircase, we mounted a ricketty
ladder to the narrow passage that leads to
Davison's chamber, so named after the English
consul at Algiers, who discovered it seventy
years ago; it is directly above the king's
chamber, the ceiling of the one forming, it
would appear, the floor of the other. The
ceiling of Davison's chamber consists of eight
stones, beautifully worked, and this ceiling,
which is so low that you can only sit cross-
legged under it, Caviglia believes to be the

floor of another large room above it, which
he is now trying to discover. To this room
he concludes the little passage leads, that
branches from the south side of the king's
chamber. He has accordingly dug down into
the calcareous stone at the further end of Davison's chamber, in hopes of meeting it;
once found, it will probably lead him to the
place he is in quest of.

And now, I am sure, if I have been happy
enough to inspire you with a tithe of the interest with which I followed every winding of
the Pyramid and of our cicerone's mind, itself
a most extraordinary labyrinth, you will be
glad to hear that there seems every probability
of his soon reaching the little passage. Leaving a servant in the excavation, descending to
the king's chamber, and shouting at the hole,
the man answered by striking on the stone —
distinct strokes — as satisfactory a reply as
could be wished for.

Here, of course, our wanderings ceased. We
regained the gallery, and from thence descended, as I have already intimated, in a direct
line, past the well, through the passage forced
by Mamoun, and up the passage of entrance to
the open air; and glad were we to breathe it;
but our first care was to don our coats and
cloaks as preventives against catching cold;
the toil-drops were falling from us like rain,
and such hands and faces were never seen, for
many a rood had we to creep on our hands
and knees, or like the king of the beggars, who
used to haunt the purlieus of the Tower when
I was a little boy, legs forward and face forward, punting with one's hands,— an attitude
somewhat difficult to describe.*

* " It is a pity no one thinks of looking for any probable entrance to the chamber in which Herodotus says
the king is buried, in a sarcophagus isolated from the
rest by the water of the Nile, which enters and flows
round it. The level of the Nile is 130 feet below the
foundation; the angle of descent always used here is

After ablutions, &c., we drank tea, delicious tea! in Caviglia's tent; a candle stuck in a bottle enlightened our repast, but dark, mystical, and unearthly was our conversation, — a sequel to the lecture he had given us inside the Pyramid, pointing out an end, a hidden purpose, a secret meaning in every nook, cranny, and passage of the structure — the scene, he told us, of initiation into the ancient Egyptian mysteries.

We had him to breakfast two or three days ago at Cairo, and I had had a long confab with him before that. Living, as he has done, so solitary, I should rather say, in such society as that of the old Pharaohs of Egypt, their pyramids his home, and that strange enigma of a sphinx his fellow-watcher at their feet, he

known, and, with these two data, it is easy to calculate the level at which any passage to it must begin, and the distance from the Pyramid. It might be fruitless, but would be worth a minute examination all round." — *Mr. Ramsay's Journal.*

has become, to use his own expression, " tout-
a-fait pyramidale" in dress, feature, manner,
thought, and language. We are told that in
Ceylon there are insects that take the shape
and colour of the branch or leaf they feed
upon — Caviglia seems to partake of their nature, he is really assimilating to a pyramid.
His history is very curious; " As a young
man," he told us this evening, "je lisais
Voltaire, Jean Jacques, Diderot — et je me
croyais philosophe " — he came to Egypt —
the Pyramids, Moses, and the Holy Scriptures converted him, " et maintenant," said
he, " je suis tout Biblique." I have seldom
met with a man so thoroughly imbued with
the Bible; the saving truths of the Gospel,
man's lost condition by the fall of Adam,
Christ's voluntary death to expiate our sins,
our inability to save ourselves, and the necessity of our being born again of the Holy
Spirit — every one of these doctrines he

avowed this evening; he seems to cling to them, and to love our blessed Saviour with the simplicity of a child (14)—he never names him without reverence; but on these doctrines, this rock, as a foundation, he has reared a pyramid of the most extraordinary mysticism —astrology, magnetism, magic (his familiar studies), its corner-stones, while on each face of the airy vision he sees inscribed in letters of light, invisible to all but himself, elucidatory texts of scripture, which he read off to us, with undoubting confidence, in support of his positions.

Every religious truth, in short, unessential to salvation, is in his eyes fraught with mysticism. His memory is as accurate as a Presbyterian minister's—every text he quoted was prefaced by a reference to the chapter and verse where it occurs. He loves the Arabs, and looks forward to their conversion and civilization as the accomplishment of the prophecies that " there shall be a highway out of Egypt to Assyria" in that day when " Israel shall be a third with Egypt and Assyria, even a blessing in the midst of the land"—when the Lord shall have " set his hand the second time to recover the remnant of his people from Assyria, from Egypt, from Pathros, from Cush," &c., and shall bless the assembled myriads, saying, " Blessed be Egypt, my people, and Assyria, the work of my hands, and Israel, mine inheritance."

He quoted these remarkable prophecies, and I had the pleasure of telling him I looked forward to their speedy fulfilment with the same interest as himself*.

---

* " Caviglia told me that he had pushed his studies in magic, animal magnetism, &c., to an extent which had nearly killed him — to the very verge, he said, of what is forbidden to man to know ; and it was only the purity of his intentions which saved him. He told me he could have the power of performing all the magical rites formerly practised, only that by the coming of our Saviour

I must wish my dear A—— good night. You can have no idea how comfortably we are lodged here. The rock is honeycombed with tombs, but this one has been cleared out, furnished with mats, glass-windows, &c., &c.

everything of minor degree was included, and it would now be a profanation to attempt such things.

" Now one is very apt to call such a man a monomaniac on this particular point, and I should not know well how to reply to any one who should do so. He gave us a sort of history of his life ; he had come out a perfect infidel to Egypt; he had curiosity about the Pyramids, and on being told that they did not make attempts at discovery, because the devil was there, ' If it's only the devil,' said he, ' I shall not trouble myself about him,' and so descended to the well, and made the discoveries he showed us. By reading, first of all, the works of the Greek philosophers, and then the Bible, he has become, as he said, ' peu à peu Bibliste et Chretien.'

" Yet he has strange unearthly ideas which seem to open up to you, as he says them, whole vistas of unheard of ground, which close up again as suddenly, so that one can hardly know what his theories are. He says it would be highly dangerous to communicate them, and looks mystical, but evidently does not like to speak on the subject, and, otherwise, loves a good hearty laugh and joke as much as any one."—*Mr. Ramsay's Journal.*

Caviglia seems really to enjoy himself in his little fortress ; the Arabs are very fond of him —he is monarch of all he surveys, knows his fame, and enjoys it — and long may he do so ! He is now sixty-six, but still hale, active, and hearty. He hates Cairo, he says, the noise and bustle distract him, and he is quite happy here with his pyramids, his mysticism, and his Bible.

Here we are at Cairo again. This morning, after breakfast, the kind Caviglia took us to Cephrenes' Pyramid — Belzoni's, as the Arabs call it with far more justice. The passage of entrance descends very rapidly ; entering backwards, it is difficult to keep one's footing except by pressing one's back against the roof, and " straddling," like Apollyon, over the whole breadth of the way. After creeping under the portcullis, which Belzoni raised so successfully, and descending the shaft by a ladder which Caviglia has placed there, we reached the chamber of the sarcophagus, beautifully cut out of the rock; the roof is composed of hewn stones, and rises in a pyramidal shape, which shews there must be a chamber above; but how to get at it? The passage, leading to the other room discovered by Belzoni, has been blocked up with stones by the Arabs. Altogether, this pyramid is much inferior, both within and without, to that of Cheops, alias Caviglia's.

Standing at the entrance, Caviglia pointed out to us a white hill, about a league and a half distant, where, he says, the base of a pyramid, three hundred feet long, is traceable, surrounded by little pyramids of pulverized granite, probably still more ancient than the pyramids of Djizeh themselves.

The rock has been cut away so as to form a spacious area to the north of Cephrenes' pyra-

mid; we rode through it towards that of Mycerinus — much smaller than its fellows, but
of workmanship far superior to that of Cephrenes. The ground is covered with dislodged blocks of the red granite with which it
was cased.([15])

—— Once upon a time, Pharaoh was presiding in his court at Memphis, when an
eagle, hovering over his head, dropped into his
lap the smallest and prettiest slipper that ever
was seen ; inquiry being made whence it came
and whose it was, it turned out to be the property of the fair Rhodope of Naucratis, and
to have been snatched by the eagle out of her
attendant's hands, while she was bathing.
Rhodope became queen of Egypt, and, on her
death, was buried by her disconsolate husband
in this Pyramid.—A pretty story — would it
were true !   Do you remember our poor friend
H—— mentioning it as possibly the original
of Cinderella? ([16])

Not less fanciful are the Arab traditions as to the origin of these world's wonders! Saurid ebn Salhouk, who ruled in Egypt three hundred years before the flood, saw in a dream the earth convulsed, its inhabitants lying on their faces, the stars falling from heaven, clashing as they fell, and, marvellous to relate! changing into white birds, which, snatching up his unfortunate subjects, hurried them between two vast mountains which closed behind them, and then the remaining stars went out, and there was thick darkness on the earth.   Springing up in horror, he summoned the wise men of Egypt, one hundred and thirty priests; ([17]) they consulted the stars and foretold the deluge. " Will it come to our country?" said the king. " Yea, and will destroy it."   " And there remained a certain number of years for to come, and he commanded in the mean space to build the Pyramids, and a vault to be made into which the river Nilus entering, should run into the

countries of the west and into the land Al Said;
and he filled them with talismans, and with
strange things, and with riches and treasures,
and the like. He engraved in them all things
that were told him by wise men, as also all
profound sciences, the names of alakakirs,* the
uses and hurts of them, the science of astrology and of arithmetic, and of geometry, and
of physic. All this may be interpreted by him
that knows their character and language.

" After he had given order for this building,
they cut out vast columns and wonderful stones.
They fetch massy stones from the Ethiopians,
and made with these the foundation of the
three great pyramids, fastening them together
with lead and iron. They built the gates of
them forty cubits underground, and they made
the height of the pyramid one hundred royal
cubits. The beginning of this building was
in a fortunate horoscope. After he had finished
it, he covered it with coloured satin from the

* Magical spells engraven on precious stones.

top to the bottom, and he appointed a solemn festival, at which were present all the inhabitants of his kingdom.

"Then he built in the western pyramid thirty treasures, filled with store of riches and utensils, and with signatures made of precious stones, and with instruments of iron and vessels of earth, and with arms which rust not, and with glass which might be bended and yet not broken, and with strange spells, and with several kinds of alakakirs, single and double, and with deadly poisons.

"He made also in the eastern pyramid divers celestial spheres and stars, and what they severally operate in their aspects, and the perfumes which are used to them, and the books which treat of these matters.

"He also put in the coloured pyramid the commentaries of the priests, in chests of black marble, and with every priest a book, in which were the wonders of his profession and of his actions, and of his nature, and what was done in his time, and what is, and what shall be, from the beginning of time to the end of it.

"He placed in every pyramid a treasurer. The treasurer of the westerly pyramid was a statue of marble stone standing upright, with a lance, and upon his head a serpent wreathed; he that came near it, and stood still, the serpent bit him of one side, and, wreathing round about his throat and killing him, returned to his place. He made the treasurer of the Eastern pyramid an idol of black agate, his eyes open and shining, sitting upon a throne with a lance; when any looked upon him, he heard on one side of him a voice, which took away his sense, so that he fell prostrate upon his face, and ceased not till he died. He made the treasurer of the coloured pyramid a statue of stone, sitting; he which looked towards it, was drawn by the statue till he stuck to it, and

could not be separated from it till such time
as he died."*

Here, then, in these sepulchres of Saurid,
his brother and his nephew, was the knowledge
and science of the antediluvians preserved, and
hence they sprang forth again into life after
the deluge. But it was a grander flight still
which attributed their construction, with Baal-
bec and Istakhar, to Gian ben Gian, the
Preadamite monarch of the world! — Well
might the Arab poet look up at them, and say,
" Ce sont des edifices que les siècles redoutent,
pendant que ceux que nous élevons redoutent
les siecles !"†

Temples or tombs, monuments of tyranny or
of priestly wisdom, no theory as to the *meaning*
of the Pyramids,

> " Those glorious works of fine intelligence,"

has been broached so beautiful, to my mind, as

---

* Greaves' Pyramidographia.—(Churchill's collection
of Voyages and Travels, vol ii. p. 660.)

† Al Ouardi.

old Sandys's, who, like Milton and the ancients, believing them modelled in imitation of " that formless form-taking substance," fire, conceives them to express the " original of things." " For as a Pyramis, beginning at a point, by little and little dilateth into all parts, so nature, proceeding from one undividable fountain, (even God the Sovereign Essence), receiveth diversity of forms, effused into several kinds and multitude of figures, uniting all in the supreme head, from whence all excellencies issue." A truth that will outlive even the pyramids.

Each of them, according to the Arabs, has its guardian spirit; that of the southern pyramid is often seen hovering round it towards sunset, in the shape of a beautiful girl—but all go mad whom she favours with a smile. ([18])

The sphinx, too, according to the ancient Arabs, was a talisman, fixed there to protect the district from the encroaching sand, that

ever-rising, never-ebbing tide of the desert—
which had already in the geographer Bakoui's
time — the 14th century, swallowed up the
palace and the city of Pharaoh, and other flourishing towns and villages to the west of Djizeh;
one marble column remained, towering over the
waste, but no one could reach it. Caviglia
cleared away the sand from around the sphinx,
about twenty years ago, but the winds have
nearly covered her again — her back, I should
rather say, for she always held her head above
water. Her attitude bespeaks the calm repose
of conscious strength, her expression of countenance, benevolence—the tout-ensemble, strange
mysterious beauty, awful in its stillness. A
monster she is indeed, but not one to tremble
at — oh no! you stand before her in awe and
reverence, as before the wise, but benevolent
Simurgh; and oh! if one could but give her a
tongue, what histories she would tell, what
wisdom reveal to us! ([19]) A little temple is built

between her paws; a lion couches in front of it, looking up at her — both now fathom deep under the sandy deluge.

There are numbers of tumuli, or barrows, around the three great pyramids, heaving the soil, like graves in a country churchyard; they look mere mole-hills from the top, but contain spacious halls and chambers.

The sphinx, by the by, Caviglia told us he believed to express, enigmatically, the doctrine of man's regeneration, as explained to Nicodemus by our Saviour, and which he supposes to have been one of the ancient Egyptian (it certainly was one of the Indian) doctrines, derived from primitive revelation. That they had much traditional wisdom is unquestionable, and Heliopolis, the On of Genesis, was the shrine where it was preserved, — I know few places of more intense interest; Potipherah, Joseph's father-in-law, was prince and priest there; there dwelt the sages of

Egypt, and there Moses, Herodotus, Plato, Eu-
doxus, successively became learned in all the
wisdom of the Egyptians.

We visited the site two or three days ago —
a range of mounds, inclosing an oblong square,
smooth and covered with corn — Selim encamped on it when he came to conquer Cairo
—one obelisk, lone survivor, still pointing to
the sky. It was erected, we know, by the
Pharaoh Osirtesen, in the eighteenth century
before Christ, in front of the temple of Vulcan,
but where, you ask, *is* the temple? I see no
propyla, no dromos, no shrine — where is the
temple? Are those shapeless fragments of
granite the sphinxes Strabo mentions? Possibly—Heliopolis was desolate even in his day.
You may search, but there is nothing more to
be seen; the corn waves in the breeze, and
you push your way through it without stumbling; all is smooth, and you are ready to
think the genies of Aladdin's lamp must have

carried off the temple and left that single obelisk to tell the tale. Alas, poor Phœnix ! wert thou to come to life again, and revisit Heliopolis ! [20]

———————

I have said that the Pyramids were building while Abraham was in Egypt ; I dare say you have been wondering on what grounds I assert this, so much dispute having always existed as to their antiquity. And when I add, that I think there is every reason to believe that they were built by the " Royal Shepherds" of Egypt, who afterwards became the Philistines, you may well call on me for my reasons.

Come, dear A——, for I know the delight you feel in such adventures — come, and let us venture, hand in hand, into this dark chasm, at the mouth of which we stand, the cavern of the past, and, with mummy-torches to guide us, let us explore its recesses. We shall find

facts, isolated facts, like carbuncles, casting a
sure light through the gloom, jewels of historical truth, worthy of being set into a neck-
lace which even Clio herself need not disdain to
wear.   Are you ready? come then......The
cave grows chillier and chillier, gloomier and
gloomier, as we descend ; do you hear the roar
of waters ? the deluge is still seething up here ;
the cave extends far beyond that dark and
stormy water, but there is no crossing it, no
reaching yon distant shore without the bark of
Noah, and the Ark has been buried for ages
under the snows of Ararat.   Here stop we——
But a truce to this nonsense, and let me to my
argument.

Yet do not mistake me ; I have no new
theory to advance ; I aspire only to dovetail
into one harmonious piece of *marqueterie* the
scattered discoveries of those learned men who
have studied the subject, and which, viewed
connectedly, lead to the results briefly ex-

pressed above. Ab initio, then, dear A——, c'est à dire, commençons par le commencement.

Of Ham's three sons, Canaan, the youngest (the only one on whom the curse was pronounced), was ancestor of the ten tribes whom Abraham found in occupation of the Promised Land, bearing the national patronymic of Canaanites — how awfully depraved in their morals, I need not remind you. Their iniquities, however, had not come to the full till four hundred years after Abraham, when the Israelites were the hammer in the Lord's hand for crushing them.

A giant race, distinct from the Canaanites, "a people great, and strong, and tall," occupied many parts of the country between the Nile and the Euphrates in Abraham's day; their punishment, probably as being earlier depraved, took place between his time and that of Moses; the Anakim, who dwelt at

Hebron in the hill-country of Judah, the
Emim, who occupied the country east of the
Dead Sea, afterwards Moab, the Zamzummim,
who dwelt in what was afterwards called Ammon, &c., being so utterly " destroyed by the
Lord," by the agency of the children of Lot,
&c., who dwelt in their country, that, in the
time of Joshua, " only Og, the king of Bashan,
remained of the remnant of the giants."

Besides these nations, the Chorim or Horites,
who occupied Mount Seir, were destroyed to
make room for the children of Esau, or the
Edomites; and the Avim for " the Philistines,
the remnant of the country of Caphtor" —
" who came out of Caphtor"—" whom," God
emphatically tells us, " I brought from Caphtor."

Caphtor is the same word as Egypt or Copt,
applied in scripture to Lower, as Pathros is to
Upper Egypt, or the Thebaid.

It is clear, therefore, from the word of

truth, that God, our Author and Disposer, " who hath made of one blood all nations of men for to dwell on all the face of the earth, and hath determined the times before appointed, and the bounds of their habitation"— brought the Philistines, after some great revolution which reduced them to the mere remnant of a once powerful nation, out of Lower Egypt into the land of Canaan.

While Canaan was peopled by the descendants of the younger, Egypt was so by those of the elder son of Ham, the Misraim. From her great natural advantages, she soon rose to civilization, and flourished till a nomadic race, surnamed the Uk-sos, or Royal Shepherds, (by some, says Manetho, supposed of Arabian origin) poured down upon the country, subdued the natives, and held the sceptre for two hundred and sixty years, till the natives roused themselves, and, after a long and bloody contest, compelled them to take refuge at

Abaris, probably Pelusium, a stronghold on
the Eastern branch of the Nile, which their
first king had fortified as "the bulwark of
Egypt" against the Assyrians, then the dominant power in Asia. After a tedious siege,
the Egyptians, in despair of getting rid of
them otherwise, allowed them to depart, with
their families and cattle, in quest of another
settlement, which they did, in the direction of
Syria.

It must have been during this usurpation
that Abraham visited Egypt, for the revolution
by which they were expelled had evidently
taken place shortly before Joseph's time, when
" every shepherd was" such " an abomination
to the Egyptians," that the pasturing Israelites
were assigned the district of Goshen, " the
best of the land," rich unoccupied pasture-
ground, for their residence, that they might
dwell there with their flocks and herds apart
from the natives ; by which providential sepa-

ration they were preserved as a distinct people. Jacob passed through Goshen, and Joseph met him there, on his road from Canaan to Egypt; the Israelites did not cross the Nile when they quitted Egypt; Goshen, therefore, lay to the east, probably along the eastern bank of the Pelusiac branch of the Nile. Why was " the best of the land" unoccupied, but because the shepherd owners had just been expelled?

Now, when we read in the Bible that the Philistines came out of Lower Egypt, and were settled in the land of Canaan before the arrival of the Israelites, from whose triumphant exodus (though Manetho ignorantly, and Josephus wilfully, confounds them) their's differed in being so calamitous an expulsion that " a remnant" only survived, though that remnant was numerous enough to subdue the Avim, and occupy their country; and when, naturally inquiring what light Egyptian history throws on the subject, we find this story

of the expulsion of the shepherd kings, in the
direction of Canaan, at a period anterior to the
arrival of Joseph; is it possible to doubt the
identity of the royal shepherds and the Philistines? — that warlike people, those " foreigners" of the Septuagint, speaking a language distinct from that of the Jews, who,
occupying the sea-coast between the Nile and
Ekron, gave it their own name, Palestina, confined by the prophet Isaiah to their pentapolis,
but afterwards extended to the whole land of
Israel, Palestine—a word, mark you, not Hebrew, but Sanscrit, and still implying, in that
language, " the shepherd's land !"

If this needed confirmation, we should find
it in the testimony borne by the Hindoo records, that a branch of the great Pali, or
shepherd race of India, whose sway extended,
from their far-famed capital, Pali-bothra, to
Siam on the east, and the Indus on the west,
the intermediate country bearing the same

name Palisthan, or Palestine, afterwards im-
posed on the land of Canaan—conquered Egypt,
and oppressed the Egyptians, in the same
manner as the Egyptian records tell us the
royal shepherds did. Nor is it less remarkable
that while Abaris, or Avaris, the stronghold of
the Auritae, or royal shepherds, in the land of
Goshen, derives its name from *Abhir*,([21]) the
Sanscrit word for a shepherd — *Goshena*, or
Goshayana, in the same language, implies
" the abode of shepherds," and *ghosha* is explained, in Sanscrit dictionaries, by the phrase
Abhiropalli, " a town or village of Abhiras or
Palis."([22])

And who, then, (to revert to the point from
which I set out), who can the *shepherd Phi-
litis*,* who fed his flocks near Memphis, whose

---

* *Bhilata* or *palita*, " a shepherd," in Sanscrit. It is
remarkable that one of the ancient Pali tribes in India
was called Rajpalli or Royal Shepherds. — *Annals of
Rajasthan, vol. i., p.* 119.

name the popular tradition of the Egyptians,
in Herodotus's time, gave to the pyramids,
built by his *cotemporaries* Cheops and Cephrenes, the tyrants who shut up their temples,
and forbade the sacrifices, and whose names
the people held in such abhorrence that they
would not pronounce them—who and what can
he be, but a personification of the shepherd
dynasty — the Palis of the Hindoo records,
who, after erecting the Pyramids, those imperishable monuments of their glory, after the
models they remembered in their native Assyria, re-appear in later years, and when fallen
from their high estate, as the Philistines, " the
remnant of the country of Caphtor," ever at
enmity with the people of God, and now, like
every nation that oppressed them, vanished from
our eyes ?

I have argued it clumsily, but do you not
now agree with me, that the pyramids were
built by the shepherd kings of Egypt, the

ancestors of the Philistines, in the time of Abraham?

And will you not sympathise with me, dear A——, when I add that the name of Pali, that once rang as the slogan of victory from the Irawaddy to the Po, — which blazed on the banner that, ages before Rome was thought of, waved as free to the wind on Mount Palatine as on the hills of Meroe, and the towers of Palibothra (what a pyramid of empire!), is now a reproach, a curse, and a hissing, to the wretches on whose outcast heads that crown of glory has descended—Pali, Pelasgi, Palatines all extinct — its sole inheritors; dwelling on the hills where erst Palibothra rose, girt round by the Rajpoots who supplanted their power and called their country by another name, and still worshipping Mahadeva, their ancestral god, who, in the twilight of Egyptian history, led their kinsmen to the conquest of Meroe and the Nile, — robbers, thieves, outcasts; of all the degraded tribes of India, there are none more miserable, one only more despised, than the Bheels, the Palis of Malwah !

Bear with me a few minutes longer. Is it too much to argue from the fact that both nations were punished only, not exterminated, by a just and discerning God — that, fearfully as both had gone astray, neither the Royal Shepherds at the period of their expulsion from Egypt, nor the Egyptians at the time of the exode of the Israelites, had reached that acme of depravity, which, at corresponding seasons in the history of the chosen people, caused the earth to swallow up the cities of the plain — to vomit forth the tribes of the Canaanites ?

And were, then, the Anakim, the Emim, the Zamzummim, the Horim, the Avim, equally depraved?   Else why were they thus exterminated ?

" The Zamzummims, a people great, and

many, and tall as the Anakims; but the Lord destroyed them before them; and " the Ammonites " succeeded them, and dwelt in their stead:

" As he did to the children of Esau, which dwelt in Seir, when he destroyed the Horims from before them; and they succeeded them, and dwelt in their stead, even unto this day;

" And the Avims, which dwelt in Hazerim, even unto Azzah, the Caphtorims, which came out of Caphtor, destroyed them, and dwelt in their stead."

—— Oh! who can sum up, who can form a conception of the misery, moral, physical, temporal, and eternal, brought into this world by sin, and laid all upon our Saviour, when the birth and death of three nations extirpated for their vices — we know nothing more of them—are summed up in three verses—a mere parenthesis in the Bible such as this!

One word more —I forget whether or not

you are a convert to the longer system of chronology, so ably advocated by our friend Dr.
Hales, by which we get six hundred additional
years before, and seven hundred after the deluge — years most welcome to the historical
antiquary, who feels himself woefully cramped
in his investigations by the common Bible
chronology, which makes Noah alive at the time
of the great apostacy at Babel, and Shem cotemporary with Abraham, Isaac, and Jacob!
May we not derive another argument for this
system from the consideration that, if God bore
with the vices of the Canaanites four hundred
years before he considered it a righteous thing
to destroy them, the Avim, Emim, Zamzummim, Horim, &c., must surely have existed as
nations at a period earlier than the received
chronology assigns to the deluge ? If not,
the Avim and Horim, to take these two as
examples, must each have become a nation,
have forsaken the patriarchal worship, sunk

into all manner of depravity, and been destroyed from the face of the earth, within six-hundred years after the deluge — judging by analogy, a manifest impossibility.

———

Adieu, dear A——; we start to-morrow for Upper Egypt.

LETTER V.

Our Dahabieh—Night-Scenes on the Nile — Pyramids of
Saccara, Dashour, &c.—The False Pyramid—Minieh—
Story of Ebn Khasib — Siout — Tombs of Lycopolis—
Stabl Antar — Traditions of the Copts — Ruins of
Abydus—Palace of Sesostris—Kenneh.

December 28, 1836.

My dear Mother,

I HAVE just been admiring our little
bark from the banks of the Nile, as she glided
slowly along, her wings spread wooing the
breeze, and a blue sky above us,

" So cloudless, clear, and purely beautiful,
That God alone was to be seen in Heaven!"

You must understand the epithet *little* as one
of endearment, according to Burke's theory of
the Beautiful; in truth, she is of ample dimensions,—come, let me describe her to you, pre-
mising that we left Siout last night, and are

now in Upper Egypt, the land of Thebes, a rapturous reality, sometimes difficult to convince ourselves of. Two crocodiles have welcomed us already; we have only just entered their territory. No hippopotami are to be seen north of the cataracts; to supply the deficiency we have named our boat " the Hippopotamus," an epithet by no means mal-appropriate to a river-riding bark like our's.

She is of the *dahabieh* class, the middle size of those employed on the Nile. Our first care, after securing her, was to have her sunk, to destroy the rats and vermin, then to have her painted and repaired; she is now quite clean, and, I hope, will last so a good while. The inner and smaller cabin is just large enough for me; the larger is furnished with a Turkish divan on one side, and William's bed on the other, with a table between and a mat below: the windows are Venetian blinds, and open or shut at pleasure, with chintz curtains drawing

across them; on the pannels we have suspended three pair of pistols, our large *far-
keeker*, straw hats, looking-glass, &c., &c. A
sword, with which we equip our dragoman,
Abdallah, when we go on shore in state, and
William's gun and rifle, occupy the corner.
Shelves are put up in both cabins; in mine I
have marshalled our little library, which looks
charmingly there.

In front of the cabin a large tent is pitched,
of double canvas, open at the mast-end, furling
upwards at the sides during the day, and
closed in at night, when Missirie, Abdallah,
and Hadji Achmet (an Arab *help*) sleep on its
cushioned divans.   Here we breakfast and
dine; we live here, in fact, during the day-
time, and after dinner (sunset) adjourn to the
cabin to drink a cup of delicious Mocha coffee,
and read till tea-time, then again till about
midnight—and Bedfordshire.

Beyond the tent, and facing the mast, is the

kitchen, a little edifice of wood and brick-work, where Missirie presides as *cuisinier*, and a first-rate *artiste* he is. Beyond the mast are the quarters of the crew, and a small cannon.

The crew consist of ten men, besides the reis or captain ; they are active, willing, good-humoured fellows, and have harmonious voices, a great lounge (to speak Etonice), as the Arab boatmen are a noisy set, constantly singing to their work, and always in chorus ; one of them leads, and the rest join in, generally line by line, alternately, neither uttering more than five or six words at a time. The chorus of each song is always the same, but the Cory-phæus, or leader, seems to sing *ad libitum*, words and air both, often deviating into a wild yell.

A curious scene was going on around us three or four evenings ago. We are now in Ramadan, the Mahommedan Lent, always rigorously kept by the Arabs, who taste no-

thing from sunrise to sunset. The sun had
gone down behind the bank of the river, but,
as they might not eat till the legal hour of
sunset, there they sat, poor fellows ! each with
an onion in his hand, their eyes fixed on Missirie's watch, by which he was to let them
know when they might conscientiously set to.
That evening was a very merry one ; squatted
in a circle, they sang unceasingly for two
hours or more — strange wild chants, keeping
time by clapping their hands, a custom handed
down to them from the ancient Egyptians, and
to the accompaniment of a rude tambour or
drum. Each song ended with two extraordinary yells, not inharmonious, in which all
joined, the voices dropping, as if from ex-
haustion, at the close. Between each song
was heard the distant chorus of a crew toiling
on the other side of the river, and the whistling
drone of a reed-pipe from a boat full of Bedouins from the west, pilgrims to Mecca,

keeping company with us ; sitting silent and
motionless, their features almost invisible —
their dark eyes gleaming from under their
massive white drapery — never saw I figures
more savagely picturesque ! The reises, meanwhile, being in the complimentary mood, guns
and pistols were going off every moment, each
followed up by the yell of all the crews, succeeded, at least on board *our* vessel, by another
song — and so on. The rolling echo of the
guns from the rocks across the river added to
the effect of this strange night-scene on the
Nile. I do enjoy these wild old airs.

We have had favourable breezes for the
most part hitherto, and have gone night and
day, the crew relieving each other ; the breeze
generally fails at sunset, when they punt the
boat, or tow it along the shore. We constantly run aground, and then they dash over
into the water, fearless of the crocodiles, and
push away, hands and shoulders, to the usual

chant of " Haylee sa! haylee sa!" till they clear her. William gets a walk and a little shooting every day, and I often accompany him as his gamekeeper. The banks, as we skim past them, are sometimes absolutely covered with wild geese — fire a gun, and they rise in myriads, as *clangingly* as Homer heard them settle on the banks of the reedy Cayster.

And what delicious weather! the morning and evening clear and transparent as the dew; but no pencil could paint, no tongue describe, the rich glow of the western sky at sunset, or the pink zone that girdles the horizon as the night falls, — pink at first, but changing from shade to shade, like the cheek of Iris, till the last, a delicate green, like chrysophraz, darkens into night. And night, how lovely! the moon riding triumphantly along, not *let into* the sky, as in the north, but visibly round and detached — you can see far beyond her, — with all her starry train around her, " the poetry of hea-

ven !" But richer sunsets and lovelier nights
are before us,—en avant !

We are pressing on for Thebes, and have
consequently left several interesting objects
unvisited till our return, when we shall be
better judges of their merit. We started
under peculiarly gratifying auspices, fairly
distancing a boat that put off in pursuit of us
from the custom-house ; had they boarded us,
a teskeray, which we had received that morning from M. Piozin, the vice-consul, would
have cleared us.

Never, dear mother, knew I what luxury
was till now ! I have realised Horace's idea of
complete repose in lying at length under a
green arbutus, (at least as shady a tree) beside
his own bright fountain at Lucretilis, but what
is that to reclining under a tent, on a Turkish
divan, in an Arab boat, ascending the Nile — a
never-ending diorama of loveliness ! villages,
dove-cots, mosques, santons' tombs, hermits'

cells, temples, pyramids, avenues of the thorny
acacia (from which the country derives one of
its old Sanscrit names), and, lovelier than all,
groves after groves of date trees,

> " bending
> Languidly their leaf-crowned heads,
> Like youthful maids, when sleep, descending,
> Warns them to their silken beds,—

all slumbrous—all gliding past like the scenery
of a dream —without effort — peacefully — si-
lently ; and yet, as when watching the stars at
midnight, you feel all the while as if the
sweetest music were murmuring in your ear.

The Pyramids of Djizeh, of Abousir, of Saccara, of Dashour — the False Pyramid, as it is
called, rising in degrees, as we are told the
Tower of Babel did, — all these have flitted
past, and minaretted Minieh, the largest town
on the Nile between Cairo and Siout : —

Ages ago, in the days of the Abbassides, to
whom Egypt bowed the knee from the middle
of the eighth to that of the ninth century, one

of the Caliphs, even the great Haroun Al
Raschid himself, was displeased with the Egyptians, and, desirous at once to punish, and
make them an example to others, picked out
the lowest of his slaves, one Ebn Khasib, the
bath-warmer of the palace, and sent him governor to Egypt, in the confidence that the
insolence, rapacity, and cruelty of such a ruler
would amply express his resentment. Never
was a man more mistaken than the Caliph;
never was Egypt happier than under the mild
rule of Ebn Khasib. His fame spread far and
wide; many even of the Caliph's immediate
courtiers, and one, especially, of his nearest
kinsmen, visited and were entertained by him;
in short, Ebn Khasib was a second Chebib.

On the return of his kinsman to Bagdad,
the Caliph, who had remarked and wondered at
his absence, inquired where he had been?
"To Egypt," replied the prince, and proceeded
to extol the humanity, justice, benevolence, and

generosity of the governor, and display the presents he had received from him. The Caliph, enraged at the failure of his scheme, sent instant and peremptory orders for his degradation, that his house should be razed to the ground, his goods confiscated, his eyes put out, and that he should be cast forth, naked and a beggar, into the streets of Bagdad.

To hear, of course, was to obey; a few weeks, and behold! Ebn Khasib, friendless, hungry, destitute, groping his way through the streets, or sitting near the gate of the Seraglio, forgotten by his old fellow-slaves, unheeded by the nobles who had eaten his bread and salt in Egypt, and whose silken garments touched as they swept past him; the summer birds flee with the summer flowers !

He was accosted one morning by a poet : — "Ebn Khasib," said he, "I was on the point of starting for Egypt with a poem in your praise; your arrival here in Bagdad saves me the trouble of that long journey, and, if you will listen, I shall have great pleasure in repeating it."

" Poor and blind, naked and miserable," replied Ebn Khasib, " what have I to give thee? Go, my friend, seek a richer patron ; *my* star has set."

" Only listen to me," replied the child of song, " and, as for recompense, God only do for you as you have done for others !"

Khasib listened, and his heart was touched ; they were the first words of sympathy that had consoled him in his misfortunes. " Cut open this seam," said he, when the song was ended, " and accept this ruby ;" it was the only valuable that he had been able to secrete on the wreck of his fortunes. The poet expostulated. Ebn Khasib insisted, and the poet accordingly carried the gem for sale to the jewellers' bazar.

" Such a stone," cried the syndik of the

jewellers, "can only belong to the Caliph,"
and before the Caliph they brought him. He
told his little story; the Caliph's eye glistened,
he sent for Ebn Khasib, owned he had done
wrong, loaded him with presents, and sent him
back to Egypt proprietor of Minieh, the spot
he was fondest of in all the valley of the Nile—
that Nile, to whose bounty the poet's fancy had
likened his own; the place is still called after
him "Minieh Ebn Khasib," and his posterity
flourished there for I cannot say how many
generations, since they were extinct when my
authority, Ebn Batuta, visited the spot in the
fourteenth century.

"As pretty a story as that of Queen Rhodope
and her slipper!" But this is *true*, dear Wee
ones! And what a commentary on the prophecy: — "Egypt shall be a base kingdom —
the basest of kingdoms!" Surely, looking
merely to the cause of Ebn Khasib's promotion,
her subjection to the warrior Mamalukes was
not so degrading! ([23])

Siout, on the west bank of the river, was
the first place we stopped at, to visit the catacombs and tombs of ancient Lycopolis, excavated in the mountain that overhangs that city,
the modern capital of Upper Egypt.   For
many hours before arriving at Manfalout, ([24])
the vast rocks that edge in the Nile to the
east are perforated with hundreds of grottoes,
some natural, others cut by the hand of man,
and often at a great height above the water —
the retreats of the Christian hermits who
treated Athanasius so kindly during his repeated exiles from Alexandria.   We often
sailed close under them, and with the glass
I could see far within the dusky portals, un-
crossed now for many centuries. The tombs of
Lycopolis, (so called from the old Egyptian
wolf-worship), were in later times appropriated
by a similar swarm to that which hived north
of Manfalout : — " They sunk," says Gibbon,
" under the painful weight of crosses and chains,

and their emaciated limbs were confined by
collars, bracelets, gauntlets, and greaves of
massy and rigid iron; they often usurped the
den of some wild beast whom they affected to
resemble; they buried themselves in some
gloomy cavern which art or nature had scooped out of the rock, and the marble quarries of
Thebais are still inscribed with the monuments
of their penance." This he says generally of
the Anchorets, but the description is peculiarly
appropriate to those of Lycopolis, who ejected
the mummies of wolves to make living mummies of themselves! Some of the grottoes,
however—those, probably, appropriated to the
wealthier human mummies, are of noble proportions; they are excavated, one above another,
in the receding face of the rocks. We visited,
I believe, all the larger, and explored with
torches some of the smaller catacombs to
which they lead; many of them end abruptly,
others seem to be continued far into the bowels

of the mountain. Every where the ground
sounds hollow under the feet, and one must
walk with caution, the floors being full of
mummy-pits and depressions where the earth
has fallen in.

The first excavation we reach'ed is called
" Stabl Antar," after the far-famed " lover of
Ibla." A lofty archway leads you into a hall
of noble proportions, once most elaborately
ornamented with hieroglyphics on the walls,
and the richest tracery on the ceiling, flowers
and diamond-shaped devices, of different pat-
terns and colours, succeeding each other in
parallel rows; they are now much defaced,
and, from the description a Danish traveller
of last century gives of them, must have
suffered much during the last hundred years.
Great pains seem to have been taken with this
chamber; we found in none of the others
such elaborate ornament or such beautiful proportions.

Leading the way up the hill, our *guides
following* us, we found, above the Stabl Antar,
a range of smaller excavations, and, above
them again, a third tier, more extensive but of
rougher workmanship than the first; a very
large hall, once ornamented with hieroglyphics, and supported by square pillars (left
standing when the grotto was hewn out of the
rock), forming a cross with an inner chamber,
narrower but longer, leading to further catacombs and passages. Regaining the face of
the mountain, which looks N. E., and turning
to the left, we came to another very large hall
on the same tier, originally entered by a vestibule between two square pillars, both now
gone; of two others, which corresponded to
them at the farther end, the one to the right
only remains. On the right, entering the
vestibule, is a large tablet of hieroglyphics,
beautifully sculptured, especially the birds,
and coloured blue; to the left, on entering the

hall, are the remains of sculptures running along the wall, three rows of warriors marching in procession, with large shields, covering nearly the whole body, and long spears or billhooks. The lower row is almost gone. Above them, and below—as it were supporting, the ceiling — runs an elegant frieze of ornaments shaped like daggers. Bones and fragments of mummies are lying here and there, wherever the riflers of the mummy-pits have thrown them—disgusting objects.

Proceeding to the left, we came to another large and loftier hall, much fallen in; many other chambers at different heights of the mountain have suffered the same fate. After visiting two or three other ranges of excavations one above another, we reached the summit of the mountain, and enjoyed a lovely view over the valley of the Nile—itself a river of verdure meandering through the desert, diversified with date-groves, the dark-foliaged fig-sycamore, and avenues of the yellow-blossoming Egyptian acacia, alternating with fields of the richest produce, every shade of green, striped with canals and water-courses; the white minarets, towering over the capital of upper Egypt, rendering a town of mud houses the most picturesque object in the landscape. ([25])

Interesting too—very interesting—is Siout, as the residence of our Saviour and his Virgin mother, after the flight into Egypt, if we may lend the ear of credulity to the traditions of the Copts, who consider the place holy, and often come here to die. ([26]) An ancient sycamore at Matarea, near the plain of Heliopolis, which sheltered the holy fugitives during the heat of noon, and opened spontaneously to conceal them from the pursuers, (so runs the legend), and a grotto in old Cairo where they subsequently found refuge — both of which we visited — share with Siout in the veneration of the Copts. Looking down on Siout, it is

pleasing to remember and believe the tradition; and the fact of there being no monkish
edifice either there or at Heliopolis, lends a
degree of credibility to both legends which
one cannot concede to many of the so-called
'loca saucta' of Palestine.

The traditions of the fathers, however, point
out Hermopolis as their residence till they
removed to the balsam-grove of Matarea, ([27])
adding, that when the heaven-born child
"was, either by design or providence, carried into a temple, all the statues of the
Idol-Gods fell down, like Dagon, at the presence of the Ark, and suffered their timely and
just dissolution and dishonour, according to
the prophecy of Isaiah: 'Behold the Lord shall
come into Egypt, and the idols of Egypt shall
be moved at his presence.'"[*] Hermopolis has
now resumed her pristine name, Asmunein;
her beautiful portico burnt for lime, poor
faded flower, no one now halts to notice her;

[*] Jeremy Taylor's Life of Christ.

we passed her by some days ago. But this
is a digression.

The modern cemetery of Siout, a beautiful
object, lies on the slope of the hill we stood
on; north of the town stands the palace of
the Pasha, and to the east, beyond the Nile,
the horizon is bounded by the Gebel Mokattam,
or eastern mountains, answering to the western
or Libyan chain, on a ridge which we were
standing; sometimes approaching, sometimes
receding from the river, they hem in the valley
of Egypt, from Cairo to the cataracts.

After examining sundry other smaller tombs,
from several of which low slanting passages,
like those of the Pyramids, now choked up,
seem to run deep into the mountain, we descended through a stony valley (not a blade of
vegetation), perforated on both sides by similar
excavations (they are really countless — there
must be thousands of them), and, turning to
the left again, arrived, to my great delight,

(for, after reaching the first excavation, the lazy Arabs left me to lead the way and explore for myself), at a portal far more magnificent than any we had previously seen, — not arched (remember, every thing here is cut out of the living rock), but flat-roofed, the sides inclining towards each other with the old Egyptian courtesy, and beautifully sculptured — a tablet of hieroglyphics inscribed on either side of the entrance, but in the hall it led us into we found none. This hall, though inferior in beauty to that of Antar, appeared larger and loftier than any we had seen; if the hills of rubbish heaped up in it were cleared away, it would be very nearly a perfect square. We observed vestiges of four square pillars, stained, as in all these larger excavations, in imitation of granite; the old Egyptians excelled in these deceptions. Arched entrances are cut in every side, and, to judge by one we entered on the right, lead to low chambers of considerable

extent.   We lighted our torches, and, creeping
along, found our way to the opening of another
smaller passage, about six feet from the ground.
We climbed up it, and found ourselves in the
first large cavern we had reached above Antar's,
a very pleasant surprise.   Our descent to the
plain was soon effected, and a pleasant walk of
about half an hour brought us to our boat —
our palace rather.*

* Dec. 29. (Two days after we visited Siout). " I
noticed this morning on, or rather *in,* the bank on the
east side, a heap of immense masonried stones, and dis-
cerned hieroglyphics on one or two with my telescope, but
there was nothing to lead one to suppose there was anything further to tempt a traveller to land.   I asked what
was the name of the village ?   ' Gow el Kebir.' they said.
So these were the last remnants (which will be swept
away next summer) of the temple, which, a few years
ago, was said to be ' perhaps the most picturesque on the
banks of the Nile.'   It was singularly appropriate to find
that the extensive plain on which it stood (formed by a
deep bay in the Mokattem range), is that on which the
combat between Osiris and Typhon, the principles of good
and evil, and which has been interpreted by many learned
men to imply the contest between the Nile and the cultivated land, is fabled to have taken place." — *Mr. Ramsay's Journal.*

January 3d, 1837.

A happy new year to my dear father and mother, and all dear to me! For some days past we have made little or no progress, but this morning we are skimming along merrily; we shall perhaps reach Kenneh to-day — to-morrow certainly, if the breeze lasts. These days, however, have been days of great enjoyment. ([28])

Yesterday we rode on donkeys from Girgeh to Arabat Madfoun, the ancient Abydus, sending on our boat to wait for us at Bellini. Next to Thebes, Abydus was once the chief city of the Thebaid, but had fallen from her high estate as long ago as the Greek geographer Strabo's time, about the commencement of the Christian era. The day was lovely, and a pleasant ride of three hours and a half, through corn and bean fields, all alive with buffaloes, camels, goats, and children perfectly naked

and as brown as bricks — alternating with
groves of majestic date-trees, sheltering generally an Arab village in the heart of each, took
us to the town and burial-place of Osiris,
where the spouse of Isis was adored in his
holiest character, and where Rameses the second, the Grecian Sesostris, built himself a
palace, which it was our chief object to
visit.*

* " Jan. 2. Our route from Girgeh lay through the
rich vale of the Nile, studded with frequent villages
under groves of dates and palms,—threading our way
through fields of young wheat just preparing to sprout
into the ear, rich clover on which the cattle, camels, and
horses were grazing, tethered in lines to certain ranges,
so that the field gradually disappeared, and was again
producing another crop where they had first commenced
it,—extensive fields of beans also, and the stubble of
large sugar plantations. The large groups of the nearly
naked, half-black, savage-looking beings reminded one
of the drawings of the natives of the South Sea Islands.
The young camels were gamboling about, and here and
there an old and stiff one, instead of supporting its character for staid and solemn stateliness, might be seen,
free from the control of pack-saddle or halter, capering

Threading a noble grove of date trees, and passing the modern village, we found ourselves on the site of the ancient Abydus, mounds beyond mounds of ruins, covered with the drifted sand of the desert, — nothing visible above the soil; think, then, of our astonishment and delight at coming suddenly on a lovely little lake,

before his astonished comrades, flying before the wind at full gallop, or playing such antics as the ungainly form Nature has assigned him might admit of." — *Mr. Ramsay's Journal.*

"— The total herd receiving first from one
That leads the dance a summons to be gay,
Though wild their strange vagaries, and uncouth
Their efforts, yet resolved with one consent
To give such act and utterance as they may
To ecstacy, too big to be suppressed —
These, and a thousand images of bliss,
With which kind Nature graces every scene,
Where cruel man defeats not her design,
Impart to the *benevolent,* who wish
All that are capable of pleasure pleased,
A far superior happiness to their's,
The comfort of a reasonable joy."

nestled in a hollow of the sandhills that form a sort of amphitheatre around it, girdled with graceful date-trees, and the doum, or Theban palm, with its fantastic head-gear, like a gay coquette by the side of a lovely single-hearted woman—of such the date-tree were a fit emblem. I cannot express to you the pleasure the discovery of this little loch gave me, and which will be as vivid years hence in recollection as when first it gleamed before me, " a vision of delight."

Antiquaries have been burrowing here, as elsewhere, and have found, 'tis said, treasures; but, oddly enough, they seem to have left the palace untouched. It is almost covered with sand, so that a step or two lands you on the flat roof, which is in perfect preservation, built of enormous stones, some of them above twenty feet long. The interior also is choked with sand nearly to the capitals of the columns, and it is very fatiguing to explore it. It was near sunset, consequently we had not time for a thorough examination, but, creeping from one compartment into another, we clearly traced the extent of the grand hall, a noble apartment, supported by pillars, and beautifully sculptured in every direction, roof, walls, pillars, with hieroglyphics: — two-thirds, at least, of it are buried in the sand. Every wall, every column, in Egyptian architecture, was painted; the colours often remain as brilliant as if they had only been laid on yesterday.

While William had found his way down into the hall, I descended to the extremity of the ruins, where I found two or three other chambers, all of them vaulted, that is to say, the span of the arch cut out of the single stones, of immense thickness, that form the roof: all but one are choked up with sand; that one, after rejoining William, and visiting the hall with him, we proceeded to examine.

Here we found the most beautiful bas-reliefs
we have yet seen, more exquisitely delicate
and highly finished than I could have imagined;
as fresh too as if finished yesterday, and yet
more than three thousand years old, for Rameses succeeded to the throne of Egypt above
one thousand three hundred years B.C. The
sculptures describing his eastern conquests are
the most interesting historical documents yet
discovered in Egypt,— those we shall see at
Thebes; these at Abydus are, I dare say,
equally curious, though chiefly mythological.
One of them, representing the sacred boat, we
uncovered — it was lovely indeed. Above us,
sculptured in the roof, we recognized a genealogical tablet, which we conclude to be that of
the ancestors of Sesostris, discovered here
some years ago by Mr. Bankes — a precious
document for ancient Egyptian history.*

* " It was formed of the ovals of hieroglyphics, which
always imply some name, in a regular list, separated by

Here, too, in the very sanctum of Sesostris
—blissful moment!—I bought a papyrus—for
about eighteen-pence English! It is in very

stars. It was evidently a genealogical chart, and must
be the one spoken of, but it is odd to call a vaulted roof a
tablet. At the end we entered, the stones were ornamented with hieroglyphics in alto relievo, very protube-
rant and marked—on one side, the characters were those
of the ordinary style, but on the other there was a specimen of a very superior style, which we deeply regretted
our time did not permit us to clear away a little more.
The ground was milk-white stone, and continued in the
same coloured stucco, over part of the darker stones forming the roof; the drawings were executed with a delicacy,
vigour, and beauty we had not yet seen, and in that particular manner which, it struck me, must be peculiar to
sacred subjects. The subject was not, at first sight, apparent, but I conjectured the various groups and objects
above the sand to be all united, and form, perhaps, a boat
or vessel, which, on having it a little cleared away, we
found to be the case,— but I had no time to draw it, and
it is impossible to describe the extraordinary forms. We
are generally inclined to attach an idea of sameness and
rigidity to these hieroglyphical figures, and the poor specimens we have at home favour the idea, but in regard to
those we saw here nothing could be more incorrect. Every
figure was varied, and quite of a different character from
the others."—*Mr. Ramsay's Journal.*

tolerable preservation, but very fragile, and no
wonder, for it must be at least two thousand
years old.

The sun had gone down before we quitted
Abydus — three hours' walk to Bellini ([29])—no
matter ; it was a beautiful starlight night,—
the path, however, was difficult to keep, being
only perceptible at a distance, like the *blind
road* over a heath in Scotland, and we soon
lost our way; inquiring at a village, a man,
after offering us hospitality for the night, vo-
lunteered to put us into the right road — not
for *bagshish,* but for love ; he walked some distance with us, smoking his pipe, and we
parted with friendly signs, though in silence—
one of those little incidents that lend such a
charm to daily life. One exchanges much
courtesy of this sort here, talking by signs, a
smile winding up each sentiment, like the little
fillip in talking with one's fingers. After
reaching the river, we had some difficulty in

finding the boat, till the cannon and pistols of those on board replying to our e-pistol-ary interrogations from the shore, we soon rejoined them.

Kenneh, January 4, 1837.

We intended visiting Dendera to-day, but, having a fair wind, have written to Isis, " postponing that pleasure," &c., &c., till our return. We have just been drinking coffee and smoking our pipes with a jolly old cock of an Arab, His Britannic Majesty's consular agent here, who wanted us to dine with him, and accept his escort to Dendera — a courtesy, which we had some difficulty in evading. On rising to depart, he mounted us on two superb donkeys, and sent a dwarf to escort us to the boat.

I have no time for more, — we are ready to start. We are both well — God bless my dear mother !

LETTER VI.

Thebes—Temples—Sculptures — Tombs — Fulfilment of the Prophecies.

Esneh — Edfou — Essouan — Ascent of the Cataracts — Nubia—Upper Cataracts—Wellee Kiashef—Disaster and detention at Essouan.

Temples of Herment—Dendera—Ombos—Tombs of Be-nihassan—Memphis—Pyramids of Saccara and Dashour — Cairo.

February 3, 1837.
Returning down the Nile.

FAR have we wandered, and much have we seen, dearest mother, during the last month and a half. We arrived at Thebes, glorious Thebes! the day after I despatched my letter from Kenneh, and fired our cannon in triumph; we always do so on reaching any place which forms an epoch in our voyage; it astonishes the natives. We saluted a Turkish Kiashef, or governor, the other evening, as he left our boat, after dining and chatting with us for three

hours; the poor man *tottered* with astonishment, he took it in very good part, however—
more of him anon.

Colonel Vyse, whose boat was moored alongside of our's, paid us a visit the evening we
arrived at Thebes. He advised our taking
advantage of the favourable wind, and proceeding direct to Nubia before it changed. It
was impossible absolutely to turn our backs on
Thebes without one glance at her, yet the
advice was not to be rejected in toto, and we
therefore took a hurried look only at the ruins,
merely to familiarise ourselves with their plan ;
on our return, we examined them minutely,
but I will say now all that I think will interest
you on the subject.

For a glance at the principal objects, two
days suffice ; the first we devoted to the western
or Libyan suburb, for the Nile divides the City
of Ammon into two portions, of which the
Eastern is the most considerable. Mounting,

therefore, a couple of Arab steeds, we started
for the ruins, Ali Massaoud, the guardiano,
leading the way, with a long spear on his
shoulder.

We soon came in sight of

" Memnon's statue which at sunrise played,"

and his companion, and in about half an hour
dismounted at Gournou, to visit the temple of
Ammon, the Theban Jupiter, begun by Osirei,
and finished, with the palace contiguous to it,
by his illustrious son, Rameses the second. It
is small comparatively, but very interesting, the
columns of the portico, lotus-stalks bound
together evidently the prototype of the Doric.
The Eastern court was the hall of assembly of
ancient Thebes. A royal palace was attached
to most of the great temples; the priests
were equally well lodged in the lateral
apartments.

Do you remember the discovery struck out
some years ago by Dr. Young, and perfected by

Champollion, of a hieroglyphical alphabet, by which they were enabled to read the names of all the kings who have recorded themselves on the ancient monuments of Egypt? It is to this discovery that we now owe the exact knowledge when, and by whom, every temple was built and tomb excavated. This alphabet gives us no insight into the wisdom concealed under the abstruser hieroglyphics, yet we owe to it many gleams of history, not the least interesting of which is the confirmation of all that ancient historians have told us — so long discredited—of the glory of Sesostris.

Memnon's statue is indeed a marvel—between fifty and sixty feet high, and originally of one block of stone; he fell asunder before our Saviour's time, but was rebuilt soon afterwards; his companion is still entire as a whole, though the features are much defaced. The name of Memnon is a misnomer;* they represent

* Corrupted from Mi-ammon, "the beloved of Ammon," the favourite title of Rameses the Great, con-

Amunoph the third, who flourished about a century before Sesostris. Hadrian and his ill-fated queen Sabina stood and gazed up at them just where we did, and, among the numerous inscriptions that prove Memnon's identity, we read, with no small interest, the names of the Roman ladies who accompanied their imperial mistress, and heard (as an in-scription which I could not find testifies), the " unseen melody" salute the ill-assorted pair *twice*, the morning they were there. And there they will sit, probably, to the end of time; looking down in the same silent austere majesty on pilgrims from lands unheard of when they were born — peoples even yet uninscribed in the muster-roll of nations. These statues marked the termination of a noble avenue, which led to the temple and palace of Amu-

founded by the Greeks with the Memnon of Homer; and applied by them indifferently to all the Pharaohs so sur-named. See an interesting note, p. 9, of Mr. Wilkinson's " Topography of Thebes."

noph, now levelled to the ground; two or three colossi, which once ornamented this grand approach, lie across it on their faces, half-buried under the soil accumulated by successive inundations.

The Memnonium, as the palace and temple of Sesostris are now misnamed, is indeed a noble ruin. The enormous granite statue of the monarch, overthrown by Cambyses, lies on its face, prone as Dagon fell, the upper half split into two or three vast fragments, the lower shivered to atoms; the workmanship is exquisite. He sat a little in advance of the temple, his hands on his knees, resting after his conquests. Judge of his stature by the breadth of his shoulders, twenty two feet! Not *quite* such a giant, either, as Gog Magog Mac Finn Mac Coull, whose mouth was eleven miles wide, his teeth ten miles square;

> " He wad upon his taes upstand,
> And tak the stars doun with his hand,
> And set them in a gold garland
>   To deck his wifis hair."

Near the colossus lie the neck and shoulders
of another statue of Rameses, better known as
that of "young Memnon," whose head Belzoni
removed to England.

I cannot express to you how delighted
William and I have been with the historical
sculptures that the temples of the age of
Sesostris are adorned with. The battle scenes
on the Memnonium have reminded every traveller of Homer, and it is not unlikely, if he
did visit Egypt, that he may have studied
them, though in his sacred character of bard
he must have seen many a noble melée — for
blind, born blind at least, he could not have
been; Schlegel has convinced me of this,
A——'s favourite critic, and mine, since she
introduced me to him. The sculptures, however, Homeric as they are, remind me as much
or more, of the glowing war-imagery of the
Prophets; lend them the eyes, the ears of your
imagination, and you have " the rattling of the
wheels, and of the prancing horses, and of the

jumping chariots; the shield of the mighty men is made red, the valiant men are dyed scarlet, the chariots rage in the streets—they justle one against another in the broad ways; the horseman lifteth up the flame of the sword, and the lightning of the spear, and there is a multitude of the slain, and a great number of carcases, and there is none end of their corpses — they stumble upon their corpses." The "horse and his rider" — the chariots of Pharaoh—all are pictured here, such as Moses beheld them.*

But, after all, is not this resemblance of Homer and the prophets to these sculptures and to each other very simply to be accounted for, by the similar state of society that pre-

* Mr. Ramsay's observations on the sculptures and paintings of Thebes, and of Egypt generally — scattered through his Journal — will be found collected together at the close of the first part of this letter; they will thus be read somewhat in the order in which he would probably have arranged them himself.

vailed in the respective countries during the
heroic ages? "Antar," is in many passages
as Homeric as the Iliad — for the same reason.
We are apt to think of none but the heroic age
of Homer, yet the world has never been without an heroic age, acting on one of her hundred
national stages. What the age of Antar was
to the Saracens, of Camillus to the Romans,
of Achilles to the Greeks, of Joshua to the
Jews, of Rustum to the Persians — that of
Sesostris was to the Egyptians.

The magnificent hall of the Memnonium
(you enter it between gigantic statues, twenty
feet high, their arms folded, tranquil and
sublime in the consciousness, it would seem,
of benevolence and power), opens into a smaller
chamber, to me by far the most interesting as
the repository of the books of Thoth — the
earliest library on record! The ceiling is
astronomical, and very interesting, as the date
of Sesostris's reign is determined by it to B.C.

1322, the year from which the grand Canicular
cycle of 1461 years, hieroglyphically veiled
under the story of the Phœnix, began. On the
northern wall of this library, Sesostris is represented seated under the Tree of Life, which
overshadows him, while Ammon-re and Thoth,
or Mercury, write his name on the leaves*—
one of the many curious patriarchal memories
preserved among the Egyptians.

From the Memnonium we rode to the ruins
at Medinet Habou—Medina Tabu, as it ought
to be written—that is to say, the city Tabu—
Thebes; for Tapo, the Sanscrit, and Tape, the
Coptic, name could only be accommodated to
Arab pronunciation by the substitution of *b*
for *p*.† We visited the smaller temple first;
the area, gateway, and propylon you enter by,

* " Her leaf hath withered on the Tree of Life."
Thalaba.—B.x. 26. And see note.
† Tapovana, or Tabenna, is the name always given to
Upper Egypt in the sacred books of the Hindoos.—*Vide*
Wilford on Egypt and the Nile (Asiatic Researches, v. 3).

and the second area and propylon — additions
of yesterday, the former by the Ptolemies and
Cæsars, the latter by Tirhaka, king of Ethiopia, the rival of Sennacherib — introduce you
to the original edifice, built by a nameless predecessor of the second and third Thothmes,
who completed it rather more than one thousand five hundred years B.C. The small six-
teen-sided pillars in the oldest part of the
building bear still a nearer resemblance to the
Doric than those we observed at Gournou.

The palace of Rameses the Third stands
contiguous to the smaller, and to the south of
the larger, temple. You ascend to it between
two pavilions — porters' lodges, probably —
built in advance of the lofty towers, but there
are no menials now to hinder your intrusion
into the most private apartments of the Pharaoh. In the sculptures of one of the upper
rooms, the floor of which has fallen in, you see
him, seated with his wife and daughters around
him—'tis like seeing their ghosts !

Beyond the palace, traversing a spacious area, two enormous pyramidal propyla (towers of entrance, that is to say — and I ought to have said it before — truncated, and connected by a curtain pierced with a doorway), introduce you into the great court of the temple, eclipsing all you have seen of previous grandeur. Do not expect architectural plans or descriptions from me—I have neither time nor patience for them — I will only say that all I had anticipated of Egyptian magnificence fell short of the reality, and that it was here, surveying those Osiride pillars, that splendid corridor, with its massy circular columns, those walls lined, within and without, with historical sculptures of the deepest interest, the monarch's wars with the Eastern nations bordering on the Caspian and Bactriana — study for months, years rather! it was here, I say, here, where almost every peculiarity of Egyptian architecture is assembled in perfection, that I first learnt to appreciate the spirit of that extraordinary people, and to feel that, poetless as they were, they *had* a national genius, and had stamped it on the works of their hands, lasting as the Iliad. Willing slaves to the vilest superstition, bondsmen to form and circumstance, adepts in every mechanical art that can add luxury or comfort to human existence—yet triumphing abroad over the very Scythians, captives from every quarter of the globe figuring in those long oblational processes to the sacred shrines in which they delighted, after returning to their native Nile— that grave, austere, gloomy architecture, sublime in outline and heavily elaborate in ornament, what a transcript was it of their own character! and where could Clio write their history so appropriately as on the walls of their temples? — And never were pages more graphic. The gathering, the march, the melée — the Pharaoh's prowess, standing erect, as

he always does, in his car — no charioteer —
the reins attached to his waist — the arrow
drawn to his ear—his horses all fire, springing
into the air like Pegasuses, — and then the
agony of the dying, transfixed by his darts,
the relaxed limbs of the slain—Homer's truth
itself; and, lastly, the triumphant return, the
welcome home, and the offerings of thanks-
giving to Amunre — the fire, the discrimi-
nation with which these ideas are bodied forth,
they must be seen to judge of it.

Here, on our first visit, we met Colonel Vyse,
and accompanied him to a place called Qoornet Murraee, to see the tomb of the elder
brother of Amunoph the third—the melodious
Memnon. The entrance is a mere hole in the
side of the hill; we crept in on all-fours:—
though inferior in size and beauty to the tombs
we afterwards visited, the paintings lend it the
highest interest, representing the chiefs of
Cush, or Ethiopia, bringing gold rings, (the

money of those times), skins, a cameleopard,
&c., tribute to Pharaoh. In an upper compartment, the sable queen of Ethiopia, throned
on her chariot, with the chattah, or umbrella
of state, and a train of attendants carrying
presents, pays a visit to the monarch of Egypt;
so attended, must the Cushite queen of Sheba
have approached king Solomon, and thus will
" the kings of Tarshish and the Isles bring
presents." " the kings of Sheba and Seba offer
gifts"—" the gold of Sheba," to " the king's
son," the " greater than Solomon," at Jerusalem. (³⁰)

After visiting another old temple called Deir
el Bahree, at the very foot of the western
mountains, which tower up majestically above
it, we retraced our steps, and, climbing over
the hills, descended into the valley of the
tombs of the kings by a narrow and precipitous
ravine—not the regular approach, but far more
impressive. The valley is desolation itself,

long and winding, shut in by lofty rocks—not
a trace of vegetation; fit scene for the funeral
processions of mighty Pharaohs — fit indeed
for the last home of the extinct dynasties of a
vanished nation ! They are temples rather
than tombs, broad passages and gorgeous
chambers opening one into another, till you
find yourself in the lofty hall of the sarcophagus, terminating each. Some of them run
three or four hundred feet into the heart of the
mountain, a gradual slope figuring the descent
into Amenti, the Egyptian Hades, or world
unseen. The most beautiful are those of the
Pharaohs who reigned from Rameses the First,
grandfather of Sesostris, to Rameses the Fifth,
in whose reign Troy was taken, B.C. 1184,
inclusive. A regular series of portraits of
the Pharaohs might be taken from these
tombs ; the likenesses are always exactly
preserved.

The spoilers have been at work in Belzoni's

tomb ; it makes the heart ache and the cheek burn to see such wanton outrage ; one whole pillar (to say nothing of partial robberies, figures cut in two for the sake of a limb or an ornament) has been stript of its sculptures, and stands a melancholy wreck, naked and dazzlingly white, amidst its companions, the chips all around it — tongues of reproach, that curse the hand that maimed it !

But, in spite of all this sacrilege, wonderful, indeed, and brilliant is this tomb : the great hall, where the sarcophagus once stood, is rich beyond conception in hieroglyphics, sculptures, and general ornament, but the unfinished chamber beyond it, where you see the simple and beautiful outlines drawn for the sculptor to work upon, and corrected by the master's hand, is to a lover of the arts by far the most interesting of the series. The whole is so fresh, and the drawing so beautiful, that you almost expect the return of the artist, and feel

it would be a shame to go without compli-
menting him on his performance. He was
embalmed three thousand years ago — for this
was the tomb of Osirei, the father of Sesostris !

In Bruce's tomb—poor calumniated Bruce !—
(I felt more pleasure in visiting it for his sake
than for the real owner's, Rameses the Third)
—we saw the paintings of harps, copied and
published by him, from which it has sometimes
been called the " Harper's tomb," but shall
not be so by me : — the harps are of the most
elegant construction, and one of the performers
seems to be damping the strings just like a
modern performer. They are respectively of
eleven strings and thirteen—or fourteen, I
could not ascertain which. I have counted
the harp-strings in almost every tomb ; there
seems to have been no fixed number. I have
seen also the five-stringed lyre, like that Apollo
played on among the Muses, the guitar, ex-

actly like the modern instrument, and held in
the same manner, a sort of mandoline, the
double flute, &c.   They kept time by clapping
hands ; Herodotus mentions this, and our
Arab-Egyptian sailors practise it, when singing in the evenings.

There are many other paintings in the side-
chambers of Bruce's tomb, of great interest as
illustrative of the manners and domestic life of
the Egyptians ; in one you have the whole
process of sowing and reaping, in another the
mysteries of Egyptian cookery ; a third is a
painted armoury; in a fourth you see every
description of Egyptian furniture, to the full
as elegant as that of Greece — arm-chairs like
our own, and of the most inviting appearance,
ottomans precisely like our's, steps for ascending to bed — at least exactly resembling
those used in England for that purpose, and
sofas, with crescents for the leg and neck to
rest upon—luxurious appendages which Cow-

per had never heard of when he wrote the
Task.

The tomb of Rameses the Fifth is peculiarly
interesting, and Champollion has described it
as a guide to the rest, the subjects represented
in it being found in most of the other tombs,
but not so detailed. The roof of the passage
leading to the principal chamber is most richly
painted, red and black, in the style of the
Etruscan vases. The ceiling of the chamber of the sarcophagus is quite beautiful, and
delightfully mystical, describing the procession of the Sun, through the hours of the day
and night — emblematical of the life of the
terrestrial luminary, Ph're, the Sun, or Pharaoh, of Egypt. The symbolical paintings are
enclosed by the double body of Nith, the
goddess of the firmament, prolonged, like the
folds of a serpent, round the ceiling and
through the middle of it, separating the day
from the night. In the east, Nith becomes the

mother of the Sun, an infant, who is carefully
placed in the bark, in which he descends the
celestial river with a large cortège of deities.
Each hour of the day is marked by a globe—
of the night by a star. They begin sounding
at the seventh hour, and a pilot comes to steer
them through the remaining hours of light, the
river growing shallower and shallower, till, at
the twelfth, the scene changes, and, veering
round in the great western lake into which the
river empties itself, they commence their
return eastwards, through the hours of the
night, towed by ropes up a branch of the
Celestial River, which terminates, like the
main stream, in the western lake. The sun is
attended only by the pilot and one other deity
during this nocturnal voyage.

I am not sure that this description is precisely correct, for the vault of this hall of
mystery was too obscure for me to see as distinctly as I could have wished. Tablets of

hieroglyphics are interspersed with the symbolical paintings, describing, says Champollion,
the celestial influences of each hour on the
several parts of the human body. In a recess,
at the end of the hall, Tethys, the wife of
Oceanus, stretches out her arms to receive the
descending bark of the Sun. In similar.
paintings in other tombs, she is represented
rising from the celestial Nile, the Oceanus of
Homer. This mysterious imagery gives one
an insight into the origin of the ancient
Grecian idea (first hinted at by Homer), that
the Ocean was a river encircling the Earth,
into which the Sun descended in the west, and
sailed round to his starting-place in the east
every night.

But the information we can gather from
these paintings as to the religious opinions of
the Egyptians is still more interesting. The
doctrines of a future state, of judgment after
death, and of rewards and punishments, are

invariable subjects of representation ; in one instance, a condemned soul is carried away in the shape of a sow, and the word *gluttony* is written over it to explain his crime ; this is probably emblematical only, but it looks like the originally Indian doctrine of transmigration, which Pythagoras is supposed to have picked up in Egypt. The punishments of the bad are frequently depicted, and the rewards of the good, who swim and sport like fish in the celestial Nile—" the rivers of the waters of life ?"

But, amidst these gleams of traditional truth, " every form of creeping things and abominable beasts, and all the idols of the house of Israel, are portrayed upon the wall round about," in these dark chambers of imagery, just as Ezekiel beheld them in the temple at Jerusalem. Serpents of the most extraordinary forms are seen in every direction—short, thick, and hooded, or long and tapering — the

latter often carried in long mystical procession, human heads surmounting their own,
or female heads growing, as it were, on their
backs, between each bearer. Belzoni's tomb
is rich in serpents; I saw there a beautiful
winged snake, with three heads and four
human legs; others had a head at each extremity, crowned with the corn-measure and
mitre, the body, curving downwards, supported
by four human legs, two looking each way;
others with four or five legs respectively. On
each side of the descent to the sepulchral chamber of Rameses V., is a most magnificent
snake with vulture's wings. How Holden,
Faber, and those other worthy men who have
written so ably and convincingly in proof of
the literal fall in Paradise through the wiles of
the serpent, arguing, among other proofs, from
the universality of serpent-worship, would
have been interested with a sight of them!
Every step I took reminded me of some inci-

dent in Indian or Grecian mythology, and convinced me more and more that every system,
eastern or western, is intimately connected in
its origin—primitive revelation and patriarchal
tradition, more or less corrupted. One subject,
frequently repeated in these tombs, forcibly
struck me—the eventual conquest of the great
serpent, Apophis, by the Gods, who transfix
him with daggers, and bind him, head and
foot, with ropes: it was impossible not to
think of the prophecies.

What a commentary are these tombs on that
most sublime passage of Isaiah, in which
Hades, the world unseen, personified, is represented as stirring up the mighty dead, all the
kings of the nations, from the thrones on
which " they lie in glory, each in his own
sepulchre," 'to behold the corpse of Belshazzar, cast forth at the mouth of their long
home, unburied, trodden under foot, and dis-
honoured :—

" Art thou also become weak as we? art thou made like unto us?

" Is thy pride brought down to the grave, and the sound of thy viols? Is the worm spread under thee, and doth the earth-worm cover thee?

" How art thou fallen from heaven, O Lucifer, son of the morning !—art cut down to the earth, thou that subduedst the nations !

" Yet thou hast said in thine heart, ' I will ascend into heaven, above the stars of God I will exalt my throne; I will sit on the Mount of Congregation on the sides of the north ; ([31]) I will ascend above the heights of the clouds; I will be like the Most High !'

" But thou shalt be brought down to the grave, to the sides of the pit !

" They that see thee shall narrowly look upon thee and consider thee—' Is this the man that made the earth tremble, that did shake kingdoms ?

" That made the world as a wilderness, and destroyed the cities thereof ? that opened not the house of his prisoners ? '

" All the kings of the nations, all of them, lie down in glory, each in his own sepulchre :

" But thou art cast out of the grave, like an abominable branch, and as the raiment of those that are slain, thrust through with a sword,—that go down to the stones of the pit, —as a carcase trodden under foot !"

In front of the tomb of Amunoph's brother, I saw a mummy that once possibly was his, and wore a crown, rifled of its cerements, black and bent double, peering, like a creature of life, over the brow of the hill, as if it watched my motions ; an Arab pushed it with his foot — it fell on its side, and the back broke,—and there it lay, " a carcase trodden under foot," soon to be redissolved into the elements that human art had so many ages defrauded of their prey. " Was this the man that made the

earth tremble, that shook kingdoms?" A
Pharaoh, probably — I could have fancied him
Belshazzar; at all events, the miserable epi-
tome at my feet had been a *Man* three thousand
years before me. Hamlet might have mo-
ralized there for hours, but we have a brighter
hope—

> " Why should this worthless tegument endure,
>   If its undying guest be lost for ever ?
> Oh ! let us keep the soul embalmed and pure
>   In living virtue, that, when both must sever,
> Although corruption may our frame consume,
> The immortal spirit in the skies may bloom!" *

How often, rambling over the ruins of
Thebes, has that noble poem sung itself to
me !

But why should the kings' tombs engross all
my praise ? Gorgeous as they are, and interesting for the study of ancient mythology,
those of the private Thebans are yet more so

* From the Address to the Mummy in Belzoni's exhibition by Delta (D. M. Moir, Esq.).

for the history of manners and daily life among
the old Egyptians. Every light and shadow,
indeed, of human life, is portrayed in them,
from the laughter of the feast to the tears of the
funeral—ointments poured on the head at the
one, dust heaped on it at the other. You see on
one side the arrival of the guest in his chariot,
white horses and a train of running footmen
betokening his consequence ; the other guests,
already assembled and seated, the men apart
from the women, wait for their dinner, and be-
guile the intervening moments with smelling
the lotus-flower, and listening to the music of
the dancing-girls. The master of the house
and his wife, richly dressed, and lovingly
seated side by side, preside at the entertainment. But the tableau would be incomplete
without side-views of the shambles and the
kitchen, and a beggar at the gate, receiving a
bull's head and a draught of water from one
of the menials. Facing this, on the opposite

wall, the mourning-women, with wailing cries and dishevelled hair, precede the coffin that bears the hospitable Egyptian to his long home ; the wife or the sister walks beside it, silent in her sorrow ; a scribe takes account of the dead man's riches, his cattle, his horses, his household chattels : Death — and then the Judgment :—the deceased is ushered into Amenti ; Horus and Aroeres weigh his merits against the ostrich-feather, the symbol of Truth ;* Thoth, the god of letters, presents a scroll, the record of his thoughts, words, and works, to the Judge Osiris, into whose presence he is at length admitted on the favourable re- sult of the scrutiny. Sad presumption for man thus to usurp his Creator's prerogative of reading and judging the heart !

And amidst all these varied scenes, as if to show how narrowly joy may be partitioned off

* " The good actions are weighed in the grand balance against a feather—a fine idea."—*Mr. Ramsay's Journal.*

from sorrow, how the merry-hearted and the
broken-hearted may unconsciously pillow within an inch of each other, and how the world
jogs on in daily routine, indifferent to the feelings of either — the occupations of every-day
life are pictured in their minutest details around
you, — scenes of industry, scenes of frolic,
parties pledging each other's healths, young
folks dancing to the music of the harp, hus-
bandmen in the fields, artificers of every trade
at their work (many of them with tools precisely like those now in use), carpenters,
smiths, glass - blowers, shoemakers, wheel-
wrights, statuaries, idolmakers — I saw a god
under the graver's hand, and thought of
Isaiah's noble apostrophe, which Sir Frederick
P——, you may remember, read so beautifully that delightful evening he spent at
Haigh last summer. The illustration was perfect.

But of all the Egyptian tombs, scarcely any

interested me so much as one I visited at Elethyiæ above Thebes. Life on the one wall — Death was pictured on the other; to the left, rural occupations, ploughing, sowing, reaping, and gathering into barns — the vigour of the year and of human life; the owner and his wife, lovingly embracing each other, entertain their friends with the fruits of their labour; servants are in attendance, young men and maidens— the heyday of youth and riches; to the right he stands erect, but stiff and lifeless — the embalmer extracts his brain with a long crooked instrument, preparatory to filling the skull with aromatics and spices; that work over, the coffin is borne in solemn procession; a figure, muffled up and shapeless — his wife (she was embracing his knees five minutes ago)—is drawn on a sledge in front of it; the sacred boat of the dead, two obelisks, and two trees like cypresses — Horace's lines came across me as I gazed on

them with an indescribable feeling of melancholy,—

> " Linquenda tellus, et domus, et placens
> Uxor, neque harum, quas colis, arborum
>> Te praeter invisas cupressus,
>>> Ulla brevem dominum sequetur !"

" Thy lands, thy home, the wife of thy
bosom—all must be relinquished; nor of these
trees that thou cultivatest will any, save the
hateful cypress, accompany their short-lived
lord !"

In another tomb at Elethyiæ, you see the
father dandling his child, and the lady's pet
monkey tied to her chair.* In the tomb of

---

* " 3 Feb. We went to see the grottoes of Elythias,
which lie on the east bank, about half a mile inland. On
the way, we came upon the walls of the ancient town,
which are of crude brick, about thirty feet high, and
twenty thick, and in a very perfect state, the square
openings for the gates in the middle of each side of the
square being quite preserved: they enclose an area a mile
long, and three quarters of a mile broad. The interior is
flat and bare, except to the west, where a range of high
mounds evidently conceal what remains of the ancient

one of the royal scribes at Thebes, the young
Princess of Egypt, Amunoph the Third's
daughter, whose tutor he had been, sits on his

town. What its antiquity may be, I do not know. The
grottoes are behind it. They are chiefly tombs, of tolerable size, dug out of the mountain-face, and extending
some distance in. They are in general in a ruined state.
The pits for the mummies are very apparent in some,
and they have evidently been all ransacked and *sacked*
by previous travellers and speculators. About six or
eight of them contain designs on the walls, in a tolerably
perfect state, of which three are highly interesting. They
contain drawings, very well done, of the whole life of the
individuals of whom they treat. One gentleman, who
was a proprietor of boats on the river, then governor of
the government shipping, and, lastly, an officer in different wars under Thothmes, has a very curious tomb ; and
next to him lay a priest of the goddess presiding here.
The history begins from childhood. The principal figures
are the person and his wife, seated together on a chair,
under which is a pet monkey ; they appear to be on loving
terms, and are entertaining a party of friends, who sit
opposite a large collection of dainties ; pages pour water
on their hands, present them with lotus-leaves, &c. Behind are all the preparations,—the butchers are killing
and cutting up the oxen (very well executed)—the process of cooking goes on—the guests come over the river
in boats. In another part, the proprietor comes in his

knees, as little Minnie might on mine, and playfully puts the lotus-flower to his nose. It is nonsense limiting our sympathies by time and space—

> " A heart hath throbbed beneath the leathern breast,
> And tears adown the dusky cheek have rolled" —

and children *have* " climbed the knees and kissed the face" of every mummy that we

car to superintend all his rural affairs; ploughing, sowing, reaping, thrashing, stowing, and weighing the corn, and selling it for money in rings, and every thing connected with agriculture, are minutely represented. The songs of the different occupations are written above, and Champollion has read them, he says. Droves of oxen, donkeys, sheep, &c. very spiritedly done, are brought up to scribes, who register them. The similarity, and, in many instances, identity of things in common use with those used now in this country is very striking. The filtering water-jars, and their wooden stands, are the very same; the plough is the same, and the head-dress also. In one place boats are represented, some sailing, others being rowed, and others getting mended, or being charged or emptied. Our sailors were in raptures with them, and found out their own likenesses in the crew. The sail used was a very strange one. Again, they are drawing large nets for wild-geese, which are no sooner caught than

trample on, scarcely regarding it as the sacred
relic of humanity it really is. Human nature
was the same then as now; she has oscil-
lated between smiles and tears ever since
Adam's fall — and philosophers may say what
they please, but I will defy the most callous of
them to visit these tombs, and deny that man
may sympathise with man, his elder by half
the world's age.

The largest of all these Theban tombs is the

plucked, dressed, and served up. The funeral is a very
conspicuous part. In some the process of embalming is
shown very clearly. The body was placed on a bier, resting on a sledge, to which a long cord was attached, the end
of which was fastened to a cow, and all the mourners had
a hold of it. In some the preparations and sport of hunting is represented. These tombs are of the period of the
eighteenth dynasty — about 3300 years ago; the colours
are as fresh as ever, and, except where the people who,
probably, live in them at times, or strangers have broken
them down, they are not in the least the worse for their lon-
gevity. The precision with which the dates of all these
places is determined is quite clear: they have the dates
inscribed, even to the day and month, in general."—*Mr.*
Ramsay's Journal.

least interesting, except from its immense extent, ramifying over more than an acre of ground — exceeding that of any of the royal sepulchres. A priest, named Petamunap, excavated it for himself, and probably his family, quite recently — in the seventh century, B.C. It is blackened with smoke and dirt; the bats flew past us in swarms, as we intruded on their dusky domains; the descent to the lower range of excavations was like the mouth of Hades itself—I never plunged into a place so dreary.

So much for Western Thebes. You may well imagine it took us some days to examine all the places I have described.   We visited the temples the first day of our first visit, and some of the principal tombs, and a day of delight it was. Colonel Vyse sailed for Cairo the moment we reached Gournou, where the boats were moored; we saluted him with our cannon, and then crossed to the other side of the river.

The next morning, we visited the temples of Luxor and Carnac. The former is a most magnificent pile, architecturally considered, but otherwise the least interesting of the four great temples of Thebes. You originally entered between four gigantic statues of Rameses the Great, and two superb obelisks, of which one only remains—the French have carried off his brother, and every lover of antiquity must regret their separation. The obelisks, statues, and pyramidal towers were additions by Rameses to the original edifice, founded by Amunoph the Third.

From the propyla and obelisks of this temple, an avenue, guarded by sphinxes, facing each other, extended northwards, to the great temple of Jupiter Ammon at Carnac, meeting it at right angles the latter extending from west to east. The road we followed lay nearer the river, and led us through a comparatively small temple of Isis, that would have detained us

longer in a less attractive neighbourhood, into
the great court of Jupiter Ammon's temple, the
noblest ruin at Thebes. A stupendous colonnade, of which one pillar only remains erect,
once extended across this court, connecting the
western propylon or gate of entrance, built by
Sesostris, with that at its eastern extremity,
leading to the grand Hall of Osirei, and the
sanctuary.—We ascended the former;—the
avenue of sphinxes, through which the god returned, in solemn procession, to his shrine at
Carnac, after his annual visit to the Libyan
suburb, ascends to it from the river,—the same
avenue traversed age after age by the conqueror,
the poet, the historian, the lawgiver, the phi-
losopher—Sesostris, Cambyses, Homer, Herodotus, Thales, Anaxagoras, Solon, Pythagoras,
Plato — and now the melancholy song of an
Arab boy was the only sound that broke the
silence; but that poor boy was the representative of an older and a nobler race than that of
the Pharaohs.

Long did we gaze on the scene around and below us — utter, awful desolation! Truly, indeed, has No been " rent asunder!" The towers of the second, or eastern, propylon are mere heaps of stones, "poured down" — as prophecy and modern travellers describe the foundations of Samaria — into the court on one side, and the great hall on the other,— giant columns have been swept away like reeds before the mighty avalanche, and one hardly misses them. And that hall, who could describe it? Its dimensions, 170 feet by 329,— the height of the central avenue of columns 66 feet, exclusive of their pedestals,— the total number of columns that supported its roof 134, — these particulars may give you some idea of its extent; but of its grandeur and beauty— none. Every column is sculptured, and all have been richly painted. The exterior walls too are a sculptured history of the wars of Osirei and Rameses.— How often I longed for

J——, and A——, while examining these noble designs ! except those I shall presently mention at Beit Wellee, I have seen nothing in Egypt that would interest them so much. In one corner, of especial interest, are represented the Jews captured by Shishak, and their king Rehoboam, with the hieroglyphical inscription " Jehouda Melek," "the king of the Jews."— This is the only reference to the Israelites found in Egyptian sculpture ; many have wondered at finding no allusions to their residence in Egypt, but I think without cause, for, except the pyramids, the tombs in their vicinity, those of Beni Hassan and a few other remains, of but little interest, I do not believe that any monuments exist, coeval with Moses and the Exodus.

Two large boats ornament one of the outer walls of the great hall ; these sacred arks are sculptured in every temple — reminiscences, evidently, like the Argo of the Greeks, the Argha of the Hindoos, &c. of Noah's. It is

very curious that Baris, the old Egyptian word
for them, is mentioned by Nicholus Damasce-
nus, a peripatetic of Augustus's time, as the
name of the mountain on which the patriarch's
bark rested.

Passing two or three propyla and two lovely
obelisks, each mourning a prostrate brother,—
(the larger — it is sweet to think of it — dedicated by Amense, to the memory of her father
Thothmes I. 3400 years ago, yet the hieroglyphics are as sharp as if cut yesterday,)—
two small granite pillars, beautifully ornamented
with the lotus-stalk and blossom — the remains of the ancient portal, introduce you to
the sanctuary — not the original edifice, for
that was destroyed by Cambyses, but the resto-
ration by Philip Aridaeus, brother of Alexander
the Great. Beyond it are the remains of the
small polygonal columns erected by the Pharaoh
Osirtesen—the oldest in this temple, indeed in
all Thebes. It is curious to trace at a glance

the progress of Egyptian architecture from
these diminutive columns to the stupendous
pillars of Osirei. Many other halls and buildings, almost buried under the accumulated soil,
extend as far as an unfinished propylon, commenced by the Ptolemies, which closes the
eastern appendages to the temple.

Returning to the great obelisk, and seating
myself on the broken shaft of its prostrate
companion, I spent some delightful moments
in musing over the scene of ruins scattered
around me, so visibly smitten by the hand of
God in fulfilment of the prophecies that describe
No-Ammon as the scene of desolation I then
beheld her. The hand of the true Jove Ammon,
Ael-Amunah, the God of Truth, has indeed
" executed judgment on all the gods of Egypt,"
but especially on his spurious representative,
the idol of this most stupendous of earthly
temples : silence reigns in its courts ; the "multitude of No " has been cut off; Pathros is

"desolate";—the land of Ham is still "the basest of kingdoms,"—so sure is the word of prophecy, so visible its accomplishment !

But oh ! that obelisk is lovely ! yet ten times dearer to me than ever mere loveliness could make it;—temples and palaces have been crumbling into dust, dynasties and nations vanishing around it, yet there it stands, pointing to heaven in its meek beauty, the record of a daughter's love — love strong as death, — stronger, for it has triumphed.   Time, surely, read the inscription, and could not find it in his heart to strike.

Or might not one fancy, rather, that when earth cried out to heaven for vengeance on Thebes, and the Lord came down as he had threatened, to "rend No asunder," he planted a guard of angels round this monument of filial piety, to shield it in the storm — to protect it against the indiscriminating zeal of the ministers he had commissioned to destroy ?

And is not the same record of filial love

written by the Spirit on the heart of every
Christian, and when " the Lord our Righteousness " comes down in his glory to take vengeance on his enemies, and on " all the people
that forget God"—spiritual Babel, and spiritual
Egypt — will he not then encircle with his
angels the faithful few on whose hearts he
reads that blessed inscription, and, amid the
crash of empires, and the wreck of all that
this world esteems most excellent and glorious,
strengthen their hearts, and stablish their
feet, and cheer them with the smile of his
love ?

Meditation " might think down hours to
moments " among the ruins of Carnac.

We returned to Luxor through the four propyla, successively built across the avenue that
connects the two temples—lined with sphinxes,
massive and mutilated, yet singularly beautiful
in design and execution ; the face of one that
we discovered in a cross-avenue near the lake

is very lovely,—a little girl's evidently—
the cheek as soft and rounded as dear little
Mayflower's.—We started that same evening.

Nothing can be more unaccountable than the
cloud of utter oblivion that hung over Thebes
till the middle of the seventeenth century. No
Frank traveller, certainly, had penetrated beyond Cairo, but that the Arab writers, who are
generally apt to exaggerate in their descriptions
of architectural remains, should take no notice
of ruins like those of Thebes, is most extraordinary.* Abd'allatif gives us no assistance ; he
was not in the upper country, and his valuable
work on Egypt is merely an account of what
he himself had seen, extracted from a larger
compilation ;—Ebn al Ouardi, who was nearly
his cotemporary, (at the beginning of the
twelfth century,) and Bakoui, who flourished

* Yet not more so than that Herodotus should pass
them over so completely.

two hundred years later, are quite silent;—
Abulfeda, who finished his work in 1321, after
bestowing just praise on the antiquities of
Oshmunein, Ensina, and Memphis—pronounces
a grave eulogium on the pottery of Luxor!
Ebn Batuta, who ascended the Nile in 1325,
mentions El Aksar, (Luxor), as one of the
stages of his journey, but says nothing, (at
least in the abridgment, which is all we possess
of his work), of its ruins.   How Leo Africanus
could have omitted all mention of them is most
surprising; he must have passed and repassed
them by night, for he expressly states that he
sailed up the river as high as Essouan.   But did
he *hear* nothing of Luxor and Carnac?   Were
there no tales current of those vast halls, that
genii might walk under with unbended brow,
—of those awful statues that, side by side, look
down on the Nile like the tutelar guardians of
Egypt — works worthy of the Preadamites —
were there no tales of mystery, no talismans

concealed there for Al Ouardi or Bakoui to record? — One would almost fancy they believed
that merely naming them would wake Memnon
and his brother from their charmed slumber,
let loose the sphinxes, and bring them down a
mighty army, to revenge the wrongs of Egypt
on her oppressors' heads.

Neither Carnac nor Luxor are to be found
in D'Herbelot's precious 'Bibliotheque Orien-
tale,' published in 1697, and he suggests that
Cous in the upper Thebaid may possibly be
the ancient Thebes.

In short, the first notice I have been able to
find of them occurs in the brief narrative, dated
1668, of Father Protais, a worthy Capucin
missionary, who, after describing Luxor and
Carnac with the simplicity and accuracy of
Burckhardt, does not appear to have been aware
he had trodden on the dust of Thebes ! (^{32})

For this fytte adieu ! *

---

* Remarks by Mr. Ramsay on the Theban sculptures.
Battle pieces at Carnac. " There is extreme spirit and

I will be brief, my dear mother, in my description of the temples of Esneh and Edfou, which we visited en route for Essouan : the

boldness in the execution, and the story is told most distinctly and plainly. Though modern artists might have more correct ideas of perspective and true proportions, yet I doubt if any of them, following those rules, could so clearly represent in the same space the subjects contained in these. The liberty used by the sculptor, of giving you ground-plans, or elevations, or both, as it suits his purpose, is undoubtedly contrary to all just rules of drawing; but one's eye soon accustoms itself and ceases to be offended, while the story is told with much greater facility and correctness."

Sculptures at Medinet Habou. "It is difficult to analyze one's feelings with regard to these drawings ; except in the hieroglyphical representations of animals, (which are *perfect*) nothing is critically correct; you confess that the drawing of every thing is most faulty, but yet the soul and fire, the animation and expression in the figures, is most wonderful! A lion wounded, for example, strikes you as the most admirably expressive and living thing ever drawn, but look again, and though the idea of a lion in agony and rage has been most forcibly presented to your mind, yet there is not a single line of the lion critically correct."

"In a neighbouring tomb to the first we saw at Qoornet Murraee, a group of oxen is splendidly drawn. I don't

names of both are Egyptian, and have survived
the comparatively modern Greek appellations
of Latopolis and Apollinopolis Magna.

think I ever saw finer execution ; the rules of perspective
are quite observed; the gambols of the calves in every
possible position, and the free touch and taste of the whole,
are admirable. Near them are a few which have been
fatted, for show, I suppose—not less beautifully done. It
is thus in almost all the tombs; here and there, amidst
the common work of routine of professed painters, a master hand has been called in to dash off a few groups. In
one it was particularly evident—two groups were unfinished
in the middle of a series of the usual representations of a
funeral — they were merely sketched in with red paint,
but with vigour and correctness of proportion, which
would have done honour to a Raphael."

" The grand Entrance-Hall is the place which stamps
Carnac as the first architectural remain in the world.
Ammon had indeed a magnificent temple for his worship !
The varied style of the columns is interesting; some are
as old as Joseph's time. On the last propylon towards
Luxor, are the torsos of two lovely statues, perhaps
twenty-five or thirty feet high; they are much mutilated,
and have no heads, but what remains of their sculpture
and contour is beautifully graceful, and yet in the Egyptian style, arms close to the sides, and left foot advanced.
The priests seem to have employed real master geniuses,

K 2

Of the former, dedicated to Kneph by the
early Cæsars, the beautiful portico only remains; fresh from Thebes, we little expected

but to have confined them to certain fixed forms, at least
in the human figure, for where they are freed from these
shackles, as in the animals in the phonetic hieroglyphics,
nothing can surpass the execution of the drawing, as
well as the finishing. Hundreds of sphinxes, statues, and
figures of all sorts, are lying about this grand approach.
One sphinx, in particular, made a great impression on me ;
they say all sphinxes are male, but the features of a
really sweet, pretty girl could not be mistaken ; and
though her nose, part of her mouth, and chin were gone,
yet one hardly missed them, what remained was so pretty
and elegant. One pitied the poor thing being tacked to
such an uncouth body as that of a sphinx and obliged to
sit in line with a hundred uninteresting fellows for ever,
as it were fascinated down by the wand of some ancient
magician."

"Off Luxor. We have revisited the temple here,
and walked as far as Carnac, which is certainly the most
stupendous thing conceivable. Every thing else sinks into
perfect insignificance in the comparison. But we could
only give a hurried glance before the sun set.—We revisited the crowds of sphinxes and broken statues on the
grand southern approach — There is a great deal that is
uncouth and unskilful, the effect of which is only to be
estimated by their situation as parts of a grand whole,

to view it with the admiration it excited. The features are so grand, and the general effect so sublime, that one almost forgets the modern mud-walls which divide it into two unequal parts, and intercept the light so much, that we looked in vain for the zodiacs sculptured on the ceiling between the walls and the last row of pillars at each extremity. Nothing would offend the critical eye were the capitals more uniform; they are variations of the lotus-leaf, and all individually beautiful; the sculptures and hieroglyphics reveal the *decadence* of Egyptian architecture, but, on the other hand, the columns are of juster proportions

and the constrained stiffness of which must be explained and excused by the despotic influence of form and custom in religious matters, studiously inculcated and preserved by the priests—but there are among them forms of eternal beauty, such as remain henceforth part and parcel of one's mind—pure and clear as truth — no mystery, no mere symbol of mystical priestcraft, but a bright embodying of the soul of genius, which speaks from mind to mind at the interval of three thousand years."

and more regular distribution than any we
have yet seen.*

The temple of Edfou, (delightful was our

* " The pillars, twenty-four in number, are magnificent.
They are straighter and more classical-looking than any
we have yet seen, somehow or other reminding one of the
Pantheon at Rome, one hardly knows why, for, except in
the absence of the usual enormous swell of the pillars,
they retain all the characteristics of the Egyptian style,
and are, to my mind, the most beautiful we have yet seen,
as well from their regularity and beautiful proportions, as
from the majestic elegance of the capitals, so different
from any thing Grecian! But nothing could be finer;
though these pillars be ponderous, they are by no means
heavy; there is nothing which offends the eye, all is in
character and keeping. The fact of being reminded of
the Pantheon, however inexplicable, makes me feel certain
that the same mind which gave birth to the one style had
influence in the formation of the other. People derive
Grecian architecture from the Egyptian, and there is no
doubt they drew much of their science and wisdom from
this country; but that the Egyptian is the coarse, rough
attempt of beginners at an art afterwards improved and
brought to perfection in Greece, is too much to say, for
two different lines have been pursued, and superlative
excellence has been reached in both, as this portico at
Esne proves. If we look solely to Egypt for the origin of
Grecian architecture, we may easily talk of cutting down

walk to it through fields of the beautiful castor-oil plant, of cotton, Indian corn rustling in the breeze, and groves of date-trees), is quite perfect — not a stone displaced, and an Arab village is built on the roof. And no wonder—it was built only yesterday. Antiquity, in our enlarged ideas, ends with the reign of Rameses the fifth, the cotemporary of Hector and Achilles. We had a hearty laugh the other day at the expression, " stupendous antiquity," being applied to a pitiful infancy of nine hundred years. The propyla, dromos, or court, portico, and cella, are richly ornamented with sculptures and hieroglyphics, but it is the

and paring away, and thus this style of Esne, of the largest pillars at Carnac, Luxor, &c., will merge into the Corinthian, and the other style used here into the Doric; but it appears to me absurd to slice off, for the sake of argument, or supporting a theory, the most essential and peculiar features of a particular style. Why, one might pare every upright thing in the world down to the Doric, as it is the simplest of all — may we not for this very reason suppose that it is the earliest, or, at least, original?" *Mr. Ramsay's Journal.*

general effect, the distribution, the proportions
of this temple, its perfect state of preservation,
and the grandeur of its outline, that render it
so interesting; the details are of inferior execution.   The court is choked with Arab huts,
and from the top of the propylon you have a
curious view of the town beneath, like an
enormous honeycomb, mud cells, for the most
part roofless, with a single minaret towering
over them—our Reis had gone there to pray.*

* "Edfou, Jan. 9.   The fields were looking very beautiful; the system of irrigation is carried on to an immense
extent here, it is every thing; at every short distance,
one sees the water raised from the Nile by men, who hand
it up in buckets one to another, into little tanks, till it
reaches the top, when it runs down the channels formed
for it.   There is one grand channel, which branches off
into smaller ones, and these again into smaller, till at last
it enters the small fields or plots, generally about ten feet
square, where it spreads and remains, each little plot
being enclosed by raised banks, on which the channels
run; when one plot is watered, the entrance for the water
is closed with a lump of earth, and the water passes on to
the next; when the whole of one division has received its
share, the connection with the grand passage is stopped,

We saw some ostriches near Esneh, others
since—they are numerous in the Eastern desert ;
crocodiles too, in abundance—William fires at

and so on. The squares are all very neatly and carefully
kept, and, in fact, in this irrigation consists the whole
system of husbandry. A plough, I suppose, is never
used, all the land requires is a rough breaking up with a
hoe for wheat—for clover, not even that. Indian corn is
now ripe, and its harvest is going on. It is sown before
the rise of the Nile, and is ripe soon after its fall ; and it
is thus calculated that this must have been the corn which
was *not* smitten in the plagues of Egypt by the hail, as
it was just sprouting above ground, when the other corn,
which is sown on the waters retiring, was ripe and fit for
the harvest. The same system seems to be pursued now
as in the early and palmy days of this country. The
drawings on the walls of some of the tombs display all
the processes of husbandry and other daily occupations—
and allusions in the Bible might have been made as to
what happens at the present day, so much the same has
every thing remained. It is called ' the country which
thou wateredst with thy foot,' and it is so now—the people
use their naked feet for stopping their water-channels,
when required. A very beautiful plant, which we saw a
good deal of to-day in the fields, is the castor-oil tree—
I never saw such a diversity of appearances on one plant
at the same time; two totally different flowers on the
same stalk, one red, the other white, berries, buds, and

K 5

them sometimes; the young ones flounce into the water in an awful fright, the old ones look astonished at our impudence, and then sink down with more regard to their dignity, but still it is a very clumsy operation. Of the other " venomous creatures bred in this river, as scorpions, water-snakes, grievous misshapen worms, and other monstrous things, which," according to old Lithgow, " often annoy the inhabitants and those who traffic on the water," I can give you no account.

The colour of the natives waxed darker and darker as we approached the tropics; the pea-sants, who were plying the *shadoof*, or pole-

fruit something like horsechesnuts, but more delicate—the young leaves also were of a deep purple, the old ones bright green." *Mr. Ramsay's Journal.*

" 2 Feb. Edfou. Since we were here last, the appear-ance of the country is very much altered. The forests of Indian corn are cut down, and the stubble is a poor substi-tute, especially when the sun is so hot as to-day; the wheat has grown to eight inches or a foot, in three weeks; the cotton-plants have withered, and the irrigation has altered its character." *Mr. Ramsay's Journal.*

and-bucket water-engine, where we landed at Edfou, were nearly black, and naked above and below the waist—the children quite so.

The vale of Egypt appears to end in a cul-de-sac as you approach Essouan, old Syene, its southern boundary since the days of the prophets, and, indeed, from time immemorial, for, though many of the Pharaohs extended their sway over Ethiopia, the two countries remained always politically, as they are geographically, distinct. We reached Essouan, one of the most beautiful spots in Egypt, on the 10th of January, mooring on the Eastern bank near the enormous granite rocks, on which the ancient Syene stood; a Saracenic succeeded to the Egyptian town, but it was visited so severely by the plague, four hundred years ago, that the survivors deserted it; the ruins at a distance strikingly resemble an old European town of the middle ages.([33])

Opposite Essouan is " the Isle of Flowers,"

ancient Elephantine, the dwelling, according
to Herodotus, of the Ichthyophagi, or fish-
eaters, whom Cambyses sent as his ambassa-
dors to the Ethiopians—those "blameless Ethiopians" eulogised by Homer, whose country,
according to the father of song, the gods
visited annually, and who appear to be the
Yadavas or Yatus of Hindoo story, a primitive
and sacred race, which, emigrating from the
east in the infancy of time, established themselves, under their monarch Yatupa, on the
mountains of Yatupeya — the Ethiopia and
Ethiops of the Greeks, who, designating these
as the Western, refer to their brethren who remained near the Indus, as the Eastern Ethiopians, describing the whole nation as " a two-
fold people, who lie extended in a long tract
from the rising to the setting sun"—Cushites,
I conceive, all of them, and whose original settlement must surely have been Khusistan,
Susiana, or Cush, between the Tigris and

Persia. But I shall weary you.—Elephantine! this was really mythic land! We crossed to the lovely island, and, walking to the rocky southern extremity, saw the Nile, no longer pent in as below Syene, but expanded a bright broad lake before us, studded with islets of granite, polished and glittering in the sun. Hence to the northern extremity, through fields of the richest verdure, irrigated by innumerable little canals, about a foot wide, of banked earth, supplied by Persian wheels with the precious water of the Nile — and groves of date-trees, that draw their nutriment seemingly from the very sand of the desert, whispering in reply to them. These little canals (opened or shut by the foot) connect my associations with the Egypt of Scripture, " where thou sowedst thy grain, and wateredst it with thy foot," as God described it to the Israelites in contrast to Palestine, " the land of hills and valleys, drinking water of the rain of heaven,"

more vividly than all the temples and pyramids.
They are often alluded to in Scripture, particularly in that most beautiful proverb of Solomon, true indeed of every man, " the heart of
the king is like the canals of waters in the hand
of Jehovah ; whithersoever it pleaseth him, he
inclineth it." Here, as elsewhere, from ignorance of eastern scenery and manners, our
translators, admirable as their version is for all
practical purposes, have failed in expressing
the minute poetical beauty of the original
imagery. These little aqueducts are more refreshing to the eye than it is possible to conceive in your frigid zone.

The temples that, till of late years, adorned
Elephantine, have all been levelled with the
ground ; two or three square pillars, some
vestiges of what is called the Nilometer, and a
solitary statue seated among the ruins, are the
only remains. But old remembrances and the
perennial verdure of Nature are still enough to

render it a little paradise for the imagination. Here was the limit of Herodotus's Egyptian travels ; the geographer Eratosthenes, (I honour his memory), probably often sauntered along the shore; I have too little love for Juvenal to feel much interest in the remembrance that he was banished to Syene — his spirit was little kindred to such a scene as this.

Now for the cataracts. Next morning (the 11th), soon after breakfast, the reis, or pilot of the cataracts, made his appearance, and, after pipes and coffee, announced that, till the wind sprung up, it was useless starting. Æolus had compassion on us, and sent a breeze so favourable that, within half an hour, we were under sail, a prayer having previously been offered up by the reis and crew for our safe passage.

Bidding adieu to Elephantine, the breeze carried us gently along between the black granite islets mentioned above, of the most sin-

gular forms, many of them sculptured with
hieroglyphics—their polished edges glittering
in the sun ; a scene strangely beautiful, almost
too wild for beauty.   A hawk, Nature's
sculpture in the living rock, springing up pro-
pitiously on the left, from the brow of the
eastern craigs, seemed to invite us to the
sacred isle of Philae, and augur a prosperous
passage of the intermediate cataracts.   The
wind freshened, and, ere long, the lovely isle
of Shehayl stole into sight, and flitted past
like a dream, its palm-trees waving in the
breeze, and children sporting under them,
naked as the day they were born ; an Isle of
the Blest it seemed — one of those happy
islands where poets tell us the shades of heroes
of old wander, under whispering groves, in
sweet converse, placid and at rest after the
turmoils of life — aptly figured by the black
rocks that, hemming in the noble river, gave so
awful a character to the surrounding scenery.

And yet this little isle had still more exalted
inhabitants; Sati and Anuki, the Juno and
Vesta of Egyptian mythology, and Kneph, the
spirit of the universe, delighted in its bowers,
and honoured it with their protection; and
hieroglyphical tablets, anterior to the birth of
Cecrops, attest its early sanctity. The whole
valley, indeed, of the Nile between Elephantine and Philae, was " holy ground " to the
Egyptians and Ethiopians.

The scenery now exchanges its character of
mingled beauty and terror for that of unmingled
grandeur ; not that the rocks are particularly
lofty, but Salvator never dreamed of such
strange unnatural combinations — sometimes
shooting into craggy pinnacles, often piled one
on another, regularly and methodically, as if in
mockery of human architecture, or wildly and
confusedly heaped like the fall of a volcano
shower—all gloom, relieved only by the yellow
sands that lie drifted, like snow-wreaths, on

the face of the western shore; if that can be
called relief which carries the imagination beyond the narrow bounds of visible desolation to
the illimitable wastè of the desert, where even
Fancy's wing must sink exhausted.　The sun,
glowing in a cloudless sky, reminded us of our
approach to the tropics, while Father Nile,
flowing swifter and swifter as we drew near
each successive rapid, dashing and foaming
over the islets, and often there most turbulent
where we were to force our passage, seemed to
bar all further progress towards his undiscoverable source.　But his opposition, like
that of the visionary waters of fairy legends,
vanished before the steady breeze of resolution;
he offered a more formidable barrier in ancient
times, if we may believe the fictions of the
poets.

　　The Arabs, who met us by appointment at
the first rapid, were of little use; the breeze
carried us up steadily and beautifully, and we

sailed on again for a while in smooth water;
but the river recovered its velocity as we approached the second, and more formidable
rapids, winding our way between the little
glittering islets, constantly expecting to fall
foul of them, but escaping always by an inch or
two, thanks to the counter-eddies,—shifting our
broad lateen sail every moment, as we changed
our position with regard to the wind; the
white-bearded reis, meanwhile, conspicuous
from afar in his brilliant robes of red and blue,
with variegated turban and cane of office, gesticulating and shouting from the rocks — the
sons of Shem, Ham, and Japhet, yelling the
languages of Europe, Asia, and Africa around
us—our last detachment of Arabs and Nubians
watching us from the opposite shore, or, cling-
ing to a log of wood, flinging themselves fearlessly into the very jaws of the cataract, swept
down like lightning, soon to re-appear at our
vessel's side, like mahogany and ebony statues,

with a request for " bagshish," a present, viz.,
in guerdon of their intrepidity — altogether it
was a strange, a savage scene, worth coming
all the way from England to witness.

Here, at the second rapid, the Nile appears
completely closed in by the rocks ; it was at
first sight difficult to conceive the possibility
of threading our way between, or penetrating
beyond them.   After one fruitless attempt, we
succeeded in crossing to the opposite rocks,
where, the natives attaching a large and strong
rope of twisted palm-fibres, we commenced
our ascent, with the chorussed song of " Halee
sa ! " " God help ! "   By dint of pulling and
poling, in which we all lent a hand, we got up
famously — to our wonder, looking back — for
the rapid we had surmounted is by far the
most difficult of ascent, owing to the narrowness of the channel where alone it is practicable.   Then we had smooth sailing for a while,
the reis, in his ample robes, heading our cor-

tege on the eastern shore, at least seventy or
eighty men and boys, efficient and inefficient,
following in his rear, laughing and skipping,
pelting each other with sand, and flourishing
their long dirks, half-earnest, half-play, till we
arrived at the third and principal rapid, where
the Nile, collecting all his waters, rushes down
in one broad sheet, smooth as a mirror and
fleet as an arrow; but we mounted it with
little difficulty, there being no rocks to defile
through: pull, pull, pull, steady and unre-
laxing, and the cataracts were past. We detached the rope, unfurled the sail (it had been
useless since our arrival at the second rapid),
and glided gently over the calm waters till, the
rocks opening, the sacred island of Philae and
its noble temple stood forth to greet us, like
the castle of some ancient Dive among the
rocks of Ginnistan. High on the eastern
bank stands a beautiful columnar edifice, supposed by some to have been once shewn as the

tomb of Osiris, but styled, in the traditions of
the country, the Bed of Pharaoh; there we
moored, and, leaving the boat, proceeded to
explore one of the most interesting spots in
the whole valley of the Nile.

Isis, her husband Osiris, and their son
Horus, were the triad worshipped at Philae.
The sacred isle is only three or four hundred
yards in length, but it was covered with shrines
and colonnades : fringed with a few date-trees,
the interior is now a mass of ruins; Nubian
huts have succeeded Ethiopian temples, and
both are deserted.

The temple of Isis is the principal ruin. An
irregular colonnade, of which the western
range, built up perpendicularly from the river,
is covered with hieroglyphics and sculptures,
while the eastern seems never to have been
completed—irregular, inasmuch as symmetry,
a charm to which the Egyptians seem to have
been little sensible, was here necessarily sa-

crificed to the limited space the architect had
to work upon — leads from the southern along
the western bank to the propylon, or pyramidal towers of entrance, similar to those at
Edfou, but on a smaller scale, and covered
with colossal sculptures of the moon-crowned
Isis, the hawk-headed deity, and a gigantic
warrior about to inflict the fatal stroke on
thirty wretches, whom he holds by the hair of
their head, back to back, reminding one of the
many-headed, many-handed monsters of Indian
mythology. These figures are repeated, as well
as the smaller row of deities above them, on
the second propylon, which you reach through
an irregular dromos or court, surrounded by
columns covered with sculpture and hieroglyphics; not only are all the capitals different, but those on the left are surmounted
by square tablets with masks of Isis—the same
sweet and mournful expression that characterises all her portraits ; perhaps suggested by

the beautiful planet with which she was identified.   The second propylon ushers you into
by far the finest part of the temple — a noble
and truly beautiful portico, supported on three
sides by lofty columns, sculptured with hieroglyphics, and painted azure and yellow.   The
walls, ceiling, &c. are also beautifully ornamented, the winged orb forming the principal
device ; this is sculptured over the entrance of
almost every temple in Egypt and Nubia—how
like *our* idea of " the Sun of Righteousness
arising with healing on his wings !"

We explored all the cells with torches, but
looked in vain for the sculptured hawk that
travellers mention.   I was particularly anxious
to find it.   Dr. Richardson supposes it was
venerated at Philae before Osiris, Isis, and
Horus supplanted its worship. If so, I cannot
but suspect that the true God was worshipped
here before the rise, as He undoubtedly was
after the fall, of Paganism, when the temples of

Philae, Edfou, Thebes, and many others were dedicated to the Saviour.

" The God," says the patriarchal Zoroaster, in his noble enumeration of the Almighty's attributes, " is (represented) having a hawk's head; He is the Best, Incorruptible, Eternal, Unmade, Indivisible, most unlike every thing, the Author of all good, the Wisest of the wise," &c.—" Here," observes Dr. Hales, we have " perhaps the first instance on record of symbolical representation blended with pure spiritual description, and in this respect it is highly curious, as furnishing, perhaps, the earliest specimen of those animal hieroglyphics, attributed to the Deity so copiously in Egypt, still to be found on their ancient monuments, and which, when the recondite or mystical meaning came to be lost, in process of time produced all that multifarious polytheism, which corrupted the primitive theology of the Egyptians, Indians, Greeks, and Romans."

Egypt was first peopled from Ethiopia; to the Ethiopians, (who considered themselves, says the Greek historian Diodorus Siculus, the most ancient of mankind), the Egyptians looked as the parents of their religion; and Philae was held equally sacred by both nations. Here, then, probably was the seat of the primeval Egyptian worship, established by Misr and his successors, the children of Ham, a race, with the exception of the Canaanites, neither blessed nor cursed by their patriarch Noah, who are mentioned without approbation in the earliest scriptural records, but who, probably, retained for some generations the knowledge, and maintained the worship, of the true God in Egypt and Ethiopia, as their kinsmen of the line of Canaan did at Salem in Syria. Originally, I conceive, familiarized to Egyptian, as well as Persian, imagination by the symbol of the hawk's head, the omnivision of the Deity was probably thus represented by the

Egyptians in hieroglyphical sculpture; and, its
spiritual meaning being, in lapse of time, forgotten in this case, as in so many others, " the
creature came to be worshipped more than the
Creator, who is above all, God blessed for
ever." Philae, then, losing its real sanctity
as the Salem of the Land of Cush and Ham,
retained, I conceive, its celebrity as the seat of
idolatry; the hawk continuing the chief object
of worship, till that of Osiris, Isis, and Horus
supplanted, and, in part, became blended with
it; the *name* of the Almighty, in fact, sup-
planting his *attribute:* for, *Osiris*, as Dr.
Hales elsewhere observes, is evidently a cor-
ruption of *Iahoh Sihor*, or *Jehovah the Black*,
the " black-clouded Jove " of Homer. Nor is
the character of Osiris, as the good principle
and judge of the dead, unlike that of the Deity :
his identification, moreover, with Bacchus, the
giver of the vine, (Iswara in India), is another
proof of his identity in name with the giver of

all good things " and fruitful seasons, filling our hearts with food and gladness " — for Iacchus, the Greek form of the name Bacchus, is simply the guttural pronunciation of Iahoh, with the Greek termination, and the mystic fan of Bacchus, represented in the Eleusinian mysteries of Ceres, (Isis) — introduced originally, says Herodotus, from Egypt, strikingly resembles that in the hand of the Son of Man, with which he is to purge his threshing-floor.

Here are theories for you, dear mother! " guesses at truth " rather ; I would not have troubled you with them, only they will tend to explain a little poem which I enclose you, begun while we were passing the cataracts, and finished afterwards in Nubia. *   I should pre-

---

* THE ASCENT OF THE CATARACTS.

The sky is clear, not a cloud in heaven,
  And blithely swells the sail,
While myriad islet rocks between
  We skim before the gale—

mise, however, that I have no authority for making St. Thomas visit Ethiopia on his way to India.

Like a black swan each on a still lake's breast,
Peacefully cradled in noontide rest.

The Cataract's roar ! around their chief,
    Each to the God of Ishmael bending,
The turbaned crew approve his prayer,
    Their lives to Allah's will commending ;
A prayer of much simplicity—
And we, too, Lord ! we trust in Thee !

Syene's rocks are far behind,
    And thy green banks, sweet Isle of Flowers !
And thine, Shehayl ! whose children's laugh
    Rings merrily through the date-tree bowers,
That erst, mysterious rites concealing,
O'ershadowed silent Pharaohs kneeling.

And yearly to the triple shrine—
    For Kneph's and Sati's equal smile
With Anuki's was courted there—
    Dark-visaged queens from Meroe's Isle,
And kings from farthest Hadramaut
Bright gems and Indian incense brought.

The Nile ! the Nile ! I hear the gathering roar—
    (No vision now—no dream of ancient years !)

One guess more—was not the eagle of Zeus,
the Roman Ju-pater, or Father Jove—the same
emblem, borrowed from the same Egyptian or

Throned on his rocks, amid the watery war,
  The King of Floods, old Homer's Nile appears!
With gentle smile, majestically sweet,
Curbing the billowy steeds that vex them at his feet.

Not so when, bursting from the matron breast
  Of central Afric, veiled from eye profane,
Ten thousand fertile streams, with foamy crest,
  Rush down to waft their monarch to the main;
  Then to those billowy steeds he gives the rein,
And, leaning on his car with simple grace,
  Speeds, like the light, o'er Egypt's thirsty plain;
The Hours, the Seasons, laugh before his face,
Fresh as the new-born sun, rejoicing in his race.

Thus, when the Sun of Righteousness, his wings
  Of healing spread, shall rise upon our woe,
The River of Life, from heavenly Zion's springs,
  As Nile o'er Egypt, o'er the earth shall flow;
  Desert no more, Zahara's sands shall glow
With purple flowers—wheree'er the floods extend
  Knowledge shall bloom, and Love enthroned below
Dwell in all hearts; and every bough shall bend
With sacramental pledge of blessings without end!

Persian source ? How unlike *its* eye, closing,
as Pindar beautifully describes it, under the
lulling influence of the lyre, to His who never
slumbers nor sleeps !

Then, Philae! (lo! the Rapids past,
　Like wrath supplanted by a smile,
'Tween opening rocks and waters clear
That murmur music to the ear,
　Steals into view the lovely Isle)—
Then, Philae ! then shall hymns once more
Resound along thy templed shore !

Shrine of old Faith, though long defiled !
　To God and man thou still art dear,
For Cushite kings of earliest time,
　And blameless creed have worshipped here,
Ere blinded man the All-seeing Eye
Degraded to idolatry.

Christ's agony ! a second blight
　That morn pale Egypt overspread ;
The hoary Pyramids, steeped in night,
　Trembled upon their rocky bed,
Foreboding judgments from on high
Fiercer than those that shook their infancy.([34])

Isis that morn, moon-crested dame,
　Sweet Philae's bowers forsook for ever,

Interesting as is the temple of Isis, and noble
as its general effect is, the sculptures and
hieroglyphics are of a very inferior style. The

Her shrine thenceforth was dumb, kings came
    To ask, but answer gat they never !
The priests, too, fled—their time was o'er,
And votaries sought her Isle no more.

Years dawned and died till, bound for Ind,
    With holy eye and snowy beard,
With scrip and staff and girdled robe,
    One autumn eve a Sire appeared ;
    More to be loved seemed he than feared,—
The children rested from their play,
And craved his blessing as he went his way.

Well might they ask it ! he was one
    That He who little children loved
Had breathed His holy Spirit upon ;
    And, by that Spirit inly moved,
He then sought out an humble pair
That dwelt in lonely virtue there.

The night in holy converse past,
    The stranger went his way the morrow,—
Long, long remembered, uneffaced,
    His words of mingled cheer and sorrow !

lovely nondescript edifice by the river-side
pleased me much more ; the eye willingly
turns from the heavy grandeur and rude sculp-

> For meek and mournful was his mien,
> As one that of himself had long mistrustful been.
>
> Me lists not to recount the tale
>   How, through that pair by truth enlightened,
> To hundreds, o'er each Nubian vale,
>   The sun of Gospel gladness brightened,
> And Philae heard once more delighted
> Hymns to the God to whom her youth was plighted.
>
> But Persecution, even here,
>   Sought out and slew them ; writ in heaven
> Their names, unread in human story,
> Shine like the morning stars in glory ;
>   In robes of whiteness, freely given,
> Palms in their hands, the Victor band
> Before the Lamb, their Saviour, stand.
>
> Uncouth inscriptions, rudely traced,
>   A sculptured cross—mute things alone
> Reveal where erst Acceptance graced
>   The prayers through which their prize was won :
>   And Philae, with a mother's moan,
> Unmindful of their happier lot,
> Weeps o'er her children that are not !

ture of the larger, to repose on the airy grace
and unadorned simplicity of the smaller ruin.
There is not a hieroglyphic on it, nor any
sculpture except the winged globe over the
portal by which it was entered from the temple;
open above and laterally, and seen from below,
it is beautiful indeed. No roof was ever added
or intended, and the intercolumniations are
built up only a little more than a third of the
height; the capitals of the columns are leaves

Rise, sweet one, rise! and dry thy tears;
    A brighter day is dawning o'er
A world for twice three thousand years
    Trodden down of man, and drenched in gore;
    Thy children thou shalt see once more,
Shalt hear their voices blend united
In hymns like those in which thy youth delighted!

Soon, O soon! may the day-star rise
    O'er Egypt's vale and Asshur's bowers,
To warn the nations, unseal their eyes,
    And guide their feet to Salem's towers,
When every hand shall an offering bear,
And every heart be a House of Prayer!

of the date-tree. Several courses of stone,
intervening between the columns and the cor-
nice, add to the singular effect, without diminishing from the beauty of this dear little
temple — as our sweet Minnie would call it.
This cannot surely be the tomb of Osiris—the
Egyptian lowered his voice, and sunk his eye,

" And pointed upwards as to God in Heaven,"
when he swore the tremendous oath, "By Him
that sleeps in Philae !" Neither edifice is
older than the day of the Ptolemies. ([35])

The sullen roar of the cataracts was our
music for the night.

This rocky range above Syene I take to be
the Hemacuta or Golden Mountains of the
Hindus, ([36]) who, considering the course of the
Nile, after issuing from the Lake of the Gods
under the *Southern* Meru, exactly analogous to
that of the Ganges, after issuing from Lake
Mansarowar under the *Northern* — assert that
each bursts through three ranges of mountains,

named alike in both countries Himalaya, Ni-
shada, and Hemacuta, before reaching its last
unfettered flow towards the ocean. Each river
is held equally sacred, as well as the points of
junction of each with its tributaries. Few
Indian pilgrims, however, in these degenerate
days, visit Egypt. Wild and grotesque as it
often is, there is a world of beauty in the old
Hindoo mythology, and more truth than we
are often disposed to allow in their geography
and history.

The next morning, January the 12th, we
started on our voyage into the Land of Cush,
gliding smoothly along between rocky hills that
confine the fertilizing influence of the Nile to a
very narrow strip of cultivable ground, often
encroached upon by the sands of the desert,
which lie in broad sheets on the western bank.
The scattered clumps, however, of date and
doûm trees (Theban palms) lend a pleasing
variety to scenery, otherwise of the sombrest

character. Once this country was rich and
beautiful and populous, till Surya, the Regent
of the Sun, being seized one morning with a
most unseasonable fit of devotion, descended
on it to say his prayers; the waters dried up
immediately, the mountains took fire, and the
inhabitants were roasted to death. Brahma
and Vishnu descended to expostulate with,
and, indeed, console, the unlucky Surya — for
he was as concerned as they were at the unfortunate issue of his zeal, and promised, with
deep contrition, to amend the mischief. "It
is I," replied Vishnu, "who must repair it,
and when I shall revisit this country, in the
character of Crishna, to destroy the demon
Sanch'asura, the land shall cool, and be re-
plenished with plants and animals. The race
of Palis shall then settle here, with the Cuti-
lacesas, the Yavanas, the Barbaras, and other
mixed tribes." — Crishna has been incarnated
—the demon Sanch'asura destroyed—the Palis

have arrived and departed,— the Yavanas, or Iaones, are forgotten even in Greece, the " ultima Thule " of their wanderings — but Vishnu's promise has been only partially performed, and the effects of Surya's approach are still visible in the blackened and scorched aspect of the hills of Nubia.

We now entered the region of the Berber language, but the children were as familiar with the magical word *bagshish*, as our's in England are with the kindred phrase *Christmas box* — which Bishop Heber thinks may have been derived from it.

We visited a temple at Dabod — the first within the tropic, and another at Kalabshe : those between the Cataracts were for the most part built by the Ptolemies and Cæsars ; many of them have been left unfinished ; they can boast, generally speaking, of but few sculptures, and those of a very inferior execution. The Augustan age in Egypt was that of the

decadence of the arts ; long indeed before the
Ptolemies, they had fallen from their high
estate under Osirei, Sesostris, and their immediate successors; there were Homers then in
the land, who celebrated the wars of those
heroic princes on imperishable stone ; but you
see few historical sculptures later than Rameses the Fifth; the national spirit had died
out — religion had sunk into a mere caput
mortuum — and the descendants of the artists
who sculptured the Memnonium had degene-
rated into mere mythological copyists, constantly reiterating a Pantheon of deities, whose
every attitude was prescribed by law — it is
only wonderful that they copied so well, but
the life is wanting.— The likenesses of the
Pharaohs, as I have observed already, whether
painted in the tombs or sculptured on the
temples, were always exactly preserved — but
once taken, they seem never to have sat a
second time for their portraits. The same

likeness is constantly reiterated; you cannot trace the gradual change—step by step—year by year — from the full cheek and brent brow of youth to the sunk and care-worn lineaments of age — that lends so touching an interest to the series of a Greek king's medals.—It would be interesting to compare the Egyptian with the medallic portraits of the Ptolemies and Cæsars, and ascertain whether any pains were then taken to preserve the resemblance.

The most spirited sculptures we have seen in the Valley of the Nile are those in the small rock-temple of Beit-Wellee, half an hour's walk from Kalabshe — founded by Sesostris to commemorate his victories over the Cushites or Ethiopians, and the Shorii, an eastern nation, according to Mr. Wilkinson (I quote his words) "apparently of Arabia Petræa, who, having been previously reduced by the Egyptian monarchs and made tributary to them, rebelled and were reconquered by Osirei and the Second Rameses." Open and exposed for three thousand years to the air of heaven and the hand of man, these sculptures are still as sharp and fresh almost as when the artist exhibited them, in his pride, to Rameses.

To the right, entering the open area excavated in front of the temple, you have the conquest of the Shorii ; to the left, the submission of the Cushites : every thing bespeaks the desperate resistance of the former, the tame cowardice of the latter. On the right wall, Rameses, alike victorious on foot and in his war-chariot, attacks the Shorii, slays their chief in single combat, and drives them to the fortifications of their town ; his son, the heir of Egypt, storms the walls, and presents his prisoners bound to his father, who, in the last compartment of this sculptured history, is represented seated on his throne reposing after his toils, the favourite lion that acccompanied him in battle couched at his feet. — On the

left wall, the Prince of Cush, his hand raised
in supplication, his son and daughter at his
side, is introduced by the Prince of Egypt to
the mighty Rameses, throned in state; rings of
gold, bags of precious stones, elephants' teeth,
apes, (but no peacocks)—the wealth of Ethiopia, are borne after him, offerings to the
conqueror; the lion, the giraffe, the bull, the
gazelle, the ostrich, figure in the procession.
The contempt of the Egyptians for their unwar-
like neighbours may be traced here, as elsewhere, in the caricatured features of one of the
tribute - bearers, whose countenance bears a
ludicrous resemblance to that of the monkey
that precedes him in the procession.

And yet they did not yield absolutely without
a blow. There is one scene of most touching
interest. The Cushites have been defeated —
they hurry confusedly to the woods for refuge,
stumbling over the dying and the dead, but one
of them has outstripped the fleetest, in hopes

of saving his friend's wife from the pursuers
—he knew not that that friend was already at
his own door — but alas! faint and bleeding,
wearily dragging on, his arms thrown round two
of his comrades' necks, who grasp his wrists
to strengthen him. He overtakes them at the
moment when his friend's *sister* and his children
recognize him — *she* stands aghast, one boy
holds up his hands in horror,— another covers
his face with one hand, and runs to clasp his
father's knees with the other,— the third runs
to tell his mother, who, unconscious of what
awaits her, is preparing her husband's meal.
But the tumult approaches — the flying Cushites, the chariot-wheels of Pharaoh and the
Egyptians—fly! oh fly! —they see only, they
hear only, the wounded man! — a minute —
and wife and husband, brother and sister, children and friend, will all be overwhelmed by the
mighty torrent; — a monkey has climbed to
the top of a tree for refuge — there is yet time

— but what are they to do with the wounded
man ? 'tis too late now — they come, they
come, rushing—crushing through the forest—
and now......let us drop the curtain.

The sculptures of the interior temple are
highly interesting, and evidently allusive to the
scenes of conquest sculptured without. A Sho-
rian and an Ethiopian, the representatives, I
presume, of their respective nations, lie at the
feet of Rameses ; with one hand he grasps their
hair, the uplifted battle-axe gleams in the
other.   Forced on his knees, but those knees
clenched together, the muscles rigid, the joints
unyielding, the brave Arab meets with un-
quailing eye the glance of his conqueror, and
raises his left arm firmly to ward off the blow
which the Ethiopian tamely submits to,— the
contrast is that of courage with cowardice —
personified in the relaxed limbs, uplifted but
shrinking hands, and averted face of the negro;
the lips of both are moving, but you need not

fancy to supply words — every limb, every gesture speaks.

The following morning we visited the gloomy and awful temple of Guerf Hassan, ancient Talmis, completely excavated in the sandstone rock, and singularly resembling, travellers say, the Cave of Elephanta, in India — I hope, my dear mother, I shall some day be qualified to judge of the resemblance! But for the name of Rameses graven on every wall and every pillar throughout the temple, one would be inclined to assign it to the earliest period of Egyptian or, more strictly speaking, Ethiopian architecture; it is almost impossible not to believe it more ancient than any other monument in Egypt except the pyramids; there is not a trace of the taste and beauty of Rameses' time. A ruined portico, (square columns, faced with colossal statues), leads to the first and largest of the excavated chambers, a noble hall, supported by six enormous square columns,

faced, like those of the portico, with statues
of Osiris, above eighteen feet high, cut in full
relief,—mild, chubby, undignified countenances,
the arms crossed, holding the scourge of power
and the crosier of peace,([37]) — the legs naked
and shapeless, more like pillars than human
stumps ;— the attitude of the lower part of the
body reminded me of the Esquimaux, their
pendent sashes of Highland sporrans, the head
of some animal projecting in the usual place,
with seven tassels below it. Statues of Phthah,
or Vulcan, to whom this temple is dedicated,
of Athor the lion-headed, (Venus), and of
Anuki, (Vesta), are sculptured in recesses behind the columns on each side of the hall.
Beyond it, are the cella, supported by two
large columns, and the adytum, or innermost
shrine, at the further end of which, on a high
platform, sit four most mysterious-looking,
colossal figures,— a large hewn stone on the
floor in front of them, perhaps an altar. In

the small lateral apartments are benched recesses, probably for embalming. All the chambers are sculptured, but they are so black with
smoke and dirt, and the rock has in many
places proved so unfaithful to its trust, that we
could make nothing of them. Negro and
Nubian boys ciceronied us with burning ropes
through this extraordinary excavation. Mithras' cave itself could scarcely have been
gloomier than the Rock-temple of Guerf Hassan !

The Persians, those Iconoclasts of antiquity,
piqued themselves on their spiritual worship
of the Deity, and certainly they never sank
into such gross polytheism as the Egyptians,
Greeks, and Romans ; yet their reverence for
fire, while it proves that *both* nations drew
their religion from one primeval source, was
no less idolatrous than that of the Egyptians
for Phthah, the Vulcan of Egypt, and all the
rest of their " divine menagerie," as William
calls it.

The sacred fire of the Persians, like that of the Jews, was originally emblematical only of Mithras, the hidden god, but when the " spiritual meaning of the visible sign" had been forgotten, they worshipped it as a deity ; and, if they regarded *it*, as we know they did the element in general, as a *living creature,* Cambyses (unless, indeed, like his father, Cyrus, he acknowledged " the Lord for his God),'' had no excuse for sheathing his sword in the bull Apis.

Again : In all ages the Egyptians revered Phthah as their earliest king, assigning no duration to his reign — in other words, ascribing dominion to him from all eternity, till his resignation of the sceptre to his son Helius, the orb of day, whose reign they limit to 30,000 years.

Surely we see the God of Light enshrined, the fire by which He will try all things gleaming, in the adyta of both caves, both creeds, at first sight so unconnected, in their actual encounter so hostile !

And whom can the pigmy Pataici — the diminutive images placed by the Phœnicians on the prows of their galleys, and to which Herodotus likens the statue of Vulcan at Memphis — whom can they have represented, and whence can they have derived their name but from Phthah? whatever was his origin, Egyptian or Chaldean, still the primeval, eternal Phthah ; Vulcan of Rome, Hephaistos of Greece, Phthah of Egypt, Mithras of Persia— with reverence be it added, Jehovah of Heaven !—the God of Light, dwelling in thick darkness as his pavilion, his cloudy cave — who, in the olden time, " looked unto the host of the Egyptians through the pillar of fire and of the cloud, and troubled the host of the Egyptians" —by fire, and wind, and water, his ministering elements, " executing judgment on all the gods of Egypt," while he " led forth the people whom he had redeemed," from an apostate land that, no longer recognising him as a spirit, no longer worshipped him in spirit and in truth.

Approaching Korosko, we sailed through a strange country, black volcanic-looking mountains on either side the river, and in many places a few yards only of cultivation intervening between it and the desert.   We moored for the night at Korosko.—Imagine our dismay when Wellee Kiashef, the Turkish governor of the country between the cataracts, resting there for the moment on one of his progresses through his little vice-royalty, sent to offer us a visit ! It could not be helped, so we entertained him—an intelligent and very inquisitive man, most anxious for information ; he said it was his great delight to make acquaintance with, and gain knowledge from Englishmen, whenever he could meet with them.   The first compliments were scarcely paid, when he pro-

duced a little Arabic treatise on geography,
printed by the missionaries at Malta, and asked
how many men formed the standing force of
Russia? We expected to be regularly cate-
chised on the resources of every state in Europe, but his subsequent questions were chiefly
geographical ; he had evidently made the most
of his little book — his sole library, he told us
—and had treasured the information he had
picked up from travellers. I gave him four
or five Arabic books, one on astronomy, the
others chiefly religious, that I had found lying
at Alexandria along with some books I bought
there, and included them in my bargain, on
the chance of finding some opportunity of
giving them away.

All his geographical ideas, except those
derived from his text-book, were very vague.
He discriminated the Abyssinian branch of the
Nile from the western river, the most considerable of the two, by calling it emphatically

Bahr el Nil, or the Blue River; I believe it is
always painted blue in the sculptures — the
word is Sanscrit too, and applied in the sacred
books to the western Nile, though the usual
name for it is Cali or Chrishna — the Black,
which corresponds in meaning with the Hebrew name Sihor: and yet, oddly enough, the
river is neither black nor blue, but a muddy
colour.   The Kiashef, in reply to our question
where the sources were, said they were not
very distant, but that the barbarous tribes and
fierce animals, with which the intermediate
country abounds, rendered them difficult of approach.   One of these tribes, he told us, is a
nation of dogs with women wives! the old
tradition, then, of the Cynocephali, or dog-
headed men, is still current here.   The same
belief prevailed in Tartary in the time of
Zinghis Khan, and Mr. Buckingham was
asked at Assalt, east of the Jordan, whether he
had ever been to the Belled el Kelb, where the

men had dogs' heads. The Nile, added the Kiashef, parts into three rivers—the Egyptian stream, another that reaches the sea near Algiers, and the third near Spain.

Naming our acquaintance, Omar Effendi (a young Turk, sent by Mohammed Ali to study in England, but now returned and settled at Cairo), he said he was from the same village, and seemed interested in hearing we had been at college with him.

Taking his departure, he sent us a couple of turkeys, and a sort of firman or order, to furnish us everything we might need between the cataracts. Nothing could be kinder than his offers of procuring us men, camels, and assistance of every sort, wheresoever we might be disposed to go. It was interesting, but painful, to see a man, evidently of talent, born and bred in intellectual darkness, and aware of his situation, struggling and catching at every ray of light. He entered at once on his inquiries, never doubting our willingness to afford him what aid we could ; the conversation seldom flagged a moment, and, in his eagerness, the pipe was often neglected. On paying us another visit on our return (to which I alluded at the commencement of this long epistle), he told us very feelingly that, since he had become acquainted with Europeans about three years ago, he had disrelished the society of other Turks ; all their conversation ran on women or dress, never on subjects of real interest. " Now," said he, " I like to know how the sun shines, how the world was created, who inhabit it, &c., and because I do so, and seek the society of those who can instruct me, my countrymen call me proud, and I am quite alone among them ;"— " solo, solo, solo ! " as Abdallah translated it : it went to my heart — poor fellow ! he must indeed be lonely, and so must every one be who outstrips his fellows, while they are still as unenlightened as the

Turks, even by the very insignificant distance that Wellee Kiashef has got before them.

We reached Wady Halfa, the limit of our Ethiopian voyage, on the 19th, passing Ebsambul, the magnificent rock-temple opened by Belzoni, without landing — our large boat could ascend no higher. I ought to have told you that, to our delight, we found we *could* take her beyond Essouan; we thought we should have been obliged to hire a small one there, and anticipated bugs, cock-roaches, spiders—all sorts of miseries.

Friday, the 20th January, we started for the second and principal cataracts of the Nile, a few miles only beyond Wady Halfa, in a small boat, manned with Nubian sailors, or Berbers, as they are called in their native tongue; and Barbaradesa is the name given to all this district in the Hindoo records. They are a very handsome race, far superior to the Arabs — of Egypt at least; almost black, but with a po-

lished skin, quite unlike the dirty hue of the
negro; the eye rests far more complacently on
their naked limbs than on those of the whiter
castes: they are tall, for the most part, and
beautifully proportioned—sinewy, no fat—the
heel on a line with the back of the leg, a noble
expression of countenance, and fine phreno-
logical foreheads; their honesty is proverbial.
Cultivation, I think, might do wonders with
them.* So much for the race in general; the

* Mr. Ramsay's Observations on the races of Nubia.
" The people here (Philae) are of the Berber race, or
Nubians, a very fine nation. No people have ever struck
me so much; they are almost invariably handsome and
elegant in their form and features, with an expression of
high intelligence and mind I never saw in other people of
their rank. Talking phrenologically, their heads are
perfect, and I cannot help thinking their capabilities for
civilization very great. They seem to have a great deal
of ready wit and humour, to judge by the constant
repartees and roars of laughter; and their songs are
beautiful."—Letter of Mr. Ramsay, Feb. 18.
" Jan. 12, Kalabshi. The natives are the most savage
uncivilized looking beings one could wish to see. They
grow darker at each village, but have by no means the

individuals on this occasion—naked except the
waist, and full of fun and merriment, punted
and rowed us up the river as far as the boat

attributes of genuine Nubians; their hue is more like that
of a very dirty collier in England, or a sweep, than the
pure, shining, polished skin of the true breed. The
little dingy naked children, running away to hide themselves, or staying to joke and laugh at us, which they do
with all their heart and soul, as different in appearance
as in manners from their neighbours south of Essouan,
have a very savage look."

" Jan. 17, beyond Derr. The country grows wider
and more picturesque. The varieties of inhabitants are
remarkable; each village appears to have a different
race — at one point, a group of thorough-bred, woolly-
headed, frightful negroes — at another, that race we call
(whether rightly or no) *Nubians*, a handsome, interesting people, not black, though nearly approaching to it—
at another, the Berbers (I suppose), a *peculiarly* fine set,
with the free independent air of the desert, and simple
elegant dress. They are considered as having the best
character of any people in every respect. The Arabs
also here and there appear, the same as in Egypt. The
women's dress in some places is peculiarly elegant, consisting of wide trowsers, drawn tight at the ankle, and
apparently continued as a sort of boots over the shoes.
These reach to the waist; the upper robe is very elegant,
formed, apparently, of a doubled cloth, square, and with

M 5

could ascend, and then, landing on the western bank, we proceeded on foot, alternately over sand and rock, to Abousir, a lofty cliff that overhangs the rapids, conspicuous from afar, and covered, we found, with the names of former travellers.

Climbing the rock, the Nile lay before us like the map of an Archipelago — so it seemed to me at first, till the eye presently discovered the main stream of the river winding between myriads of little black islets, tufted with the Egyptian acacia, and glistening in the sun-beams like those near Philae — themselves washed by hundreds of collateral streamlets

a hole for the head, which is passed through it, and it then falls gracefully over the whole body. Their hair is always in layers of curls, with something black on the top. The whole dress is of coarse unbleached linen cloth, and has a thoroughly different appearance from that of the Arab women, which is always deep blue or black. But I have seen none of them near; they never show themselves, nor ever appear in company with the men, who come in troops down to the banks."—*Mr. Ramsay's Journal.*

that glitter, foam, and roar in emulation of
their parent. Ten miles in length and two in
breadth, are these rapids. It is the lower
cataract on an infinitely larger scale, but the
impressions excited are widely different; there
you feel an interest in every rock as you pass
it, you admire their savage grandeur individually, and the rapids the while are dashing away
under your feet—there you thread a labyrinth
—here you look down on one, quite bewildered.

The prospect, miles to the eastward, is
bounded by the prolongation of Gebel Mokattam — to the south, by the mountains of
Dongola — it was something to have seen
them! It was a sad thought, that I had
reached the limits of my southern excursion;
sad—though now every step I took would bring
me nearer to my happy homes in England and
Scotland! From one of the western craigs
I had a partial view over the Libyan desert—
a dreary sight.

While William carved our names on the
rock, where many a future traveller will read
them in association with those of Belzoni,
Burckhardt, Irby and Mangles, &c., I enjoyed
half an hour's delightful rumination, on a most
commodious natural seat that overhangs the
Nile beyond the rock Abousir, and on which,
before departure, I cut my cypher by way of
claiming it as my own; Coutts will perhaps
one day find it there, and add his own to it.
Nowhere else have we attempted to immor-
talize ourselves in this way. At Petra, if we
ever get there, we have a plot *in petto* — to
carve our names, "Ramess'," and "Lindess',"
(they are actually written so in many ancient
charters), on some conspicuous rock or wall,
in hieroglyphical characters within king's
ovals; "what a splutter" will this make
among the antiquaries!

Our Nubian sailors entertained us with some
most extraordinary Berber songs, as we re-

turned to Wady Halfa—much more melody in
them than in the Arab airs. One of them
ended in the wildest and shrillest single yell
I ever heard—single in its effect, though de-
composable into a rapid reiteration of the same
high note, springing from the throat like stones
from the mouth of the Geisers, followed by a
second yell of one single note, every voice
joining in it—two or three heathenish laughs,
liker the neighing of a score of horses than
aught human, finishing off the melody.

We started northward on regaining the
" Hippopotamus," rowing now to expedite
our motions, floating down stream between
two and three miles an hour. From Alexandria to Wady Halfa, the distance is nine hundred and sixty miles.

Words cannot express to you how much
I have enjoyed my trip hitherto, but this
expedition within the tropic I shall always
remember with peculiar delight. How you

would both enjoy Nubia ! the weather is lovely, the mornings and evenings exquisitely beautiful, fresh breezes tempering the heat; the sky, by day, transparent as crystal, at sunset, a sea of molten gold, rich beyond conception, and at night, lighted by a moon and stars so brilliant and clear ! I finished Cowper's Task one evening, lying on the divan in the tent, with no light but the fair moon to read by; the air was balm, and the musical dash of the oar shed a thousand sparkles of broken light as we glided along.

Thursday, however, the 26th of January, dawned on us the gloomiest morning we had seen in Egypt — now, at last, for an adventure ! Few travellers have been shipwrecked in the cataracts of the Nile !

The Reis made his appearance, and we started on our descent to Essouan immediately after breakfast. The first rapid we passed prosperously, with the exception of one bulge,

but the rope attached to the vessel, to retard
the rapidity of her descent, breaking as we
approached the second and more difficult one,
we were hurried off by the torrent, and struck
against a rock under water, the same which
Ibrahim Pasha ran against some years ago,
when his whole crew perished. We, most
providentially, struck sideways, or we should
probably have suffered the same fate. The
force of the blow drove us on a shoal near an
isolated rock in the middle of the river; the
vessel grounded — our men leapt on the rock,
and secured her with ropes. Our first idea
was to lighten her by landing the heavy boxes,
&c., but the water (for we had sprung two or
three leaks), gained on us so fast, that all
hands were set to work to remove the luggage
to the island — every thing was hurried out,
pell-mell; I was in the cabin, giving out the
last handful of books, after pocketing one or
two that I valued, and a bag of gold pieces, on

the chance of being able to save nothing else,
when the cry rose that we were going down
the stream again! I sprung out, the vessel was
edging away from the rock — I leaped and
caught by my hands, my feet in the water;
the Arabs pulled me up, and I was safe, thank
God! Twice did the boat nearly escape us,
the current was so violent; at last we got her
safely lashed to the rock with all the ropes we
had, and for an hour, or more, the men were
occupied in landing every thing portable, first,
our things, then the oars, planks, &c., of the
boat, lastly, their own stores of dates and
biscuits, which they would not touch, honest
fellows! till our's were safe. We expected
every minute to see the ropes break and the
boat topple over, lying sideways as she did,
the deck half under water.

Here we were then, and a most extraordinary scene it was to be in! wild and picturesque at all times, doubly so now, dark

purple clouds lowering around us, rain pouring, (a wonder of itself in Upper Egypt), lightnings flashing, and thunder outroaring the rapids that were dashing past on either side our islet, covered as it was, with boxes, books, pipes, pistols, guns, crockery, pigeons, fowls, lambs, goats—and, last and least, two chamelions, poor little things ! we had bought them at Derr, the capital of Nubia, and had had great fun with them.*   Our Arabs and Nubians—

* "Jan. 22. Gave half a piastre for a couple of chamelions, which we have been trying, unsuccessfully, to tame.   Their natural colour appears to be a fine green, which is changed into a deep brown or black, and varies between the two.   It is a very curious animal, like a lizard in general appearance, but much slower in its motions, and differently organised.   The body is about four inches long, and the tail, which is long and tapering, about double that length.   It has a large head and enormous mouth ; the eyes are covered with a skin the same as its body, with a small hole in the centre, which they have the power of directing to any point they chuse, so that they can see in all possible directions, without moving the head ; each eye is moved quite independently of the other, so that one is often pointed forward while

some were sitting idle on the baggage, others
unloading the vessel; a messenger every now
and then catamaraning it from the shore on a
log of wood, or fearlessly dashing through the
rapids, calculating his distance, and the necessary allowance for the force of the current,
with the most unerring precision. Our captain,
meanwhile, sitting on the edge of the rock,
bare-headed, and almost naked, was raving
like a madman, now rocking backwards and
forwards, now stretching out his hands, apos-
trophising his boat, and crying like a child;
one of the sailors covered his head, exposed as
it was to the rain, and robed him — he was
quite unconscious of the attention; I never

the other looks backward. The feet are divided into two
parts, of the same size and form, with three sharp claws
on each part, and they have the power of grasping with
the two divisions, as well as hanging by the tail; the
division and action of the feet are on much the same
principle as those of our hands and thumb, only as if
there were two hands thus united, with three fingers
each." *Mr. Ramsay's Journal.*

saw a man so utterly unnerved. The crew, too, were blubbering at first, but afterwards they worked like men. Abdallah was active and useful; Missirie, a host in himself, was packing up this, tying up that, stowing away the books, and preparing every thing for the re-embarkation which we hoped to effect, though we were not unprepared for the necessity of making the rock our bed for the night; a situation, altogether — what with the war of elements, the wreck, our uncertainty how we were to get off, if at all — as impossible to describe as to forget.

We had ample time, three hours or more, to reflect on the kindness of Providence in directing us against the rock we struck on; had we missed it, we should have been hurried down the cataract, at the certainty, almost, of being dashed to pieces; had we grounded nearer the first rapid, we must have swum for our lives—we should have had no islet to take refuge on, such as proved our safety this morning.

Having sent to Philae and Essouan for help, both messages took effect in due time, the former producing a small boat, the latter our friend of Korosko, Wellee Kiashef! who, we found afterwards, was just stepping into his boat for Esneh, when he heard of our misfortune, and came forthwith to our assistance, with his Armenian secretary, and the dragoman, or interpreter, of a German baron, bound on the Pasha's service, to the gold mines in Sennaar.

The Philae boat was beautifully manœuvred; it darted past us, and down the rapids, like an arrow, and then veered round under the rocks, and was towed up by the Nubians, swimming from rock to rock, till they brought it alongside our Islet. After getting all our valuables on board, we embarked with Missirie, Abdallah, Achmet, the Captain of our boat, the portly

Reis of the Cataracts, and the surviving chamelion, for the other, drooping for some days past,
had died on the island — altogether a tremendous freight. We started, held back for
a while by a rope till we reached the line of
the rapid; then they let go, and, without rope
or guidance except the helm, we rushed down
between the rocks, cleared them to a wish, and,
in a few seconds, reached still water, and rowed
to the shore, where we were kindly greeted by
the Kiashef. The baggage landed, Missirie
arranged a mat and divan, and we sat down
and talked with him for an hour or so, waiting
for the camels which he had sent from Essouan
to carry our baggage. He had also brought
donkeys for us, and we accepted a most cordial
invitation to dine with him, and lodge in his
apartments at the Government House. No
camels appearing, and the day wearing, we
started for Essouan on the Kiashef's own donkeys, for this good Samaritan would not suffer

us to mount the hired beasts, or to pay for them
on our arrival. We had ridden but a few
minutes when we met the camels towering
along at their stately slow pace. — I should
have mentioned, by the bye, that, on landing,
we let the little chamelion go ; Missirie took it
to a grassy spot where I dare say it has
been enjoying itself, after the fashion of chamelions, ever since. Poor little thing ! its
adventures surpass even those of the " Travelled Ant," in the Evenings at Home!

Our road to Essouan lay just within the
edge of the eastern desert, through the wildest
scenery : —a ravine, which we could only thread
our way through one at a time, opening into a
broad sandy plain, like the dry bed of a river—
both edged in by rocks of the most extraordinary shapes, piled one on another like the
fragments of an earlier world — black and
massy—not a blade of vegetation,—contrasting
strangely with sheets of the finest white sand,

sparkling as snow, and rippled all over by the wind, lying here and there in broad wreaths between them,— and a clear evening sky above us, for the day had brightened after the storm. The sandy valley ends in the cemetery of old Essouan, the Saracenic town, depopulated (as I mentioned above) centuries ago, by the plague, and deserted ever since. Hundreds of tomb-stones, carved with inscriptions in the old Cufic character, lie on each side the road; ruined mosques, and the shattered walls of the old town, crown the hills on the left, and had a most singular appearance, relieved against the sunset sky. I could scarcely have imagined any thing more dreary than the desert, that death-bed of nature; but a cemetery in the desert, and that the forgotten one of a deserted town, strikes cold to the heart.

It was dusk by the time we dismounted at the Kiashef's harem, the first house we came to; he brought out a couple of arm-chairs, and gave us a most acceptable cup of coffee, and then, leading the way to the government-house, ushered us into the presence-chamber, as I suppose I must call it, where the Bey gives audience during the summer.

Here we again smoked our pipes, and drank the coffee of our hospitable friend. William and myself, seated in arm-chairs of state,— the Kiashef, (as grave and silent as a judge now he was among his countrymen), and a Turkish officer — on two plain chairs — and the Armenian secretary cross-legged on his mat, formed our party, and a very pleasant one it was, for nothing could be more cordial than their attentions.

Dinner at last made its appearance. Napkins were first given us; then raisins and a fiery liqueur of aniseed were placed on the table as a whet; then came the dishes drest à la Turque, which we partook of à l'Anglaise; the Turks eat after their fashion, dipping in the dishes very neatly, with pieces of bread for spoons : little was said during the meal, for the Turks don't talk on such occasions; lastly, a servant brought water to each of us, to wash our hands, pouring it over them ;—then coffee again. We had a good deal of conversation afterwards, through Abdallah and a Nubian, who had travelled with Lord Belmore some years ago, and spoke a little Italian. The officer spoke highly of his own achievements in the chace, of having killed (and eaten ?) a lion, &c. &c. A lion, he told us, would never attack a woman, even armed :—

> " 'Tis said that a lion will turn and flee
> From a maid in the pride of her purity "—

I did not expect to hear a sentiment of chivalry in this part of the world.

About nine, we rose and wished the party good-night—Missirie, we found, had made our rooms comfortable in the extreme, putting up the camp-bedsteads, making a divan of the

cushions of the boat, and putting the things in
order ; every thing almost had been saved.
We were much the better for our tea, as you
may suppose, and read and wrote afterwards
till bed-time, by the light of an immense
Turkish candle stuck in the orange-basket.

Next morning, before we were up, Wellee
Kiashef had been to see us, and had smoked
three pipes ; he returned about ten, and breakfasted with us ; he drank his tea and ate his
omelet with great apparent satisfaction, and
afterwards smoked his pipe again, seated on
the divan, and cherishing his foot.   The Armenian secretary also came to see us.   An
Abyssinian boy attended, the Kiashef's page,
and apparently a great favourite,— respectful,
but without servility ; the Kiashef spoke kindly
to him, and the boy made his observations
freely, though modestly :—the henchman stood
at the door, like Evan Mac Combich in Waverley.
— William gave the Kiashef a musical snuff-

box, which he seemed pleased with. After staying about an hour, he again inquired whether he could do any thing for us, and protested, on our reiterating our gratitude for his past kindness, that really it was 'nothing — nothing.' He then rose to go, and, with kind wishes and salams, we parted.

We then started, with Abdallah, for the Cataracts, to see after the boat. It was a lovely day, but so hot that we had almost resolved on giving up the walk, when the appearance of some donkeys that we had countermanded determined us to proceed. I was glad to see the Saracenic tombs again in broad daylight; the head-stones are in perfect preservation, many of them lying quite loose—dear A——would have enjoyed a walk among them, — she is tout à fait Saracenique, as Caviglia would say.

We followed nearly the same route as yesterday, and were equally delighted with the extraordinary scenery. Before descending to the river, we took a last look at Philae in the distance, and its beautiful temple.— The boat, we found, had kept its place during the night; the Reis of the cataracts was there with his men, and they were stopping up the leaks in order to bring her to the bank, that they might get her ready for coming down to Essouan the next morning. Swarms of Nubian children clustered around us with curiosities for sale; we bought some necklaces and bracelets of red and white beads and straws, (they show beautifully on a black skin), and several fetiches or amulets, which they wear generally under the right arm — the dagger under the left; the latter even the children carry. William dissected one of these fetishes afterwards, and found a long roll of paper inside, covered with Arabic writing and mystical diagrams, magical and astrological apparently.

The fearlessness of the boatmen, their intimate acquaintance with every eddy of the river, and their dexterity in manœuvring, struck us with admiration; while we were standing there, a vessel, in full sail, every oar plied, ascended half the rapid, landed some of the crew on a projecting rock, and then floated back again, the broadside to the stream; the most graceful, lady-like retreat imaginable.

After sauntering about, identifying the scenes of our first and second passage, we returned by a Nubian village built on the shore in a grove of date trees, — plenty of women and children — no reserve in the former, though one of them, whenever we looked at her, hid her face like the Arab women, for fear of the evil eye probably; the boys were naked, most of them; the little girls wear belts of small leathern thongs. One of the children danced before us, naked, and brandishing a short spear, a thorough young cannibal.

Next morning we crossed to Elephantine,

and had another delightful stroll over the
lovely island. — It was a heavenly day — still
and thoughtful ; the broad Nile lay before us,
sparkling as if with a thousand eyes ; the fish-
ermen were paddling about on their catamarans
—I have called them so, inadvisedly perhaps,
but they much resemble those used at Madras,
if the descriptions I have read be correct ;
they consist of a log of wood, fixed between
two bundles of reeds tied together at the two
extremities ; the fisher sits on it, not astride,
like the Indian, but as on a sledge, and with
his single paddle strikes twice or thrice on
each side alternately, zigzagging it like a water-
fly.—I thought the Isle of Flowers lovelier than
ever !

Sunday morning, we had a delightful walk
along the heights beyond old Syene. A solitary forsaken minaret, or watchtower, crowns
the brow of one of the hills ; we climbed up it,
and read the service there — some boys who

had followed us the whole morning with curiosities for sale must have thought us magicians. We extended our walk much further. Every hill is crowned with a mosque; in one of them that we entered, the arches were all pointed—it is among the tombs and mosques of Old Essouan, that Mr. Wilkinson thinks the earliest specimens may be found of that style of architecture. The oldest known at present is the mosque of Sultan Ahmed e' Tayloon at Cairo, erected A. D. 879.

I was reading, most comfortably disposed on the divan, that afternoon, when William entered with a gentleman from India, one of a party of three who had started from Philae in the morning—his friends by land, having heard of our disaster—himself, more adventurous, by water. The Reis presumed to pilot the boat without a rope; the consequence was, that she was hurried by the current against the rocks, and her bottom completely and

irreparably stove in. The captain went as
frantic as our's did, forgot even his child, which
was left in the boat; Mr. Clarke, our new
acquaintance, caught it up and swam to land.
William met Mr. C. on the shore, and advised
his applying for rooms in the government-
house, which were granted immediately.

Soon afterwards, the other gentlemen arrived; we asked them, of course, to dinner.
Mr. Clarke, a very pleasing gentleman-like
young officer, proved to be the son of Dr.
Edward Clarke, the celebrated traveller; his
companions were Dr. Mac Lennan, the distinguished physician, chef d'hôpital, I believe —
at Bombay — so kindly mentioned by poor
Victor Jacquemont in his last letter to his
brother,—and Mr. Southhouse, also in the Indian service. We spent a very pleasant evening,
and, at night, sent them some cloaks and the
cushions of our divan to sleep on, none of
their things having arrived from the wreck.

Messrs. Mac Lennan and Southhouse breakfasted with us next morning; Clarke, like a
man of his word, had gone betimes to the boat,
having promised the men to do so. He found
them very hungry, and yet they had not touched
their master's provisions, nor attacked the
fowls in the hencoop; one poor fellow being
quite naked, he arrayed him in a shooting-
jacket and knee-breeches; a strange figure he
must have cut!

They all three dined with us, and, after another agreeable evening, we parted on the stair-
head—such a night it was! I stood long there
watching it,—brilliant, and yet inexpressibly
soft and lovely, the stars, varying in tint and
apparent distance, twinkling through the whispering date-trees, or crowning them like diamonds on the forehead of beauty.

Enfin, on Tuesday morning, the 31st of
January, A. D. 1837, we started for Thebes,
after bidding our Indian friends farewell. They

felt most kindly on the subject of the trifling attentions we had paid them, and expressed it not only by words but deeds; think of Clarke's sending us half a dozen of Hodson's ale, an Indian luxury, and Dr. Mac Lennan a dozen of Madeira, and four bottles of Constantia! What sunshiny days such are in human life !

And so we bade adieu to Essouan—sorrowfully, at least on my part; I had received kindness there, and had shared with William in showing it to others : I took more than one last look at the noble rocks, and the minaret we visited on Sunday, conspicuous from afar on the hill beyond them, and the lovely Isle of Flowers—never, probably, to greet her again ! They had become "things familiar" to us, and it was painful

"Even from their lifelessness to part."

Since that morning we have been leading our Nile life again, the old routine ; the vessel is all right, and every thing goes on as it did before our wreck. What mercies all these are to be grateful for !

P. S. I find, on looking over " fytte the second " of this interminable epistle, (I hope you will not consider it a *romance*), that I have omitted all mention of our visit to the magnificent temple of Re, ([38]) or the Sun, at Ebsambul, near Wady Halfa, discovered by Burckhardt, and opened by Belzoni, Irby, and Mangles ;—two words only—I must not pass over the most stupendous excavation in the whole valley of the Nile.

You enter between four enormous statues of Rameses the Great, about sixty feet in height, seated—the expression of countenance almost feminine in its mild beauty ; they are admirably sculptured, in full relief, their backs scarcely resting against the rock ; looking up at them from the southern and shadowy angle of the excavation, their sublimity was, indeed, almost overpowering.

The doorway is surmounted by a beautiful

sculpture of the hawk-headed deity Osiris, and that by a frieze of hieroglyphics, above which—strange finish for such a work! sit a row of monkeys—but nothing, however quaint or extraordinary, is out of character in Egyptian architecture.

Descending between the colossal statues, you enter the great hall, supported on each side by four columns, faced with gigantic statues reaching to the ceiling, similar in dress to those we saw at Guerf Hassan, but, in proportions and execution, far finer; nor are they so awful—you have room to look at these—there you felt the passage between such monsters too narrow.

The temple was excavated soon after the accession of Rameses, and the sculptures seem to refer chiefly to his earliest campaigns. On either side of the door, inside, is a gigantic figure of the Conqueror holding by the hair a group of kneeling captives, back to back, and about to slay them; they are of different

nations and colours—you distinguish blacks of
various castes, and the same Shorii, with the
forked beards and aquiline noses, who die so
nobly at Beit Wellee. The sculptures on the
south wall appear to record his victories
over this people. Standing on his chariot,
drawn by two horses, with the usual feathers
on their heads, the reins fastened to his girdle
behind him, his bow in his hand—a perfect arc
— Rameses pours his unerring arrows on the
enemy, many of whom have already fallen, and
others vainly try to avoid them ; farther on,
dismounted and trampling on one of their
chiefs, he seizes another by the arm, and
pierces him with his lance. On the opposite
or northern wall, are sculptured battles on a
smaller scale, spirited, but inferior to those of
Thebes ; the preparation for the battle ; the
parting of a warrior and his wife ; the clash of
chariots and riders, and horses falling under
the arrows of the Egyptians all the tumult of
war and bloodshed. After all, these war-

scenes are composed in the very spirit of a Highland pibroch; the gathering, the advance, the battle, the song of triumph, the welcome home, and the coronach for the dead, you hear and you see them all.

Beyond this noble hall, there are a second, supported by square columns, a cella, and an adytum, with four deities seated at the extremity, and an altar before them, as at Guerf Hassan; besides many lateral chambers of inferior interest.

There are several other temples of much interest between Wady Halfa and Essouan; but I will only mention one of them — that of Hermes Trismegistus at Dakke — beautiful! beautiful! What fame such a visit would have conferred on us in the good old days of astrology, alchemy, and diablerie ! *

————————

* "Dandour, Jan. 24. The temple is a small one, and hardly mentioned in the books, but is very interesting.

" Fytte the Second " has kept upon the whole so free from antiquities, that I shall make no apology to my dear mother for reverting to that seducing subject in the present, after which it will be

> " Adew, ye get nae mair of me,"

on the subject of Egypt.

Thebes I have said more than enough about already; but there is a little temple at Herment, old Hermonthis, a few hours' sail to the south of it, well worth mentioning, as a rich mythological museum, and invested, moreover, with peculiar interest as having been built by the unblushing Cleopatra, to commemorate the birth of Cæsarion, her son by Julius Cæsar. I was much struck at finding it a perfect Augean

---

The turn of the ornaments on the doors, &c. is elegant, and the hieroglyphics, though not of the palmy days of Rameses II. are of that substantially good style, which never offends the eye by any glaring defects or false drawing and taste."—*Mr. Ramsay's Journal.*

stable, disgustingly filthy within, and without
plastered with cakes of dung, drying for fuel.
The accouchement of the Goddess Ritho, symbolical of Cleopatra's, is sculptured in the
adytum, and the scheme of young Cæsarion's
nativity on the ceiling. † (³⁹)

† "Feb. 5. Rose off the temple of Hermonthis, which
we visited before breakfast. It is interesting, and differs
from any we have yet seen in style and appearance, which
are such as to have induced Dr. Richardson, and other
travellers before the hieroglyphical discoveries were made,
to consider it as one of the oldest in Egypt. It seems
never to have been completed, at least the ovals for the
names have never been filled up in the interior of the
temple, and very few on the outside. The portico is
composed of tall pillars in the style of that age, but not
very graceful, from being too near each other. The interior is very simple, consisting of two chambers, very
lofty and very gloomy; the furthest and smallest one
seems merely a slice of the whole building, built off, and,
consequently, its length is the breadth of the temple, its
width not above three yards, and its height equal to the
other. A window at the top throws light on the roof,
which has been called a zodiac, and bears some appearance of being so. It is a strange device, in all probability
an astrological scheme of nativity of the young Cæsarion.
On the walls are represented the birth, education, &c. of

Nor must I wholly pass over the far-famed temple of Dendera, a most extraordinary pile, unlike anything we had seen in Egypt, at once grotesque in its details and magnificent in its general effect, and in perfect preservation. The ceiling of the portico is covered with astronomical subjects, representing, for the most part, the processions of the Sun and Moon, in their barks of state, through the signs of the

the same child, or rather of the young God Haphré, his patron, I suppose. Astronomical subjects cover the ends of the room. In the larger apartment is a strange series of designs; the child is presented to all the different gods, and the whole show of the divine menagerie is exhibited—cats, dogs, crocodiles, &c., as well as the hideous figures of Typhon and his consort. A winged scarabaeus, with the globe, also the winged hawk, are conspicuous objects over the door, where the child is seated on the horns of the bull Apis. The demon Typhon is the only one I have ever seen represented with his face towards the spectator, and his body turned half so, between front and profile—and this only in one other place, where he is made of enormous size and hideous deformity. A house is built on the top of this temple, and it stands in a dung-yard."—*Mr. Ramsay's Journal.*

zodiac; each zodiac is involved within the interminable body of that celestial boa, Nith, the mother of the Sun, whose beams are represented, at the moment of his birth, illuminating the disk of the moon. Strange mythological fancies are sculptured here — snakes, for instance, with human arms or legs, or erect on their tails, presenting offerings, &c. When the sepoys were here, they recognised the gods of India in those sculptured on the walls, and worshipped with the same ceremonies they would have performed at Benares. This of itself proves the first-cousinhood of the two religions.* ([40])

* " Dendera. However grand and stupendous this temple may be, it is not worthy of the lavish encomiums most travellers indulge in — perhaps, because it is the first they see in Egypt, whether in ascending the Nile, or coming overland from India. It bears extreme evidence of the great decadence of art at the period of its erection. The spirit which animated the early ages in this country had long passed away, the forms only remained — these were preserved scrupulously by the in-

A deadly feud raged whilom between the crocodile-haters of Dendera, and the crocodile-worshippers of Ombos; one of the latter having fallen into the clutches of the Tenty-rites, "they eat him up, baith stoup and roup," as the devils are said to have served the victor of Culloden. Near the temple at Ombos (a noble relic) is a large wall of crude brick, on which, Dr. Richardson supposes, the sacred crocodile took his daily airing, and, below it, the tank in which he bathed — poor wretch, to be debarred his own imperial Nile!

terested zeal of the priests, and under the Roman rule, which considered all religions equally useful, were dignified by such dedications as this. But the peculiar turn of spirit which breathes from even the most insignificant remains of the Pharaonic period, is quite wanting here; it is dead, formal, and in details quite uninteresting—or, if one's curiosity be excited by the zodiacs and planispheres which are one of the peculiar features of this temple, the fact again recurs to the mind, that they are, after all, but priestly imitations of what we have already seen in the tombs of the Pharaohs; made to be stared at, not felt and understood."—*Mr. Ramsay's Journal.*

The quarries at Hadjar Silsili are wondrous indeed ! What think you of squares a hundred feet deep, and as spacious as those of London, cut out of the mountain, and communicating with each other by long winding streets or passages ?

At Beni Hassan we visited the oldest tombs we have seen in Egypt, excavated in Osirtesen's time, seventeen centuries B.C. The owner of one of them seems to have been a regular sporting character; his dogs stand by his side in the full-length portrait drawn of him, as is usually the case, in one corner of the tomb ; hunting, fowling, and fishing scenes are represented in other compartments; a mock-fight, and the successive rounds of a wrestling match (or, probably, of several, for there are scores of groups, exhibiting every attitude and vicissitude of the struggle), adorn the extremity of the tomb. These wrestling matches are found in most of the tombs at

Beni Hassan ; it was evidently a science in Egypt at a very early period.

The game of draughts, two seven-stringed harps, tossing up and catching three balls successively, the pirouette with extended arms, practised by figurantes in the modern opera, and the attendance of dwarfs on the Egyptian nobles, are among the note-worthy objects depicted in these curious sepulchres. The columns that support them are of two orders, both extremely primitive; polygonal, like those of Thebes, slightly fluted, and very elegant ; or, simply, four lotus-stalks tied together by a broad band under the buds.

And now, my dear mother, I have almost done. You must be sick of temples and tombs ; I fear that many things I have expatiated on, in the hope of their amusing you, must have failed to do so ; but all I can say in excuse is, that I have spared you much. I shall continue, however, to write *lengthily*, for I think

you and A—— will be pleased to follow me,
step by step, throughout my pilgrimage.
Memphis is the only place we have now to
visit; in two or three days we shall arrive at
Cairo, but shall be very very sorry to bid adieu
to the little bark that has been our home so
long, and in which we have become so
thoroughly domesticated.

Port of Cairo, 23d Feb.

We arrived here this evening, but do not
intend landing till to-morrow; this is the last
night we are to spend on board the Hippopotamus !

We have spent the whole day in visiting the
site of Memphis and the pyramids of Dashour
and Sacara. Mounds and embankments, a few
broken stones, and two colossal statues, dis-
interred a few years ago by our friend Caviglia,
are the solitary remains of the ancient capital
of Lower Egypt. We rode for miles through

groves of palm and acacia, cultivated fields, and wastes of sand, over what we knew must be the site of Memphis, but every other vestige of her ancient grandeur has disappeared. Noph is indeed "waste and desolate."

The colossus of Rameses the Great, forty feet in height, lies on its face — the workmanship beautiful, the features (mild and benignant) in perfect preservation. This was, without doubt, one of the six statues (of himself, his wife, and four of his sons) erected by Rameses in front of the great temple of Vulcan, which, from the descriptions of the ancients, must have been a wonder of the world. A short distance to the south, lies a small statue, about ten or twelve feet high, we thought, which, perhaps, belonged to the edifice where the bull Apis was kept and exhibited, and which lay in that direction, according to Herodotus. This is all — how truly has the prophecy been fulfilled, " I will destroy the idols, and will cause their images to cease out of Noph ! '' ([41])

Near the temple of Vulcan, the site of which is now completely overgrown with date trees, lay the Lake Acherusia — whence the fictions of Charon and his boat, and the Elysian fields. We crossed the dry bed on our way to Sacara. The Sheikh and his friends were enjoying *otium cum dignitate,* under an acacia, as we rode past the village. The groves of acacia near Sacara and Mitraheni are mentioned eighteen hundred years ago.

The principal pyramid at Sacara is built in five degrees, or steps, like the tower of Babel; there is another, some degrees to the south, similarly built, and called the False Pyramid; magnificent at a distance, it loses its grandeur in proportion to the nearness of your approach.

The two great Pyramids of Dashour are very beautiful, each about 700 feet square, but of much lower elevation than those of Djizeh.

We descended into the northern one by a steep
and sloping passage, for 200 feet, and, crawling
on our wrists and feet some yards farther, on
a level, found ourselves in the first of two
lofty chambers, connected by a low passage,
and leading to a third by another passage, the
entrance to which was too high for us to
reach it without a ladder. The structure of
these apartments is very remarkable, each successive course of stone, beginning from about
ten or eleven feet from the ground, projecting
about six inches beyond the one below it, till
the two walls meet. It is said to resemble the
inside of a Cyclopean or Pelasgic building at
Argos, popularly called the Treasury of Atreus.

We rode between many other pyramids,
some of them still preserving their shape,
though partially covered with sand, others
already sinking into tumuli, or enormous barrows; these latter are perhaps the oldest of all.

A curious root, transparent and juicy as a

white radish, grows here under the sand, betraying its existence by a tiny stalk, as thin as a blade of grass, shooting above the surface. Southey, I think, alludes to it in one of his poems.

The ride from Sacara to the point where we regained the boat, about an hour north of a place called Sheikh Etmin, was very beautiful —through extensive palm-groves clustering round Arab villages, and Bedouin encampments —wandering Ishmaelites — the pyramids of Djizeh, cotemporary with their father Abraham, towering in the distance.

February 24.

Once more at Grand Cairo—soon, I hope, to leave it for Mount Sinai, Petra, and Jerusalem — for such is the route we intend attempting. We shall travel on camels and dromedaries, and sleep in tents, like the patriarchs.

Adieu, my dear mother!

P. S. You will be glad to hear that I have
sent our friend the Kiashef, a little Arabic
library, consisting of Robinson Crusoe, two
or three books on history, the Arabic atlas
I mentioned in my last letter from Cairo, a
summary of the Old, and the whole of the
New Testament. Adieu, once more.

March 2.

P. S. (bis.)   We revisited the pyramids yesterday, and were most kindly received by
Colonel Vyse, who is carrying on his researches
there in person, Caviglia having quitted the
field.   He has attacked the three Pyramids
and the Sphinx, all at once, with a troop of
nearly two hundred Arabs.   In Cheops's —
he is in hopes of discovering the chamber
above Davison's, and an entrance on the
western side, corresponding to that on the
northern in its degree of distance from the
centre, calculating that, the one being so many

o 2

feet to the left, the other will be as many to the right of it. We saw an immense stone, that his workmen had dislodged, roll down the side of the pyramid; it was sad to see the sleep of four thousand years so rudely broken!

Colonel Vyse is cutting right into the heart of the third pyramid, but as yet has found no chamber; when he reaches the centre, he intends boring right up and down. He has bored thirty feet into the sphinx, in expectation of finding the chamber said to exist inside it —as yet without effect. He has many other ideas experimenting, and I should not be surprised if he make some curious discoveries.*

We dined with him, and returned to Cairo, much gratified with his kind attentions, the same afternoon.

* Colonel Vyse's success subsequent to our visit to him at the Pyramids has indeed been most gratifying.

EDOM AND THE HOLY LAND.

LETTER VII.

Journey to Mount Sinai. Desert of Suez — Mara — Route of the Israelites — Wady Shellal — Wady Mokatteb — Wady Feiran —Ascent to the Sinaite Mountains — Ascent of Mount St. Catherine — Of Gebel Mousa —Of Gebel Minnegia, possibly the real Sinai.

Convent of St. Catherine, Mount Sinai,
March 21, 1837

My dear A ——,

Finding a Polish pilgrim here, about to return to Cairo, I seize the opportunity of letting you and my dear mother know, a month sooner than otherwise I could, how well we have got on hitherto, and under what peculiarly favourable auspices we are likely to ·continue our journey by Petra to Jerusalem.

On Monday, the sixth of March, we started
on our voyage through the desert, (¹) a caravan
of ten camels, with two tents, one for our
followers Missirie and Abdallah, the other (an
Indian one, of bamboos) for ourselves. We
arrived at Suez on the fourth day. The hot
kamsin, or southerly wind, blew violently all
Monday, bringing clouds of sand, and pelting
us with small pebbles, which made our Arab
gillie-comstrains skip, as they rattled against
their naked legs — never was I in a heavier
hail-storm; luckily, I had provided myself at
Cairo with a Turkish scarf, which protected my
eyes; my lips were parched and chapped for
several days afterwards, and a book in my
pocket was scorched as if it had been held to
the fire. But we were fairly in the desert—delightful thought ! pilgrims following the steps
of the Israelites to the Promised Land.

We halted a little before sunset, and pitched
the smaller of our two tents, (the wind being

too high for the other), in a hollow between
two mounds, which afforded a few thorns and
tufts of arid grass for the camels, and tolerable shelter for ourselves. I really felt ashamed
when we were fairly established in the tent,
seated on our iron bedsteads, with a table, our
old ship-mate on the Nile, between us — far
too comfortable. It blew quite a storm the
first part of the night, and we thought the
tent would have flown away, but it weathered
it :—we were covered with sand when we woke
on Tuesday morning; much rain succeeded,
but it cleared up before we started, and the
day turned out delightful ; there was little sun,
but the wind had changed to the west, a fresh
exhilarating breeze.

The weather, indeed, has been charming
ever since. I always commenced the day with
a long walk ; nothing can be more enjoyable ;
—the desert, half gravel, half sand, crunches
under the feet like snow ;—sometimes bounded

by low hills, sometimes it stretches out into
an interminable plain, but always of the same
unvaried hue. We passed skeletons of camels
repeatedly, and scattered bones bleached to the
whiteness of snow; and, one morning, prowling
about near our encampment, I found an open
grave and a skull grinning up into my face
within it—the relic, doubtless, of some hapless
pilgrim. Melancholy memorials these! but
all was not death there; a frog, a species of
grey lizard, some quails and vultures, were
symptoms of animal — and various thorny
plants, a few wild flowers, and a strongly
scented plant, (a species of wild camomile
we thought it), called by the Arabs *behharran*
— of vegetable life; nor should I forget a solitary tree, long conspicuous on the horizon,
with the apparent dignity of a palm, but which
dwindled, long before we reached it, into a
stunted thorn, covered with rags streaming in
the wind, hung there by every pilgrim as he

passes *en chemin* for Mecca. The half-eaten carcase of a camel lay beneath it, and the vultures that had been garbaging on it flew heavily away at our approach.

I should have told you that the route we took was that by Mataria, north of Gebel Ataka, a long and picturesque ridge of hills, which we coasted all the third day ;— of a clear pinky grey in the morning, it assumed a deep iron-grey after sunset, as the rays died away ; it slants to the southward, as you approach Suez. The Israelites arriving at Etham, on the edge of the wilderness, from the north-west, the land of Goshen, turned southwards, a day's journey, to Pihahiroth, " the mouth of the ridge," i. e. of this very mountain Ataka :—closed in by the mountains on each side, with the sea in front, and Pharaoh behind, they could only be saved by such a miraculous interposition as that which is still traditionally remembered in the Arabic name Ataka, or Deliverance.

On Thursday we started, with the Arabian
mountains, and, as we conceived, the Red Sea,
in front of us ; it was the mirage !   A ship,
too, was curiously refracted in the clouds before
we came in actual sight of either ship or sea.

Kodsy Manoly, a Candiote Greek, the East-
India Company's agent at Suez, and a shrewd
intelligent man, received us with great hospitality, and we found there — and this is the
news that I think will please you — the celebrated Hussein, who accompanied Laborde to
Petra ten years ago. We struck a bargain
with him to convey us to Sinai, and have since
engaged him to accompany us during the rest
of our travels in Arabia.   " An excellent warrior and hunter," says Laborde, "and renowned
for his generous hospitality, he unites in himself all the qualities which render a Bedouin
respectable, especially those of so much impor-
tance to the traveller, unimpeachable integrity,
discretion which always deserves to be confided

in, and, what is very rare, genuine fidelity."
He is the principal of the three guardians, or
protectors, of the Convent of Mount Sinai, and
is known and respected wherever he goes;
Laborde made all his arrangements with the
other tribes through him, and so shall we.

Hussein and I have become great friends;
many a kind pat on the back have I had from
him. Our intimacy commenced with a long
walk one morning, that he and I took one road
while the caravan went the other; we had a
great deal of pleasant and most animated conversation; acting, gesticulating, drawing with
my stick on the sand, and the judicious use of
the *very* few Arabic words I have perforce
picked up, were generally sufficient to make
myself understood. We outwalked the camels,
and sat and chatted a quarter of an hour or
twenty minutes under the shadow of a projecting rock, before they came up. My recollection of the names and 'countries' of certain

of the Arab clans, allusions to Antar, and
such-like scraps of Arab tradition, have stood
me in great stead.   I have got much information from Hussein, through Abdallah, for whatever interesting point I asked him about,—(do
not mistake me—I don't believe I am master of
more than a dozen words of Arabic)—I always
repeated through the interpreter.

Hussein provided us with eleven camels,
those of Arabia not being so strong as the
Egyptian breed, besides two dromedaries for
riding ;—a dromedary is to a camel what a race-
horse is to a dray-horse — there is no generic
difference ; the Bactrian camel only has the two
humps commonly attributed to the dromedary.
Most of the camels were accompanied by their
owners, all of whom, two excepted, were of
Hussein's tribe, which, I should have told you,
is the Waled Said, the principal branch of the
Zoalia, the first in consideration of the Tora,
or Sinaite, clans.   The political constitution

of these Bedouin tribes strongly resembles that of our own clans in Scotland; each is divided into several septs, governed by subordinate Sheikhs or Chieftains, under whom the clansmen rally without prejudice to the patriarchal supremacy of the High Chief of the whole race, to whom the chief*tains* owe the same deference that the clansmen in general pay themselves. My heart warms to these Bedouin Highlanders, and the Tora tribes are a peculiarly fine race; the whole party, indeed, were good-humoured, hearty fellows.

All of us, masters and men, were armed to the teeth, William with rifle and gun, myself with holster pistols; every Arab had his *sikkeen*, or short sword, and some of them long match-lock guns, ornamented with pebbles, shells, and Turkish coins, which they use very expertly. One of them, unpoetical villain! shot a young gazelle one morning, and had the barbarity to press me to eat it.

Their attire was very simple, — the *kefia* or kerchief of the desert, loosely and gracefully tied round the head by a piece of rope, or a turban,—a long white robe of rather cumbrous drapery, sometimes of lighter material, secured by a girdle, — a long blue cloak, (peculiar, I believe, to the Arabs of this peninsula), and sandals of fish-skin, secured across the instep, and by clasps at the ankles, exposing the foot as in Scripture paintings ;—a small kneading-trough or bowl, a leathern bottle for water, a short pipe, tobacco-pouch, and sometimes the short crook-headed stick, represented in the hand of Osiris in the Egyptian sculptures, completed their equipment. Throw away the pipe and tobacco, (many of the Bedouins, how-ever — our friend Hussein for instance, never smoke),— substitute a lance or a sword for that ignoble weapon the gun, and any one of them might sit for a portrait of the Caliph Omar;—you cannot but remember the striking picture your favourite Ockley draws of him, on his journey from Mecca to Jerusalem.

So much for our guides, — a word or two on our own mode of travelling. I walked generally, for the first three or four hours, in advance of the caravan, resting every now and then under a shadowy rock or shrub, where such was to be found, till it came up, and then off again. Mounted — I read, mused, talked with William, or with the Bedouins through Abdallah, and took notes, till near halting-time, when I generally took another walk. We soon got accustomed to the camels' pace, which we were told was so fatiguing. (²) The caravan advances at a regular and certain pace, about three miles an hour; but the individual animals proceed very irregularly, stopping every now and then to graze on the thorny shrubs and scented plants, with which the Arabian desert, (particularly,) abounds; the drivers humour them in this, and are constantly leaving the road, and even scrambling up the rocks for a handful of any herb the animals are fond of. The first *taib* I received from my friend Hussein was for feeding a camel tied behind mine, which had not time to crop for itself.

We generally halted about sunset, on some smooth spot under the rocks or hills, made our camels kneel down, unloaded—and then let them go free to browze *à discretion* ; in half an hour more, the tents were pitched, fires blazing around, and the stars above us, for in these countries there is little or no twilight. The camels were then tethered down, and the Bedouins, their frugal meal and merry chat over, wrapped themselves up in their *abbas,* and went to sleep. We also dozed from dinner till tea-time, and then, after a cheerful cup or two, followed their example. Evenings as peaceful, and cups as cheering as those im- mortalized by Cowper, yet how different in their accessaries!—no newspapers, no politics, no prose of the present to mar our meditations on the past.

We all lent a hand in the tent-pitching; this Bedouin life is quite to my taste; 'tis the realisation of one of my childish day-dreams, when I used to pitch a tent on the nursery floor at Muncaster, and call it my home. And yet I *have* a lingering touch of European prejudice; there is something very melancholy in our morning flittings; the tent-pins are plucked up, and, in a few minutes, a dozen holes, a heap or two of ashes, and the marks of the camels' knees in the sand, soon to be obliterated, are the only traces left of what has been for a while home. There are a thousand allusions to this primitive mansion in Scripture, almost unintelligible, till familiarity with the tent, the camel, and the desert, explains them. I never drive in a tent-pin without thinking of Jael and Sisera.

Now for our journey. M. Manoly accompanied us to the shore of the Red Sea, and
saw us embark for Asia. We crossed in about
half an hour. I read the sublime description
of the Passage of the Israelites, the song of
Moses, and the seventy-seventh Psalm, with
the scene before my eyes; for it was a little
to the south of Suez that they crossed the
gulf. It was a strange and thrilling pleasure to
look down on those waters, now so placid, and
remember their division—to look up at that
azure and spotless sky, and figure to one's-self
the cloud by day and the pillar of fire by
night, that guided the chosen race to the Land
of Promise.([3])

The view from the shore of Asia is very
beautiful; Gebel Ataka, and Gebel Deradje,
each running into a long promontory, stretch
along the shore of Africa, and nearly opposite
the "mouth of the ridge," is Ras Mousa, the
promontory of Moses; *ras* and *ros* mean the

same in Arabic and Gaelic. We did not mount till near four, two of the camels not having arrived. The sun set superbly behind Ataka, and the crescent moon was shining brilliantly, when we encamped at Ain Mousa, the Fountains of Moses. There are many palm-trees scattered around them, neglected, and grown thick and bushy from want of pruning. Frogs, shrill and musical as the rings in Lady Minnatrost's Castle, serenaded us all night.

Next morning we proceeded for three hours over the desert, sandy and stony alternately, the Red Sea, of the deepest blue, on the right, and the chain of the Gebel Tih, on the left ; the country beyond it is called El Tih, 'the desert of the wandering' — Israelites. (') Between the third and fourth hour, we entered on a boundless plain of desert, called El Ata, white and painfully glaring to the eye; the wind, too, began to blow from the south, and

rendered the heat very oppressive. El Ata is
probably the Etham of Scripture, though the
desert, so called, extended, as we may gather
from the Mosaic account, round the head, and
perhaps for some distance along both sides, of
the gulf.

After seven hours' ride and a half — a short
day's journey, we encamped for the night in
Wady Seder, on a bed of sand as smooth
almost as a ball-room.—*Wady*, you must remember, means a valley, and is applied indifferently to a craggy mountain-glen, and a mere
depression in the flat expanse of the desert,
as in this instance. The Spanish *Guadi* is the
same word.—Seder is supposed to be a cor-
ruption of Shur or Sdur, the ancient name of
the desert that separates Egypt from Palestine ;
it was to this desert, you will recollect, but to
a more northerly district of it, that Hagar fled
with the ancestor of the Northern Arabs : the
shrub under which she cast him—the leathern

bottle (or *zumzummia*, as it would now be called) empty — the spring, which in these wilds lies often deep in the ground unseen, till you are close upon it—(unless we are to believe that Hagar's fountain was produced miraculously),—I cannot express to you how vividly that most beautiful scene paints itself to me now. The ground hereabouts is covered with beds of the finest chalk, caked by the sun into large flakes of pure white; the whole of this low country is under water during the rainy season.

Next day, starting at a quarter past seven, we reached the bitter well of Howara at half past two, and watered the camels there. The Arabs never drink of it themselves; I tasted, and at first thought the water insipid rather than bitter, but, held in the mouth a few seconds, it becomes excessively nauseous. It rises within an elevated mound, surrounded by sand-hills, and two small date-trees grow near it. The sky was shining with great heat as we approached, and a pale hue diffused itself over the landscape, like the eclipse one may fancy overshadowed it when the Israelites murmured against the Almighty,—for there can be no doubt, I think, of this well being the Mara of Scripture, sweetened by Moses. The name Mara, implying 'bitter,' seems to be preserved in that of the Wady Amara, which we crossed shortly before reaching it. There is no other well, Hussein tells me, on the whole coast, absolutely undrinkable.

I asked whether they had any means of sweetening bad water, and he mentioned the *munn*, a gum that exudes from the tamarisk tree, and the juice of the *homr*-berry; to this latter inquiry I was guided by Burckhardt's expression of regret that he had not made it; he, too, was informed that no other well, bitter enough to be identifiable with that of Mara, exists, as far as Ras Mohammed.

The *homr*-plant and *tarfa*, or tamarisk-tree,
grow in great abundance in Wady Gharendel, two hours beyond Beer Howara, where
we halted for the night; the former bears
small, red, juicy berries, which they squeeze
into water; the munn has a strong aromatic
taste like turpentine;—one of our guides had
a piece of it, which I tasted; they keep it in
casks, melt it when required, and spread it on
their bread like honey. Some have taken it
for the miraculous manna—too absurd an opinion to be confuted.*—Are we to understand
that the effect produced on the bitter waters
of Mara, by casting in the tree showed to
Moses by the Almighty, (or 'something of a
tree,' as the Arabic translation runs), was also
miraculous? If not, it has been suggested that

* See Mr. Conder's observations in his volume on Arabia
in that most valuable, judicious, and—considered as the
work of one man—astonishing compilation, the Modern
Traveller.

the munn or the homr-juice may have been the
specific employed :—the homr is, however, a
mere shrub, and had the whole valleys for miles
round been full of tarfa-trees or homr-bushes,
there would scarcely have been enough to
sweeten water sufficient for such a host as that
of Israel. Moreover, the Israelites were here
within a month after the institution of the
Passover at the vernal equinox, whereas the
munn-harvest does not take place till June;
this, I think, must decide the question in favour
of the miracle.—The tree that Moses threw
in is called the *alvah ;* (⁵) I think, sometimes,
I have discovered it in the *elluf*, a species of
acacia, with very small leaves, and very large
thorns, which grows abundantly in the valleys
more to the south; it bears bunches of long pods
twisted together, of the size and appearance of
French beans, slightly bitter, but not unpalata-
ble when chewed. The radical letters of the
words are the same, and Hebrew and Arabic

are ,languages so nearly allied that the resemblance cannot surely be accidental. But, whatever the tree was, it can have had no more inherent virtue in it for sweetening the bitter well of Mara, than the salt had, which produced the same effect, when thrown by Elisha into the well of Jericho.—But you will be tired.

Between Beer Howara and Wady Gharendel, the country becomes more mountainous, and assumes a more picturesque character. Two divisions of the Waled Said were encamped near the Wady ; one of the Bedouins quitted us, and disappeared, diving down a small ravine that seemed to end in nothing. One could scarcely fancy human inhabitants of such wilds. We halted among the tarfa-bushes under one of the hills of Wady Gharendel, but at too great a distance from the wells to admit of our visiting them. This, probably, is the Elim of Scripture. ([6])

Soon after starting next morning, (at half
past seven), we met a man driving a flock of
goats, the first human being we had encoun-
tered since leaving Suez. Our road lay through
Wady Ussait, west of which, Hussein told me,
Moussa and the Beni Israel crossed, and Fa-
raoun was drowned in the Bahr Souf, or Weedy
Sea—the name has little changed from the
Yam Souf of Moses! We came in sight of
Gebel Serbal that morning, a magnificent mountain of granite, N.W. of Mount Sinai.

At a quarter past one, half an hour after
watering our camels at the wells of Wady Sal,
we reached the spot where the roads to Mount
Sinai, by Wady Mokatteb and Sarbout el Kadem,
diverge ; we took the former, by far the most
interesting as the route of the Israelites. Turning westwards, therefore, at this point, we
entered Wady Taibi, the sea-breeze warning
us of our direct descent to the sea-shore.
The scenery of this valley is very striking.

During the rainy season a torrent flows down it, of the height of two men, i. e. ten or eleven feet deep ; the bottom, as in most of these valleys, is sheeted over with white mud, caked so hard as to receive no impression from the camels' feet,—in fact, in progress to stone. Rock-salt, of the purest white, and perfectly clean, is dug up plentifully hereabouts ; they showed us some, fit for an Emperor's table.

After passing a little forest of tarfa and wild date trees—winding round a black volcanic-looking—mountain defiling through a narrow ravine, where we heard a blackbird cheerily singing amidst the solitude, and leaving ano-ther black mountain to the left, we turned the angle formed by it with the valley, and the bright sea suddenly burst on us, a sail in the distance, and the blue mountains of Africa be-yond it, a lovely vista ;—But when we had fairly issued into the plain on the sea-shore, beautiful indeed, most beautiful was the view ;

P 2

—the whole African coast, from Gebel Ataka
to Gebel Rrarreb, lay before us, washed by the
Red Sea, a vast amphitheatre of mountains,
except the space where the waters were lost
in distance between the Asiatic and Libyan pro-
montories. It was the stillest hour of day;
the sun shone brightly, descending to " his
palace in the Occident,"—the tide was coming
in with its peaceful pensive murmur, wave
after wave;—It was in this plain, broad and
perfectly smooth from the mountains to the
sea, that the children of Israel encamped after
leaving Elim; what a glorious scene it must
then have presented, and how nobly those rocks,
now so silent, must have re-echoed the song of
Moses and its ever returning chorus, " Sing ye
to the Lord, for he hath triumphed gloriously;
the horse and his rider hath he thrown into the
sea !"

The plain narrows into nothing at the southern extremity, where the hills end in a detached

headland, jutting into the sea, and concealing a deep bay. I expected something beautiful, but the reality far surpassed my anticipations ; we stopped half-way through the gap ;—a large lake, so it seemed, of the deepest blue, lay slumbering before us, hemmed in by mountains, variously tinted by the evening sun, and of the most singular appearance, worn away and crumbling, as if of very old age,—with the blue heights of Gebel Serbal towering in the distance ;—a scene and hour never to forget ; the warm tears rushed to my eyes as I gazed there ; not a sound broke the silence,—the caravan was far before us,—the waters lay all unruffled, scarce rippled by the evening breeze.

Twenty steps more—and, the headland disappearing behind us, the lake vanished, and the bay opened in full beauty. The rocks, as we advanced, descended into the sea so abruptly as to cut the path quite off ; we waded round them on our dromedaries,—at high tide the passage would scarcely be practicable. As soon as we reached the little plain beyond them, the sun set behind the mountains of Africa, and night came on in her calm loveliness; the "sea of Edom" retained for a while the roseate hue that it can only boast of at such an hour, (⁷) but all ere long was grey, and by the time we had pitched our tents, the moon and stars were brightly gleaming over us. We rode ten hours and a half this day.

Starting at 10 m. p. 7, next morning, we continued our route along the narrow track under the rocks, broad enough only for one camel at a time. Winding round another headland, we entered El Murcha, a large triangular plain, covered with shrubs, and affording a well of very bad water—formed by the intersection of two ranges of mountains, the most southerly, black as if they had been only quenched yesterday, ending in Gebel Zizezzat, the same promontory as that marked Jas Jehan in Laborde's map, nearly opposite to Gebel Rrarreb in Africa. A lower range of lime-stone hills, crumbling away with age, runs parallel with them ; we pierced it through a ravine called Wady Luggum, and then, turning to the right, ascended the valley formed by the two ranges.

The *lussof* grows here abundantly—a beautiful green plant, with large juicy pods ; at the proper season it produces a fruit as large as one's finger and good to eat. We observed another fruit, of a very different character but equally useful—medicinally, the colocinth, or, as the Arabs call it, *humvul;* might not this fruit, golden as an orange externally, but bitterness itself within, and retaining its fair exterior long after the inside has all dried up, have given rise to the story of the apples of Sodom? It grows, they say, as large as a small melon, and they use the rind, dried, for holding water, butter, &c. Ostrich eggs are used for the same purpose in Egypt.—Two other shrubs I will men-

tion here, though we chiefly noticed them more
to the south, — one edible, the *hemmar*, a
bunchy plant, the leaf juicy, and bitter when
chewed—William thought it tasted like sorrel,
—the other ornamental, the *sekarran*, bearing a
very pretty flower of blended purple and white,
on a thick leafy stem ; its general appearance
reminded me of the lotus in Egyptian paintings.
—I need not apologize to my dear A—— for
this little floral episode.

In this black chain of mountains is an extraordinary ravine, called Wady Shellal, or the
Valley of the Cataract. Hussein took us
through it, while the caravan went on by the
usual route; the valley is not a stone's jerk
wide, but the scenery is awfully grand: not
a sound was heard except the sugh of the wind
among the rocks, and the solitary chirp of a
bird. Hussein and I walked on quicker than
William, who was looking out for partridges
and quails ; as we ascended the Wady, enor-

mous rocks, fallen from the heights, of every shape, and in several instances inscribed with the same unknown characters that I shall have to mention presently, lay on either side of the way, becoming gradually more numerous, till, at last, they formed a little valley of themselves within the large one, which, gradually diminishing into a narrow winding passage, brought us to a perpendicular rock, beyond which there seemed to be no passage. It is impossible to describe the extraordinary appearance of this finale.

Hussein and I sat down in the shadow, and talked after our fashion, till William and his attendant Arab overtook us; Hussein then started up, and, climbing up the rocks, led the way to an upper valley, of which I had not suspected the existence, broader than the lower, but quite as extraordinary; the ground in some places was as smooth as a gravel walk. In the rainy season the torrents pouring down it, and over the rocks into the lower valley, form the magnificent cascade, from which the Wady takes its name.   We walked on some distance to a well, which we found full of sand; Hussein scooped it out with his hands, and the water rose ; all of us drank—I never tasted anything so delicious, always excepted the water of the Nile, to which no other beverage is comparable; but then I was very thirsty, for the day was by far the hottest we had yet travelled on.   Returning a few steps, we climbed over the hills, and across two or three small ravines, till we reached Wady Boodra, where we saw tracks of the camels.   It was well we had drunk at the spring, for the ascent and descent of the hills was dreadfully hot work ; my tongue felt in my mouth like a parrot's, the sides of my throat clove together, and I could scarcely articulate when we overtook our caravan.   One of the most delightful walks, however, I ever took ! What a blessing

water is ! None can appreciate it, who has not
thirsted in the desert. It is bad policy to
drink during the march, if one can possibly
avoid it. ([8])

All the mountains of Wady Boodra are more
or less volcanic-looking ; some of them resemble the heaps of cinders thrown out from an
iron-foundry—utter silence and lifelessness.
At half past two, we passed, on the left, the
entrance of Wady Magara, one of the mining-
stations of the Pharaohs, whose hieroglyphics
are to be seen sculptured on the rocks,—and,
nearly opposite, on the right, a Bedouin burial-
ground ; soon afterwards, the valley opening,
we had a beautiful view of the distant Gebel
Serbal, standing nobly alone, a King among the
hills.

We now entered Wady Mokatteb, a spacious
valley, bounded on the east by a most picturesque range of black mountains, but chiefly
famous for the inscriptions, from which it

derives its name of the Written Wady, cut probably by the early pilgrims on the rocks that line the valley,—inscriptions too—and here is the mystery, in a character which no one has yet decyphered ; there are thousands of them. William copied a few, and afterwards sketched the valley, with our tents, camels, &c., for we encamped here for the night, after nine hours' ride.

Our next day's journey, (starting at half past six, and quitting Wady Mokatteb at half past eight), was through the noble Wady Feiran : P and F being cognate letters, always interchangeable, there can be no doubt, I think, that Feiran is the ancient Paran ; the wilderness, however, so called, like those of Shur and Etham, extended far and wide beyond the spot to which the ancient name has since been limited.——

It was noon—past. For some hours we had been anxiously looking out for the palm-trees

and gardens which were said to render Wady
Feiran the prettiest spot in the peninsula, but
nothing had hitherto appeared, except the usual
shrubs and plants of the Arabian desert, and an
occasional elluf-tree. Notwithstanding our
guides' repeated promises of *nackel*, (date
trees), I began to doubt whether we should
ever come to them, when suddenly, at half past
one, turning an angle of the valley, we found
ourselves in a Paradise; date trees, like the
fair ones they always remind one of, so much
more graceful by cultivation, rustling in the
breeze, *sidr* and tarfa-trees, gardeners' huts,
and dogs barking; I could not have conceived
such a transition. We dismounted, climbed
over a garden wall, let down our zumzummia
into a well under a palm tree, and drank copiously of the delicious water, re-mounted, and
in ten minutes, turning another angle of the
valley, were in the desert as before, with the
torrent-ploughed peaks of Gebel Serbal directly

in front of us. The change suggested a thousand comparisons ; it seemed as if we had been
dreaming.

We now came to the ruins—overgrown with
tarfa trees, and crowning a lofty rock in the
middle of the valley—of the ancient town of
Feiran, the seat of a bishopric in the early days
of Christianity—the Phara of Ptolomy the
Geographer, in whose time it gave its name to
the Sinaite promontory, and to its inhabitants
the Pharanitæ—and, as one learned traveller
has remarked, not improbably the El Paran
in the wilderness, to which Chedarlaomer and
his associate kings chased the Horites of Mount
Seir.—It has now nothing of magnificence to
boast of. On both sides of the vale beyond it
are seen deserted houses, some perched at a
great height,—and ancient tombs cut in the
rocks.—The gardens of Wady Feiran I fancied
were past, but the sight of a few date trees,
and a stream of water crossing the road, as we

wound round the ruin-crowned rock, showed I
was mistaken; indeed, it was now only that
we had fairly come to them. The large river,
that once flowed through the valley, indignantly
sank into the ground and disappeared, when
a Frank presumed to write a description of it,
but one of the loveliest little brooks I ever saw
supplies its place, overrunning the rocky path,
the bed of the summer torrents, in tiny crystal
rivulets; I drank repeatedly as I walked along,
wherever the pebbles at the bottom gleamed
clearest—just deep enough to use one's hand as
a cup; the camels were constantly stopping to
drink and browze on the tarfa trees. The
burnie became at last so copious that I was
obliged to mount my dromedary to avoid
being wet-footed.

For two hours and a half, every winding of
the valley revealed new loveliness; it would be
beautiful even without a single tree. At the
first turning, after passing the ruined town, a

most superb view of Gebel Serbal opened on
us,—every craig and pinnacle of his five peaks
relieved clearly against a sky of the most delicious blue, and perfectly cloudless,—the pale
moon, about half-full, sailing in the pure ether
above us—the eye could pierce far beyond her.
Gebel Serbal was of a bluish grey, but the
jagged rocks of the valley, forming the fore-
ground of the picture, were black, the bright
lights and deep broad shadows rendering them
perfectly beautiful.—I sat on my dromedary
under a tarfa tree, enjoying the shade and a
delightful breeze, and talking with the Bedouins,
while William sketched this lovely scene.

And was not that Mount Paran !

" God came from Teman,
    And the Holy One from Mount Paran.
    His glory covered the heavens,
    And the earth was full of his praise.
    His brightness was as the light,
    Rays streamed from his hand,
    And there was the hiding-place of his power.
    Before him went the pestilence,
    And flashes of fire went forth after him.

He stood—and measured the earth,
He beheld—and drave asunder the nations,
And the everlasting mountains were scattered,
The perpetual hills did bow,—
The eternal paths were trodden by him.
Thou sawest the tents of Cushan in affliction,
The curtains of the land of Midian trembled!

Was the Lord displeased against the floods,
Was thine anger against the rivers?
Was thy wrath against the sea,
That thou didst ride upon thine horses,
And thy chariots of salvation?
Thy bow was made bare,
According to the oath unto the tribes, even the promise.

Thou didst cleave the streams of the land,
The mountains saw thee and trembled,
The overflowing of waters passed away;
The deep uttered his voice,
And lifted up his hands on high.
— The sun and moon stood still in their habitation;
In their light thine arrows went abroad —
In their brightness the lightning of thy spear!

Thou didst march through the land in indignation,
Thou didst thresh the heathen in anger:
Thou wentest forth for the deliverance of thy people,
Even for the deliverance of thine anointed ones."

Following the windings of the valley, alternately through sun and shade, under lofty rocks and umbrageous date-trees, whispering in the breeze, and shedding the most delicious coolness, we heard from time to time the chirping of birds, the barking of dogs, and the merry voices of children—generally unseen, though occasionally we caught a passing glimpse of them and of their dusky mothers and sisters under the thick foliage embowering their huts and tents. We exchanged cordial *salamats* and *bissalams* with some of the natives that we met on the road, particularly with one aged white-bearded patriarch. Our guides, too, were constantly meeting their acquaintance, receiving their welcome and striking wrists with them : their greetings struck me as remarkably low-voiced, though cordial as between brothers. ([9])

The blending of greens in these gardens is exquisitely beautiful,—a regular gradation from the pale transparent foliage of the tarfa to the darker hue of the date towering over it, and the still deeper green of the sidr or nebbek, as dark as that of the orange and citron. Our Bedouins brought down the fruit with stones, and gave them to us as we rode along; it was delicious. In twenty days the sidr harvest will be quite ready; they sell the greater part of it at Suez, — part they keep and dry in the sun, press and reduce it to flour, which, with water or milk, they make into small cakes.

In the proper season, the Zoalia Arabs, the owners of these gardens, who entrust the cultivation to the Tebenna, a branch of the Gebali tribe, (who receive three out of every ten dates for their trouble), hold a sort of har-vest-home in the valley,—and a merry scene it is then, by all accounts. These Gebali are the descendants of a Christian colony, trans-ported by Justinian from the shores of the Black Sea, to act as servants to his monastic establishment at Mount Sinai. They have long since become Moslems and Bedouins, though the pure tribes never intermarry with them, and, as their daughters are the prettiest girls in the peninsula, many a sad tale of the course of true love thwarted is current in the glens.

About four o'clock we lost sight of the last palm, and, after riding awhile through a wood of tarfa-trees, they too ceased — adieu for ever to the gardens of Wady Feiran ! I shall never probably see them again, but often, often will they gleam in loveliness on my waking and sleeping visions. We encamped at a quarter to five, about ten minutes beyond El Boueb, "the Mouth," a remarkable defile in the valley, not more than eight paces broad in the narrowest part, and beyond which the valley takes the name of Wady Sheikh.

The Waled Said encamp for the present about half way between this spot and Mount Sinai. Notwithstanding that the day after the morrow was the second Bairam, a great feast among the Mahometans, Hussein most hospitably invited us to visit his tribe in the hills and share his tent the following evening, and proceed the third day to the convent. We were anxious to press on, and therefore declined his invitation; but, on reflecting that our visit, so kindly urged, would have excluded him, and all our other Bedouins, from participating in the festivity of their tribe, we could not but feel equally delighted at having received such an invitation, and at having declined it.

Thursday morning, the 16th of March, we started at half past five, commencing a continual ascent towards the elevated district of Sinai ; the rising sun was just lighting up the peaks of the mountains — it was very cold at first till he had fairly risen — the birds were singing their matins merrily ; again and again did I look back on the valley, closed directly behind us by the noble peaks of Gebel Serbal,

at this early hour of a reddish brown, with deep
blue shadows; there are five peaks, or perhaps
six; at least from this point there appeared to
be so many — each composed of several pinnacles; the mountain is prolonged westwards,
displaying another peak of lower elevation, but
very beautiful. William sketched it from this
point, the best, I think, that could be chosen
— he is verily an admirable draughtsman.

Soon afterwards, leaving to the left the usual
circuitous route to Mount Sinai by Wady
Sheikh, we turned up Wady Selaff, a long valley, broader but far less picturesque than Wady
Feiran, yet affording rich pasturage for sheep
and goats, which were feeding there in considerable flocks, tended by Bedouin shep-
herdesses. The *rattam*, a species of broom,
bearing a white flower, delicately streaked with
purple, afforded me frequent shelter from the
sun, walking on in advance of the caravan, and
two other shrubs, the *selleh* — thorny, with

leaves of the lightest tint of green, bearing a very pretty flower of a light pink colour, beautifully streaked inside, — and the *ooraga*, deep green, with hairy pods, ending each in a thorn, instead of leaves, and bearing a small pink flower, five petals with yellow stamina—delighted me with their simple beauty. Hundreds of little lizards — the colour of the sand, and called by the Bedouins *serabani*, were darting about, and altogether I hardly felt myself in the desert.

We reached the foot of Gebel How about half-past eleven. I mounted my dromedary there, having walked ever since starting, but soon got down again, for it was as much, we found, as the animals could do, to cross the mountain. Two of them, indeed, knocked up, and were left behind; the Arabs took them back that evening, returning to the camp of their tribe. This route through the Wady How — one of the wildest and most extraor-

dinary defiles I ever saw, leads in a direct line
to Mount Sinai. The path, rudely paved in
the steepest part, winds among fallen rocks,
many of them of enormous size, and some
bearing inscriptions in the same unknown character as those in the Wady Mokatteb. One
rock, worn deep by the torrents of ages before
it thundered down from the heights, singularly
resembled a human skull. All the fallen rocks
in these valleys — eaten into by the winds and
torrents, have a ghastly look. A few shrubby
date-trees and occasional patches of coarse
grass refreshed the eye from time to time, and
two or three sparkling mountain burnies the
parched throat—one of them I discovered myself.
The groups of camels slowly defiling along,
at different heights of the ravine, and sometimes
in different directions, were highly picturesque.

We reached the summit about two : the
Mountain of Sinai, its northern prolongation
rather, called Gebel Shereyk, stood nobly out,

as we descended the broad plain El Raha, that slopes to its foot, the scene of the encampment of the Israelites. On the left, after about an hour and a half's gradual descent, we passed the opening of Wady Sheikh, which, had we not crossed Gebel How, we should have had to go round by, and to retrace going to Akaba,— and soon afterwards, on the right, a stone on which, according to the monks, Moses broke the tables of the Law, on coming down from the Mount, and seeing the calf-worship. Hussein called it simply *Hadj Mousa,* "the stone of Moses." Hassan, another of our Bedouins, who had been praying as he walked, saluted it with his hands.

In a few minutes more, advancing up a narrow ravine at the extremity of the plain, and passing the garden with its lofty cypresses, we arrived under the walls of the Convent of St. Catherine, a regular monastic fortress — it has exactly the appearance of one, and is, indeed, defended by guns against the Arabs.   A window, under a projecting shed, was presently opened, and a rope (Sir Frederick Henniker calls it a halter) dropped, by which, first our luggage and letter of introduction from the Greek Convent at Cairo, and then ourselves, were hoisted up by a windlass; there was a door, but it is walled up, for, whenever it was opened, which only took place on the arrival of the Archbishop, the Bedouins have the right of entrance.   For this reason the Archbishops always reside at Cairo.

The monks are obliged to supply the Bedouins with bread *à discretion*, and an ample provision in that kind was lowered to them after our ascent.   No Arabs are ever allowed to enter, except the servants of the convent.([10]) The maxim " quis custodiat ipsos custodes" is l iterally acted upon here; our conference with Hussein, the Sheikh, o r chief protector of the convent, about conveyance to Akaba, was carried on through a hole in the wall; we squatted on one side, and he stood at the other; it was like talking through a key-hole.

We were received by the Superior and some of the monks on the landing-place, but could not answer their greeting, nor make ourselves understood, till Missirie came up, not one of them, apparently, speaking any language that we were acquainted with. Modern Greek and Arabic seem to be the only tongues in use here. The Superior, a fine old man, with a mild benevolent countenance, a long beard and immense mustachoes, (sadly in need of Princess Parizade's scizzars), showed us to our apartment, carpeted and divanned in the eastern style, and adorned by a print of the Virgin and Child, with a lamp burning before it; we sat down with him, and he welcomed us kindly to Mount Sinai. He is a Greek from Candia; I had the pleasure of informing him a day or two afterwards, when he told me of his birth-

Q 2

place, that an ancestor of mine, Sir Alexander
de Lindesay of Glenesk, a brave and adventurous knight, died there on his pilgrimage to
the Holy Sepulchre, in 1382.   Dried fruit and
rakie, a strong brandy made from dates, were
presented to us while dinner was in preparation—*maigre*, it being Lent.

Father Dimitri ciceronied us over the Convent two or three days afterwards.   It resembles a little fortified town, irregularly built on
the steep side of the mountain, and surrounded
by lofty walls ; the passages and courts are
kept very neat and_s clean ; balconies with
wooden balustrades run round each area, on
which the doors of the several apartments
open ; texts of Scripture are inscribed on the
walls in every direction—in inextricably contracted Greek.

The principal church, built by the Emperor
Justinian, the founder of the Convent, is really
beautiful ; the richly ornamented roof is sup-

ported by rows of granite pillars barbarously whitewashed,—the pavement of marble;—the walls are covered with portraits of saints, the Virgin and Child, and scenes from the Bible, in the old Greek style of the middle ages; most of them are modern, but some very ancient and very interesting for the history of the art; they are almost all in good preservation. The dome of the choir displays in Mosaic work, said to be contemporary with Justinian, the transfiguration of Our Saviour. The chapels are also full of paintings, some of them Russian, but in the same style. The nave is lighted by a superb silver chandelier, presented by Elizabeth of Russia, and I saw several candelabra of great beauty. The reading-desks, &c. are of tortoise-shell and mother-of-pearl inlaid. In the choir is preserved the coffin in which Saint Catherine's bones are said to repose, and the silver lid of a sarcophagus, embossed with the portrait of Anne of Russia, who intended being buried here. ([11])

We put off our shoes from off our feet, before approaching the most revered spot on Mount Sinai, or rather Horeb (as they call this part of the mountain),—where Our Lord is said to have appeared to Moses in the burning bush. This little chapel is gorgeously ornamented; a New Testament in modern Greek, with superbly embossed covers, lies on the altar,—behind it, they show—not exactly the burning bush, but a shrub which they say has flourished there ever since, its lineal descendant. The kind, hospitable monks are not to blame —they believe as the tale has been handed down to them; but on what authority, we must again and again ask, are these spots pointed out as the scenes mentioned in the Bible?

The monks are summoned to their different services by striking with a mallet on a piece of wood suspended in one of the upper galleries. Two small bells of Russian manufacture, and very sweet tone, hang there also.

Close to the church rises the minaret of a
mosque! built, for the nonce, three centuries
ago, when the Convent was threatened by the
Paynim Soldan of Egypt; he spared the Convent for its sake. It is plain and unornamented
—the contrast of a Scotch kirk to an Italian
cathedral, and is seldom used unless some
Turkish pilgrim of rank visit Mount Sinai.
The refectory is a spacious apartment, a world
too wide for the shrunk body corporate of Saint
Catherine's votaries. There are only twenty
two monks now. ([12]) One of them reads to
his companions, while they dine; I saw a large
folio " Synagogue," as it is called, of passages
from the Fathers, printed at Venice, lying on
the desk, and several other religious volumes
in a small bookcase.

In the archbishop's apartment, now used as
the Treasury, we were shown a most beautiful
manuscript of the Gospels in Greek, on vellum,
in uncial, or capital, letters of gold; I thought

the good Father would never have done turning over the preliminary leaves of illuminations, and arranging the silk screens interposed between them. Would that it were in the British Museum! I wonder whether it has ever been collated.

I was disappointed in the Library of the Convent, finding no very ancient Greek manuscripts, or valuable printed books; a manuscript of Saint Chrysostom, in a great number of folio volumes, all, apparently, in the same hand-writing, interested me most. There are many MSS. of the Scriptures in Greek, and some in Sclavonic of portions of the Bible; many Arabic manuscripts also, all of which were examined by Burckhardt. The books are arranged alphabetically in large cases.

Wedn. March 22.

Enough of the Convent; now for the environs. Yesterday I ascended Gebel Mousa, commonly called Mount Sinai, and the day before, Gebel Katerin, a much loftier peak of the same mountain ; neither of them agree with the Sinai described in the Bible.

With one exception, all the travellers that I am acquainted with, from Frameynsperg in 1346 to Belon in 1548, call Gebel Mousa—Horeb, and Gebel Katerin—*Sinai*. Since the middle of the sixteenth century that hallowed name has reverted to Gebel Mousa—reverted, I say, because, from Justinian's time till the beginning of the fourteenth century, the tradition identifying it with Sinai appears to be uninterrupted. In very early times, Gebel Serbal seems to have been the chief place of pilgrimage under the belief of its being the Mount of God. Such uncertainty hath tradition ! ([13])

Both days were clear and beautiful. Starting on Monday morning, at 20 m. to 10—descending the valley of the Convent northwards into the great plain El Raha, and then turning to the left, and winding round Gebel

Q 5

Shereyk, the prolongation of Gebel Mousa that, as I mentioned above, juts into it—I found myself ascending the El Ledja, a deep ravine, running southwards, nearly parallel with the valley of the Convent, and separating Gebel Mousa from Gebel Katerin ; it is filled with fallen rocks, one of which, a large block of granite, to the left of the path, is pointed out as the stone from which Moses struck water ; there are above a dozen holes like mouths, from which the stream is said to have issued ; it did not appear to me that they were the work of art, chiselled, as some travellers have described them, but certainly this El Ledja, abounding, as it does, in springs of water, cannot be the Vale of Rephidim. ([14])

I reached the rock at a quarter to eleven, and, shortly afterwards, climbing over a low wall, entered the gardens of the Convent El Erbayn, or of the Forty Martyrs; I should have mentioned that, to the right, at the en-

trance of the El Ledja, I passed another Convent and garden called El Bostan, and, before
reaching the stone of Moses, a beautiful orchard,
with seventeen cypresses towering, like obelisks,
over apricots and other fruit-trees in full blossom. Nothing can be more refreshing to the
eye than these little paradises in the wild.

I entered the Convent El Erbayn,—a rude
building, quite deserted. Pilgrims, for two
centuries and more, have scrawled their names
there; the earliest I saw was, if I recollect
right, of 1598, the latest that of Professor von
Schubert, a German savant, who had been
here, with a large party, on his road to Petra,
this very month. I looked into the church; a
picture of the Virgin glittered through the
gloom,—I saw nothing else. The garden, or
rather orchard, attached to this Convent, is
delightful. Olives seem to thrive there; it
was pleasant walking under their shade, enjoying at the same time the full grandeur of the

scenery, clearly discernible through the transparent foliage. The pomegranate-trees were quite bare. The white blossoms of the apple and damascene trees presented a lovely contrast to the funereal gloom of three superb cypresses that stand in advance of the Convent. ([15]) Under its walls grow two magnificent orange trees ; would that a wish could transport them to your greenhouse !

Leaving the Convent about 5 m. to 11, and turning westwards, I began the ascent of Gebel Katerin by a steep ravine, between Gebel Djeraigni on the left, and Gebel Lehummar on the right, for every craig of the mountains has its peculiar name among the Arabs. About ten paces from the garden-wall lies a large stone, inscribed with the same unknown characters of which we saw such numerous specimens in Wady Mokatteb. I observed others here and there as I ascended. At 10 m. to 12, turning out of the path and climbing over the

rocks, I reached a platform overshadowed by
Gebel Djeraign, which is scooped out, as it
were, above it, like Mac Duff's Cave at Earls-
ferry. At the very foot of the rock rises a
small spring of the coldest water, called Beer
El Shonnar, "the well of the partridge;" we
drank of it, filled our zumzummia, and then
re-commenced the ascent.

Nothing can surpass the rude and sombre
grandeur of these valleys ; utter silence reigned
around us, though now and then, the report of
a gun from the neighbourhood of Mount Sinai
murmured around us like distant thunder.
Odoriferous shrubs grow in great abundance
among the loose stones, as high as the peak
of St. Catherine's,—which is easier to climb
than to descend, the solid granite being split
into thousands of diminutive pinnacles and
ledges, smooth and slippery, and in some
places so nearly perpendicular that a false step
would be broken bones, if not worse.

I reached the summit—stood, indeed, above it—on the roof of the chapel, (hut, rather) built on the spot whither St. Catherine's remains are said to have been carried by angels, at 5 m. past 1, exactly two hours after leaving El Erbayn, and well—well was I repaid for my toil! The gulfs of Suez and Akaba, with the mountains of Africa and Arabia Deserta bounding the horizon behind them, the white and double chain of the Rua and El Tih mountains running across the peninsula, like an isthmus separating the desert beyond them from the sea of mountains at my feet,—this is Sir Frederick Henniker's simile, and none could give a juster idea of their extraordinary appearance; "it seems," he says, "as if Arabia Petræa had once been an ocean of lava, and that, while its waves were running literally mountains high, it was commanded suddenly to stand still"—

"And who commanded—and the silence came—
Here let the billows stiffen and have rest!"

such are the principal features of this superb
panorama ; condescending to particulars, I recognised Gebel Mousa or Sinai considerably
below me,—Gebel Shomar to the South, higher
than St. Catherine's,—to the S. W. the plain of
El Kaa, intervening between the Sinaite mountains and the low range called Gebel Hemam,
bordering on the Red Sea—(Tor is not visible)
—and to the N. W. Gebel Serbal, far less picturesque from this elevation than from the
Wady Feiran. The direction of the principal
valleys was clearly discernible from this great
height. On an immense scale, the view
strongly reminded me of General Pfyffer's
models of Switzerland. The Gulf of Akaba—
if I am right in believing I saw it—was of the
deepest blue ; a very few clouds, but high above
the horizon, a bright sunny sky, and breezes
fresh and exhilarating as spring, rendered this
excursion one of the most delightful I ever
took.

The ascent of Mount Sinai is as fatiguing almost as that of St. Catherine's. Starting from the Convent, the walk commences by the ascent of what is now called Mount Horeb, the general name in Scripture for the district in which Sinai stood, but here considered as the breast from which the peak of Sinai rises. Rude steps have been laid by the monks, very wearisome to climb ; the only relief is where they have been broken, or where a sheet of granite occurs. Two arched gateways, with a steep ascent between them, lead to a small plain, surrounded by rocks, the scene, according to Mahometan tradition, of Moses' interview with the Almighty : a noble cypress tree towers in the centre, with a well of excellent water at its feet. A rude building, called the convent of St. Elias, or Elijah, commemorates his visit to Horeb. ($_{16}$)   From this plain begins the still more fatiguing ascent of Sinai.   On the summit stand a chapel and a mosque.   I climbed to the top of the former, the more elevated of the two, and from thence enjoyed a superb prospect, similar to that from Mount Catherine, but inferior to it, the Gulf of Akaba being totally concealed. ([17]) The echo of a pistol there is most extraordinary ; mountain after mountain takes up the tale, answering each other across the deep valleys. I descended the other side of the mountain direct to El Erbayn, by a precipitous ravine, nearly opposite that by which I had ascended Mount St. Catherine ; and, after resting in the garden, while my cicerone and two or three Arab hangers-on took some refreshment, (a delightfully fresh breeze driving the white blossoms before it like snowflakes,) returned to the convent. The temperature of these valleys is most delicious.

I have said that neither Gebel Mousa nor Gebel Katerin answer the Scriptural description of Mount Sinai; William pointed out to me a hill this morning,—Gebel Minnegia, or Limnegia the Arabs called it—which he had a strong impression was the real mountain; and, on careful examination, I think he is right. Your kind attention, if you please :—

There can be no doubt, I think, that the Israelites encamped on the plain El Raha; it is the largest, indeed the only large plain in all this district,—a noble expanse, covered with shrubs fit for pasturage, and a gentle slope.

The mountain in question rises directly in front of you, as you descend El Raha, closing the vista formed by the valley, on the slope of which the convent of St. Catherine stands.

The Israelites, encamping in El Raha, would camp directly in front of Gebel Minnegia, as we are told they did before Mount Sinai.

There is not space enough in the narrow precipitous ravines from which alone the peaks of Gebel Mousa and St. Catherine are visible, or in any other plain or valley in the whole district, for the people to have encamped with such regularity and comfort, as it is evident they did, (Exod. c. 32,) nor for their having removed and stood afar off, as they had apparently ample space to do, when trembling at the thunderings and lightnings,—nor, after the golden-calf idolatry, for the tabernacle having been pitched without the camp, afar off from the camp,—when all the people rose and stood, every man at his tent-door, and looked after Moses, till he was gone into the tabernacle.

Moses went up to the "*top* of the mount"— and God came down upon Mount Sinai, "on the top of the mount," and the glory of the Lord was "like devouring fire on the *top* of the mount," "in the eyes of the children of Israel," "in sight of *all* the people." Neither Gebel Mousa nor Gebel Katerin are visible from the plain, but the Israelites could have seen the *top* of the mountain, and the cloud, and Moses' entrance into it, from every part of the plain, supposing that William's conjecture be correct, and Gebel Minnegia be really Sinai. I climbed up it this afternoon—the highest point is a sheet of dark sun-burnt granite, and from thence I looked over the Convent, directly up the El Raha: the mountain stands single, isolated by deep ravines, on three sides very precipitous.

It would appear, moreover, from the account of Moses, that he went and returned, communicating between the people and their God, without much difficulty of ascent; a hale old man, as he was till his death, could easily ascend and descend this mountain twice or thrice in a day—certainly not either Gebel Mousa or Gebel Katerin.

There is nothing in the Bible to lead us to suppose Mount Sinai a very lofty mountain; ([18]) yet that it was some distance from the camp, though visible from it, we may gather from the account of Moses's return with the two tables; " Moses turned and went down from the Mount, and as soon as he drew nigh unto the camp, he saw the calf and the dancing," &c.

The directions to Moses, before the audible utterance of the commandments, were that bounds should be set unto the people round about, " that they go not up to the mountain or touch the border of it," on pain of death. And, on the third day, Moses brought forth the people *out of the camp* to meet with God— (probably leading some of them up the valley of the Convent, and sending others by a more circuitous road to the other side of the mountain,)—and they stood at the nether part of the mount, &c.—and when the people heard the voice out of the midst of the darkness, &c., they removed, and stood afar off, retreating, I take it, to the plain, from which they could see just as well; indeed the divine command was, " Get ye into your tents again."

Yet what, after all, avails the inquiry, if we think merely of the stage and not of the action performed on it? This is the wilderness of Sinai—there can be no doubt of that; and, whichever the individual mount was, every hill around heard the thunder and quaked at the sound of the trumpet, waxing louder and louder as God descended in the cloud,—and trembled at the "still small voice," that, deeper than the thunder, and high above the trumpet, spoke to every man's ear and heart that fiery law—holy, and just, and good— existing from all eternity, which requires of man that spotless obedience which he cannot yield, and at the first transgression, even in thought, of its purity, lays him under the curse of eternal death—" Thou shalt love the Lord thy God with all thy heart, and thy neighbour as thyself."

One only of Adam's seed, the man Christ Jesus, has fulfilled that law ; we must travel to

Jerusalem—we must look to the cross on Calvary, to know how His righteousness may become our's.

Well, dear A—— ! time is flying—'tis eleven at night ; Hussein arrived this evening with the camels, and the sheikhs of the Eastern tribes of the Peninsula to whom they belong ; the bargain is struck, and we start betimes to-morrow morning.   Adieu !

Your's, my dear A—— !   I have now a right to subscribe myself

HADJI LINDSAY.

NOTES.

Note 1, Page 17.—Missirie.

I feel great pleasure in bearing testimony to the merits of this excellent man. During the whole time he travelled with us as courier, we never once had occasion to find fault with him, except for exerting himself too much. He kept our boatmen, muleteers, native servants, &c. in perfect order; we had not the slightest trouble with them. With other gentlemen he has travelled over most parts of Europe, in North America, and Mexico. He speaks Greek, (his native tongue), Turkish, Russian, Walachian, Arabic, English, (which he has taught himself to read and write), French, Italian, Spanish—and, I believe, can make himself understood in some other languages.

Of his personal character, intelligence, activity, energy, and those more important points — honesty, sobriety, and Christian principle—it would be impossible for me to speak too highly.

I cannot refrain from mentioning, (what would never have come to my knowledge directly), his having ransomed from Turkish slavery, and sent home to their native country, (Argos), a mother and a daughter. Nor is this the only instance, as I have reason to know, of his having stood the friend of the fatherless, and caused the widow's heart to sing with joy.

Note 2, Page 26.—Cleopatra's Needle.

Its companion lies beside it, almost covered by the sand. Both appear to have been standing when Abd'allatif wrote his account of Egypt, A.D. 1203.

Note 3, Page 27.—Pompey's Pillar.

" Nulla sane columnarum huic similis !"

EDRISI.

This noble column appears to have stood in the court of a large quadrangular edifice, popularly called the School of Aristotle, and supposed to have been built by Solomon, till the reign of Saladin, when the governor of Alexandria destroyed it.—*Abd'allatif.*

Edrisi, about the middle of the twelfth century, describes this building as supported by sixteen columns at each extremity, and by sixty-seven at either side; and Benjamin of Tudela, the last writer who speaks of it as an eye-witness, (A. D. 1160), says it contained twenty Colleges, divided from each other by marble columns, " whither men flocked from all parts of the world to learn the philosophy of Aristotle."

Abd'allatif saw the remains of the columns on the shore, * whither they had been carried by the governor, and traces of them all round the pillar, within thirty years after their destruction.†

The central pillar was cut in the quarries of the Said, or Upper Egypt. " Il en existoit originairement," (says an Arab writer of the twelfth century, cited by Langlès), " sept, de la même dimension, qui servoient d'ornement à un palais immense nommé *Maison de la Sagesse,* qui n'avoit pas son pareil sur la terre."— " Sept géants de la famille de Aad apporterent chacun un de ces colonnes sous leurs bras, depuis le Mont Bérim au midi d'Eçouan jusqu'à Alexandrie."—*Notes to Norden's Travels,* vol. 3. p. 181.

Pompey's pillar has at different times been represented as a monument erected by himself to his own glory, (*Breydenbach*), and a memorial of Cæsar's triumph on his rival's defeat. (*Belon, Sandys*). In 1507, when that "pious, honourable, and magnanimous knight," Martin à Baumgarten, visited Egypt, it was popularly supposed that Pompey's head was buried under it.

" Elle étoit surmontée, je crois, d'une statue colossale d'airain, placée sur un énorme stylobate, et qu'on nommoit *chérakhyl;* elle regardoit la mer, et avoit le doigt dirigé vers Constantinople. Un receveur général des impositions d'Egypte, Açameh ben-Zeid, demanda au khalife El-Oualyd ben-Abdoul-melik ben-Merouan, la permission de faire fondre cette statue pour en frapper une grande quantité de *fels,* petites pièces de billon."—*Langlès.*

This sacrilege must have been perpetrated between A.D. 714 and 717—the duration of El Walid's reign.

Every one has heard of persons ascending Pompey's pillar by means of a rope-ladder and a kite, but perhaps the most extraordinary achievement of the sort was that of a famous *voltigeur,* who climbed up by a knotted rope with a donkey on his shoulders, left it there to pass the night, and brought it down again the next morning.—*D'Arvieux, Memoires,* vol. 1, p. 191.

* " Je découvris au pied des murailles, sur le bord de la mer, plusieurs blocs de porphyre, qu'il seroit fort facile d'enlever pour en faire d'excellens ouvrages. Il y en a qui pesent assurément deux ou trois milliers; j'en enlevai un de 150 livres, que j'ai envoyé en France, et on peut juger par cet échantillon de la beauté du porphyre, et de l'usage qu'on en pourroit faire." —*Troisième Voyage de Paul Lucas,* (1714), tom. 2, p. 29.

† See *Edrisi,* Geogr. Nubiensis, p. 214.—*Ben. Tud.* Itin. p. 214, ed. Elzev. 32mo.—*Abd'allatif,* Relation de l'Egypte, and a very interesting note of M. de Sacy, p. 182, and pp. 230 sqq.—or in Pinkerton's Collection. vol. 15, p. 828.

Some beautiful porphyry columns were standing at a little distance from the pillar in 1658, when D'Arvieux visited Alexandria—perhaps the same as the "six pillars of marble; twenty spans about, and three fathoms high without the ground," mentioned in Grimstone's 'Estates, Empires, and Principalities of the World,'—London, fol: 1615*—a work, the title-page of which, engraved by Elstracke, is even more beautiful than that of Purchas's Pilgrims.

Note 4, Page 29.—Remains of Alexandria.

" Je vis aussi, en passant dans le milieu de la Ville, un rang de colomnes de marbre granite, d'une hauteur et d'une grosseur extraordinaires, dont il y en a encore une qui conserve son chapiteau ; ces colonnes, qui sont sur une même ligne, s' étendent près de 500 pas, et ne sont pas aujourd'hui dans une égale distance l'une de l'autre, parce que la plus grande partie en a été enlevée ou abbattue, et l'on en voit encore beaucoup de renversés. Entre celles qui subsistent, il y en a qui ne sont eloignées que de dix ou douze pieds, ce qui fait juger qu'il y en avoit sur chaque rang plus de 150. Encore faut il supposer que la première et la dernière de celles qui se trouvent sur cette ligne etoient effectivement aux deux extrémitéz de ce rang; ce qui n'est pas vraisemblable, puisque vis-a-vis de ces colonnes on en voit à deux cents pas delà d'autres semblables qui leur sont opposées ; et quoiqu'il n'en reste aujourd'hui que trois ou quatre, il est visible, par la disposition des lieux, par le même ordre, la même grosseur, qu'elles ne faisoient qu'un même tout avec celles dont je viens de parler. Il paroît aussi par d'autres colonnes, qui sont à une égale distance de ces deux rangs, qu'il y avoit autrefois en cet endroit une superbe fontaine ; l'édifice de brique, et les bassins ou l'eau tomboit, se voient aujourd'hui manifestement. Ainsi on peut conclure qu'il y avoit là une place superbe, dont la figure composoit un quarré long, large de 200 pas, et long de 500. Les principaux Palais de la ville faisoient sans doute les quatre faces de cette belle place, puisque derrière ces colonnes, du côté où il en reste un plus grand nombre,on voit quantité de murs de brique, les uns renversés, les autres encore entiers, qui laissent juger de la grandeur et de la beauté des edifices qui étoient en cet endroit. On distingue même, parmi les masures, des bains presque entiers, et j'en ai vu un dont les murs étoient faits d'un ciment si dur, qu'il ressembloit à du marbre. Les Turcs en détachent tous les jours quelques morceaux pour faire servir à leurs bâtimens. Mais comme ces ruines sont presque entiérement couvertes de sable, ils n'enlevent que ce qui paroît en dehors; et s'ils vouloient se donner la peine de creuser jusques aux fondemens, ils decouvriroient bien des choses curieuses."—*Troisième Voyage de Paul Lucas*, vol. 2. p. 31, 199.

" Proh dolor ! illustrem, maximam, habitatoribus refertissi-

* Translated from the French of P. d'Avily.

mam, pulcherrimam, opulentissimamque quondam Ptolemaeorum sedem, Alexandriam, collapsam, dirutam, majori ex parte desertam, miserando spectaculo, deploravi. Heu infelicem ! quae et quanta mœnia, quales et quàm amplae ejus urbis stratae viae, quàm conspicuæ domorum frontes ad cœlum tendentes, qui portarum fornices ! Sed in cinerem versa domorum interna omnia prætereuntes conspiciebamus."—*Petri Martyris Legatio Babylonica* (1502), *printed after his Decades*, fol. 80, verso, ed: 1533.

Note 5, Page 29.—Racotis.

M. Langlès, however, claims much higher consideration for Racotis:—

"Alexandre ne fit que relever les ruines et changer le nom d'une des plus anciennes et des plus grandes villes de l'Egypte. Cette ville se nommoit Raqouth, ou Raqoudah, suivant les auteurs Arabes, mais plutôt Rakhoty, suivant l'orthographe Qopte; mot dont les grecs et les Latins ont fait Racotis."—*Notes on Norden*, t. 3, p. 158.

Murtadi, in his curious legendary history of Egypt, says it was built by Masar, grandson of Ham, and his thirty followers, with whom he came to Egypt on the dispersion of nations. His paternal grandfather was the wise priest Philemon, who, being deputed by Pharaan, the last antediluvian King of Egypt, on a religious conference with Noah, was converted by the Patriarch, and admitted into the Ark with his daughter, afterwards married to Misraim son of Ham. Philemon, returning to Egypt with his grandson and his thirty followers, reopened the pyramids, taught them the secret writing of the *birbas* or temples, the knowledge of the talismans concealed in them, and how to make new ones, and also the rules how to subject spirits. " Ils bastirent plusieurs villes sur la mer Romaine, et entre autres celle de Racode, au lieu où est maintenant Alexandrie."—*Merveilles d'Egypte*, p. 119.

Others attribute its foundation to Shedad the son of Aad, illustrious in the annals of the East for the gardens of Irem, which he planted in rivalry of the celestial paradise. A third account states that he merely rebuilt it after its destruction by the Amalekites, or Shepherd kings.

Note 6, Page 34.—Daniel's prophecies.

" These prophecies of Daniel, foretelling the sufferings and persecutions of the Jews, from Alexander's successors in Syria and Egypt, till the end of the reign of Antiochus Epiphanes, during a disastrous period of 160 years, are, if possible, more surprising and astonishing than even his grand prophetic period of 2300 years, and the several successions of empire, or the four temporal kingdoms, that were to precede the spiritual kingdom of God upon earth. The magnificence of the whole scheme, comprising the fortunes of all mankind, seems to be an object suitable to the Omniscient Governor of the Universe, calculated to excite awe and admiration; but the minuteness of detail, exhibited in this part, exceeds that of any existing history of those times. The prophecy is really more concise and comprehensive, and yet more circumstantial and complete, than any history. No one historian has related so many circumstances, and in such exact order of time and place, as the prophet; so that it was necessary to have recourse to several authors, Greek and Roman, Jewish and Christian, for the better explaining and illustrating the great variety of particulars contained in this prophecy.— The astonishing exactness with which this minute prophetic detail has been fulfilled, furnishes the strongest pledge, from analogy, that the remaining prophecies were and will be as exactly fulfilled, each in their proper season."—*Dr. Hales' Analysis of Chronology*, vol. 2, p. 556.

NOTE 7, PAGE 42.—Interview with Mohammed Ali.

We entered unannounced—in our plain Frank clothes, and found no one in attendance on the Pasha. It is curious to contrast this unceremonious reception with that of foreigners on the same spot in Mandeville's time, about 1330.

"And before the Soudan comethe no Strangier, but zif he be clothed in clothe of gold, or of Tartarye, or of Camaka, in the Sarazines' guise, and as the Sarazines usen. And it behovethe that anon at the firste sight that men see the Soudan, be it in wyndowe, or in what place elles, that men knele to him and kisse the Erthe: for that is the manere to do reverence to the Soudanne of hem that speken with him. And whan that messangeres of straunge contrees comen before him, the meynee of the Soudan, whan the straungeres speken to hym, thei ben aboute the Soudan with swerdes drawen and gysarmez and axes, here armes lift up in highe with the weapenes, for to smyte upon hem, zif thei seye ony woord that is displesance to the Soudan. And also no straungere comethe before him, but that he makethe him sum promys and graunt of that the straungere askethe resonably, be so it be not azenst his lawe. And so don othere princes bezonden. For thei seyn that no man schalle come before no prynce but that he be bettre, and schalle be more gladdere in departynge from his presence thanne he was at the comynge before him."
—*Voiage and Travaile of Sir John Maundevile, knight*. p. 47, ed. 1727.

NOTE 8, PAGE 50.—Streets and houses of Cairo, in 1634.

" Some of those streets I have found two miles in length, some not a quarter so long; every one of them is locked up in the night, with a door at each end, and guarded by a musketeer, whereby fire, robberies, tumults, and other disorders are prevented. Without the city, toward the wilderness, to stop sudden incursions of the Arabs from abroad, there watch on horseback four Sanjiaks, with each of them a thousand horsemen.

" This city is built after the Egyptian manner, high, and of large rough stone, part of brick, the streets being narrow. It hath not yet been above one hundred years in the Turks' possession, wherefore the old buildings remain; but, as they decay, the new begin to be after the Turkish manner, poor, low, much of mud and timber; yet, of the modern fabrics, I must except divers new palaces which I have seen, both of Turks, and such Egyptians as most engage against their own country, and so flourish in its oppression. I have oft gone to view them and their entertainments, sometimes attending the Illustrissimo" (Signor Santo Seghezzi, of Venice), " with whom I lived; otherwhiles accompanied with some of his gentlemen. The palaces I found large and high, no state or flourish outwardly; the first court spacious, set with fair trees for shade, where were several beasts and rare birds, and wonderful even in those parts; the inner court joined to delicious gardens, watered with fountains and rivulets; beside the infinite variety of strange plants, there wanted no shade from trees of cassia, oranges, lemons, figs of Pharaoh, tamarinds, palms, and others, amongst which pass very frequently camelions. The entry into the house, and all the rooms throughout, are paved with many several-coloured marbles, put into fine figures; so likewise the walls, but in mosaic of a less cut; the roof layed with thwart beams, a foot and a half distant, all carved, great, and double gilt; the windows with grates of iron, few with glass, as not desiring to keep out the wind, and to avoid the glimmering of the sun, which in those hot countries glass would break with too much dazzling upon the eye; the floor is made with some elevations a foot high, where they sit to eat and drink; those are covered with rich tapestry; the lower pavement is to walk upon, where in the chief dining chamber, according to the capacity of the room, is made one or more richly gilt fountains in the upper end of the chamber, which, through secret pipes, supplies in the middle of the room a dainty pool, either round, four-square, triangular, or of other figure, as the place requires, usually twenty or twenty-four yards about, and almost two in depth, so neatly kept, and the water so clear, as makes apparent the exquisite mosaic at the bottom; herein are preserved a kind of fish of two or three feet long, like barbels, which have often taken bread out of my hand, sucking it from my fingers at the top of the water.

" But that which to me seemed more magnificent than all this was my entertainment. Entering one of these rooms, I saw at the upper end, amongst others sitting cross-legged, the Lord of the Palace, who beckoning me to come, I first put off my shoes, as the rest had done, then, bowing very often, with my hand on my breast, came near; where he, making me sit down, there attended ten or twelve handsome young pages, all clad in scarlet, with crooked daggers and scymetars, richly gilt; four of them came with a sheet of taffety, and covered me; another held a golden incense with rich perfumes, wherewith being a little smoked, they took all away; next came two with sweet water, and besprinkled me; after that, one brought a porcelain dish of coffee, which, when I had drank, another served up a draught of excellent sherbet. Then began our discourse. ......In their ques tions and replies, I noted the Egyptians to have a touch of the merchant or Jew, with a spirit not so soldier-like and open as the Turks, but more discerning and pertinent."—*Voyage into the Levant, by Sir Henry Blount, of Tittenhanger, Knight. Harleian Voyages*, vol. 1, p. 525.

NOTE 9, PAGE 53.—" Foule-fat-fool-Saint."

" Another of their Saints went about the Citie continually starke naked, covering neither head, foot, nor any part of his foule fat bodie ; yet I have seene divers as hee passed along, at divers times, (yea, women), kiss his naked armes and hands. On a time, at Bullaco, going over Nilus, he going in a passageboat, in which I, with others, went over, a Moore in the companie, seeing him come, layed him a piece of an old coat to sit on; but when he felt it under him, he layd it aside, and sate on the bare boords; so hee ever did on the stones, earth, and sands. This man was in Cairo before I came thither, and I know not how long after.

" This great fat lubberly beast would goe through the streets and take off the stalles to eat, bread, little baked meats, and fruits, and roots, and no bodie denied him, but counted themselves happie that he would do so. He would not touch money of any sort, a very kinde of scorched bacon hogg, hee was fat as he could goe.

" Other of those saints of Cairo goe but half-naked, and some of them are very leane rascalls."—*Sundrie the personall Voyages performed by John Sanderson, of London, Merchant, begun in October*, 1584. *Ended in October,* 1602.—*Purchas's Pilgrims*, vol. 2, p. 1616.

NOTE 10, PAGE 54.

" Here I may fitly take occasion to teach those that purpose to travel into Turkey how to behave themselves. If they be set upon by thieves, they may defend themselves, if they be strong enough ; but if they be polling officers, they must not be contradicted. But neither in their cities, nor in their travels, may they strike again, though they be abused and beaten by any man, except they be thieves and robbers, for if they do, they shall either be put to death, or have their hand cut off. Neither if a man receive a box on the ear at any of their hands, must he give one bad word, or look frowning upon him that smote him; for then he will strike him again, and say, 'What, Goure; dost thou curse me ? and wish the devil had me ?' But he must kiss his beard, or the skirt of his garment, and smile upon him, and then

he will let him pass."—*Biddulph's Travels of four Englishmen,*
&c. 1600—11.   *Harleian Voyages,* vol. 1, p. 812.

Note 11, Page 57.—Isle of Roda.

"Ce fut sous le vézyrat de Chahan-Chah, surnommé *El
Afdhal,* et fils du celebre Bedr el-Djemaly, qu'elle reçut le nom de
Raoudah, ou Jardin.   Ce prince avoit affectionné cette isle, et en
avoit même acquis une portion assez considérable, qu'il avoit em-
bellie avec soin, et où il se promenoit fréquemment.   Il l'appeloit
son jardin; cette dénomination est restée à l'isle entière :
cependant le véritable *Raoudah* ne paroît pas avoir subsisté
longtemps après la mort de Chahan-Chah, assassiné en l'an 515,
(A. D. 1121-2.)   Le khalife el Amar Behhakâm-Allah, que l'on
soupçonne avec beaucoup de vraisemblance d'avoir été l'insti-
gateur de ce crime, s'empara de toutes les propriétés du mal-
heureux vézyr, de son trésor qui renfermoit plusieurs millions de
pièces d'or, de ses pierreries, de ses chevaux, et de ses armes : la
maison de plaisance située dans l'isle en faisoit aussi partie ; et
si le khalyfe négligea de l'entretenir, c'etoit pour lui en substituer
une infiniment plus vaste et belle, et sur-tout plus analogue au
gout le la personne qui devoit l'occuper.

"Ce prince avoit un penchant particulier pour les Arabes
Bedouynes.   Ayant appris qu'il y en avoit une, célèbre par sa
beauté, dans le Said, il y alla déguisé en Arabe Bedouyn, et après
beaucoup de courses et de démarches il parvint à la voir. Sa passion
en devint alors plus violente ; de retour dans son palais, il envoya
auprès des parents de la jeune fille un négotiateur chargé de la
demander en mariage pour le khalyfe.   On imagine bien que la
proposition ne fut pas rejetée.   Arrivée auprès de son auguste
époux, environnée de toute la pompe des grandeurs, la jeune Bedouyne n'en sentit pas moins vivement la perte des jouissances,
ou plutôt de la liberté à laquelle elle étoit accoutumée, et peut-
être aussi l'absence d'un jeune Arabe de ses parents.   Par con-
descendance pour cet amour de la liberté ; qui devoit lui paroître
fort éstrange dans une femme, le khalyfe fit bâtir dans l'isle de
Roudah, sur le bord du Nil, auprès du *Mokhtar,** une maison de
plaisance d'une étendue et d'une magnificence étonnantes, et
que l'on nomma el *Houdedje†.*   Peut-être ce nom fut il imaginé
par la jeune Bedouyne, qui, dans ce vaste palais, se trouvoit aussi
à l'étroit que dans ces litières où les Arabes enferment leurs femmes pour les transporter sur des chameaux quand ils changent
de campement.

* Al Mokhtar, "the preferred"—a magnificent garden, planted in the
island, A. D. 937.

† "Le *houdedje* est une litière dans laquelle les Arabes transportent leurs
femmes quand ils changent de campement ; c'est une espèce de caisse, garnie
de planches ou de l'étoffe ; elle est quelquefois decouverte, ou surmontée d'une
impériale, à laquelle pend un rideau, pour cacher les femmes dans la marche.
Le *houdedje* est porté par un chameau : ce nom convenoit assez bien à une
demeure dans laquelle, malgré toute son étendue, notre jeune Arabe devoit
se trouver aussi gênée que dans une litièie."—*Langlès.*

" Le Khalyfe rendoit des visites si assidues à cette belle cap-
tive, que les Bathenyens, * qui avoient formé le complot de
l'assassiner, se mirent en embuscade, dans un four situé à
l'extremité du pont du côté de l'isle; ils fondirent sur lui au
moment où il passoit, et le poignarderent. Après sa mort le
houdedje fut abandonné, et vers le milieu du quinzième siecle de
l'ere vulgaire on n'en connoissoit plus l'emplacement.

" Les contes que l'on a faits sur la jeune Bedouyne, sur ebn
Mobahh son cousin, et sur le khalyfe El Amar Behhakam Allah
sont aussi nombreux que ceux d'El Bathal et des Mille et une
Nuits." — *Langlès, Notes sur Norden, Voyage, &c.*, tom. 3,
pp. 207-9.

This story will probably remind some of my readers of the
song of Maisuna, the Bedouin bride of Moawia, who, sighing
for the desert amidst the pomp of Damascus, found her greatest
comfort in singing its melancholy strain in private; Moawia
overheard her, and sent her back to Yemen.

> " The russet suit of camel's hair,
>   With spirits light and eye serene,
> Is dearer to my bosom far
>   Than all the trappings of a queen.
>
> The humble tent and murmuring breeze
>   That whistles through its fluttering walls,
> My unaspiring fancy please
>   Better than towers and splendid halls.
>
> The attendant colts, that bounding fly
>   And frolic by the litter's side,
> Are dearer in Maisuna's eye
>   Than gorgeous mules in all their pride.
>
> The watch-dog's voice, that bays whene'er
>   A stranger seeks his master's cot,
> Sounds sweeter in Maisuna's ear
>   Than yonder trumpet's loud-drawn note.
>
> The rustic youth, unspoiled by art,
>   Son of my kindred, poor but free,
> Will ever to Maisuna's heart
>   Be dearer, pampered fool, than thee!"
>
> *Carlyle's Specimens of Arabian Poetry*, p. 38.

---

* " Les Bathenyens étoient une secte hérétique de Musulmans, partisans,
pour ne pas dire adorateurs, de Aly. On les nommoit aussi Nossaïrytes,
(Abulfeda). Les ecrivains des croisades les nomment *assassins.*"—*Langlès.*

Note 12, Page 75.

Yet it would appear to have been open in Abd'allatif's time:—
" Cette ouverture mène à des passages étroits, à des conduits qui
s'étendent jusqu'à une grande profondeur,, à des puits et à des
precipices, comme l'assurent les personnes qui ont le courage de
s'y enfoncer ; car il y a un grand nombre de gens qu' une folle
cupidité et des espérances chimériques conduisent dans l'intérieur
de cette édifice. Ils s'enfoncent dans ses cavités les plus pro-
fondes, et arrivent enfin à un endroit où il ne leur est plus possible de pousser plus avant. Quant au passage le plus fréquenté,
et que l'on suit d'ordinaire, c'est un glacis qui conduit vers la
partie supérieure de la pyramide, où l'on trouve une chambre
carrée, et dans cette chambre un sarcophage de pierre."— On a
second visit, he plucked up courage to enter the pyramid in company with a large party—but he shall tell his own story :—" Dans
un autre visite que je rendis aux pyramides, j'entrai dans ce
conduit interieur avec ¦plusieurs personnes, et je pénétrai
jusqu' aux deux tiers environ ; mais ayant perdu connoissance
par un effet de la frayeur que m'inspiroit cette montée, je
redescendis à demi mort."—*Relation*, &c., p. 175.

" A most dreadful passage and no less cumbersome, not above
a yard in breadth, and four feet in height, each stone containing
that measure, so that, always stooping and sometimes creeping by
reason of the rubbish, we descended, (not by stairs but as down
the steep of a hill,) 100 feet, where the place for a little circuit
enlarged, and the fearful descent continued, which they say none
ever durst attempt any further, save that a Bassa of Cairo, curious
to search into the secrets thereof, caused divers condemned persons
to undertake the performance well stored with lights and other
provision, and that some of them ascended again well nigh thirty
miles off in the deserts. A fable devised only to beget wonder.
But others have written that at the bottom there is a spacious
pit, eighty and six cubits deep, filled at the overflow by concealed
conduits ; in the midst a little island, and on that a tomb containing the body of Cheops, a King of Egypt and the builder of
this Pyramis, which with the truth hath a greater affinity.
For since I have been told by one out of his own experience
that, in the uttermost depth, there is a large square place, (though
without water,) into which he was led by another entry opening
to the south, known but to few, (that now open being shut by
some order,) and entered at this place where we feared to descend."
—*Sandys*.

" Au fond de ceste descente y a une espace à main gauche,
de laquelle se void une autre descente, qui va beaucoup plus
bas sous la Pyramide, mais l'entrée en est murée."—*Relation des
Voyages de M. de Breves*, &c., Paris, 4to, 1630—p. 277. *

---

* De Breves, French Ambassador at the Porte, visited the Pyramids on
his return to France in 1605.

I transcribe from Murtadi's "Merveilles d'Egypte" the following specimen of the popular Arab traditions regarding the Pyramids.

"Après que la Pyramide fut ouverte, le monde la vint voir par curiosité pendant quelques années, plusieurs entrant dedans, et les uns en revenant sans incommodité, les autres y perissant. Un jour il se rencontra qu'une troupe de jeunes hommes, au nombre de plus de vingt, jurerent d'y entrer, pourvu que rien ne les en empeschast, et de pousser tant qu'ils fussent arrivez jusques au bout. Ils prindrent donc avec eux à boire et à manger pour deux mois. Ils prindrent aussi des plaques de fer et des barres, des chandelles de cire et des lanternes, de la mesche et de l'huile, des haches, des serpes, et d'autres tranchans, et entrerent dans la Pyramide.

"La pluspart d'entre eux descendirent de la premiere glissade et de la seconde, et passerent sur la terre de la Pyramide ou ils virent des chauve-souris grandes comme des aigles noires, qui commencerent à leur frapper le visage avec beaucoup de violence. Mais ils souffrirent constamment cette incommodité, et ne cessérent d'avancer jusques àce qu'ils parvindrent à un lieu estroit d'ou il sortoit un vent impetueux et froid extraordinairement, sans qu'ils peussent reconnoistre d'où il venoit, ny où il alloit. Ils s'avancerent pour entrer dans ce destroit, et alors leurs chandelles commencerent à s'esteindre, ce qui les obligea de les enfermer dans leurs lanternes; puis ils entrerent, mais le destroit se trouva presque entièrement joint et clos devant eux. Sur quoy, l'un d'eux dist aux autres, 'Liez moy avec une corde par le milieu du corps, et je me hazarderay de passer outre, à la charge que, s'il m'arrive quelque accident, vous me retirerez aussi-tost à vous.' Il y avoit à l'entrée du destroit de grand vaisseaux vuides faits de pierre en forme de bieres, avec leurs couvercles à costé, ce qui leur fist connoistre que ceux qui les avoient mis là les avoient preparez pour leurs morts, et que pour parvenir jusques à leurs thresors et à leurs richesses, il falloit passer par ce destroit. Ils lierent donc leur compagnon avec des cordes, afin qu'il se hazardast de franchir ce passage.

"Mais incontinent le destroit se ferma sur luy, et ils entendirent le bruit du fracassement de ses os. Ils tirent les cordes à eux, mais ils ne le peurent retirer. Puis il leur vint une voix espouvantable du creux de cette caverne, qui les troubla et les aveugla si bien qu'ils tombérent immobiles et insensibles.

"Ils revindrent à eux quelque temps apres, et chercherent à sortir, estant bien empeschez de leurs affaires. Enfin ils revindrent apres beaucoup de peine, horsmis quelques uns d'eux qui tomberent sous la glissade. Estant sortis dans la plaine, ils s'assirent ensemble tous estonnez de ce qui leur estoit arrivé, et alors voicy que tout d'un coup la terre se fendit devant eux et leur jetta leur compagnon mort, qui demeura d'abord immobile, puis deux heures apres commença à remuer, et leur parla en une langue qu'ils n'entendoient point; car ce n'estoit pas de l'Arabe; mais quelque temps apres quelqu'un des habitans de la Haute

Egypte le leur interpreta, et leur dit qu' il vouloit dire cecy, ' C'est icy la recompense de ceux qui taschent de s'emparer de ce qui ne leur appartient pas ! ' Apres ces mots leur compagnon leur parut mort comme auparavant, c'est pourquoy ils l'enterrerent en la mesme place."—*Merveilles d' Egypte*, p. 55.

NOTE 13, PAGE 78.

Cheops is doubtless the " Priest Saiouph" of Murtadi, who lived till the time of King Pharaan, under whose reign the deluge took place. "Il faisoit sa demeure dans pyramide maritime (ou septentrionale) laquelle pyramide estoit un temple des astres, ou il y avoit une figure du Soleil, et une de la Lune, qui parloient toutes les deux "—*Merveilles d' Egypte*, p. 19.

NOTE 14, PAGE 84.—Caviglia.

" His " pursuits have unsettled many of those notions which he probably received in childhood, and have given him, I suspect, no consoling equivalent. I remembered, however, that there lay in his cottage" (at Memphis,) " one of the finest uninspired volumes ever penned,"the ' Thoughts of Pascal,' " and I could not help wishing that, while looking for the Temple of Vulcan, he might find a nobler prize."—*Scenes and Impressions in Egypt and Italy*, 1824, p. 197. The wish—the prayer of the kind and excellent writer has been answered.

NOTE 15, PAGE 89.

The granite casing of the Pyramid of Mycerinus appears to have been entire in Belon's time,—1548. " La troisiesme Pyramide," he says, " est encor en son entier, n'ayant aucune tache de ruine. Ceste troisiesme Pyramide n'a non plus d'ouverture en toute la masse, que si elle venoit d'estre faite : car la pierre dont elle est faite est d'une sorte de marbre nommé Basalten, autrement appellé lapis Æthiopicus, qui est plus dur que le fin fer. Ceste sorte de pierre est celle dont pour la plus grande partie tous les sphinges Egyptiens ont esté mis en sculpture, tels qu' on voit à Rome au Capitole, et qui ont esté autrefois entaillez par les Egyptiens."—*Observations de plusieurs singularitez*, &c.—c. 45, fol. 204, verso. (edit. 1555.)

The exterior coating of the other two pyramids was entire at the commencement of the thirteenth century :—" Ces pierres sont revêtues d'écriture dans cet ancien caractère dont on ignore aujourd'hui la valeur. Ces inscriptions sont en si grand nombre que, si l'on vouloit copier sur du papier celles seulement que l'on voit sur la surface de ces deux pyramides, on en emploiroit plus de dix mille pages."—*Abd'allatif, Relation* &c., p. 177.

All the early Arab writers bear witness to the existence of these inscriptions :—see the passages collected by De Sacy, Notes to Abd'allatif, pp. 221 sqq., or in Pinkerton's Voyages, &c., vol. 15,

p. 825. Mandeville, about 1330,* and Baldensel,† in 1336, mention them, but in Bakoui's time—1403, they would seem to have totally disappeared. "On pretend," says he, "que sur ces pyramides qui étoient couvertes de sculpture il y avoit une inscription en caractères *mousnads*, (anciennes lettres Hemyarites) par laquelle il étoit dit que leur construction étoit une preuve de la puissance des Egyptiens, et qu'il était plus facile de les détruire que de les élever." *Notices des MSS. de la Bibliothèque du Roi*, tom. 2, p. 457.

Yet Vansleb, in 1672, asserts that he saw upon some of the Pyramids hieroglyphic characters, but he had not time to copy them.—*Present State* &c., p. 84.

" To reconcile the silence of the Greek and Latin writers, on the subject of the inscriptions on the pyramids, with the testimony of the Arab writers, Mr. White makes a judicious observation which I transcribe: 'Such abundance of hieroglyphical characters were seen in every part of Egypt that they would fail of ex-

---

* Mandeville's whole description is curious :—" Now I schalle speke of another thing, that is bezonde Babyloyne, above the flode of Nyle, toward the desert, betwene Africk and Egypt,—that is to seyn, of the Gerneres of Joseph that he lete make, for to kepe the greynes for the perile of the dere zeres. Thei ben made of ston, full welle made of masounes' craft, of the whiche two ben merveyllouse grete and hye : and the tothere ne ben not so gret ; *and every Gerner hath a zate for to entre withinne, a lytille highe fro the Erthe*. For the lond is wasted and fallen sithe the Gerners were made. And withinne thei ben alle fulle of serpentes. *And aboven the Gerneres withouten, ben many scriptures of dyverse languages*. And sum men seyn, that thei ben sepultures of grete Lordes that weren somtyme : but that is not trewe: for alle the comoun rymour and speche is of alle the peple there, both fer and nere, that thei ben the Gerneres of Joseph. And so fynden thei in here scriptures and in here Cronycles. On that other partie, zif thei weren sepultures, thei scholden not ben voyd withinne. For yee may well knowe that tombes and sepultures ne ben not made of such gretnesse, ne of such highnesse. Wherefore it is not to believe that thei ben tombes or sepultures."—*Voiage* &c. p. 63. Does Sir John intend to intimate that the Pyramids of Cephrenes and Mycerinus were open in his time?

† Baldensel also found a Latin inscription of six lines, sculptured on a stone in one of the Pyramids, and beginning in the following affecting strain :—
" Vidi pyramidas sine te, dulcissime frater !
Et tibi, quod potui, lacerymas hic maestas profudi,
Et, nostri memorem luctus, hanc sculpo querelam."
The concluding lines, as given by him, are unintelligible.—*Hodoeporicon &c. ap. Canisii Lectiones Antiquae*, t. 4, p. 342.
Ludolf, rector of Suchen, who performed his pilgrimage to Jerusalem the same year as Baldensel, furnishes another copy of this inscription, which is found, says he, along with other Latin inscriptions, on the wall of one of the two larger pyramids ; its second, third, and fourth faces being similarly sculptured with inscriptions in Greek, Hebrew, and an unknown character. Ludolf's work being extremely scarce, I transcribe the original passage from the folio edition printed by Eggestein at Strasburgh, (but without name, place, or date, paying, or signature,) in the fifteenth century :—" Item, juxta Babiloniam Novam, trans fluvium Nyli, versus desertum Egypti, stant quam. plurima mire magnitudinis antiquorum monumenta, ex lapidibus sectis facta; in quibus sunt duo maxima et olim pulcherrima sepulchra quadrata, in cujus unius pariete uno Latine, in secundo Graece, in tertio Hebraice, in quarto multa quae ignorantur scripta sunt et sculpta. Sed in primo pariete quo scripte erant Latine, in quantum pro vetustate discerni potest, hi versus sunt insculpti, &c. . . . Haec monumenta ' horrea Pharonis' ab incolis vocantur."

citing admiration in the observers, and be deemed unworthy of particular relation, Owing to this it is, that, in the description of the obelisks, which from the ground to the very summit are covered with hieroglyphics, this circumstance has remained unnoticed by the greatest part of the ancients."—*De Sacy.*

NOTE 16, PAGE 89.

Do we not recognise another well-known tale in Bakoui's account of the great and ancient city of Ansina (Antinoopolis,) to the East of the Nile, where the inhabitants had all been changed into stone, and were to be seen, some asleep, some awake, each in the different attitude and occupation he had been engaged in when the spell took effect? Ansina was called, in Edrisi's time, (A. D. 1153.) the City of Magicians, those opposed to Moses by Pharaoh having been summoned by him from that town.—*Geogr. Nub.* p. 41. I wonder they did not refer the transformation to the rod of Moses.

Ebn Haukul, however, in the tenth century, brings Pharaoh's magicians from Bouseir.

NOTE 17, PAGE 90.

" L'Egypte étoit alors, disent ils, partagée en quatre-vingts-cinq provinces, dont il y en avoit quarante-cinq dans la partie basse et quarante dans la haute. Et en chaque province il y avoit un gouverneur, du nombre des princes des prestres, qui sont ceux dont Dieu parle dans l'histoire de Pharaon, quand il dit, ' Envoye par les villes des herauts, qui amenent vers toy tous les scavans magiciens ;' il entend ces Gouverneurs. L'on dit que les villes des Princes des Magiciens avoient esté basties par Busire. Le Prestre qui servoit les astres estoit sept ans en charge, et quand il estoit parvenu à ce degré, on le nommoit Cater, comme qui diroit *Maistre des Influences,*[*] et alors il prenoit seance avec le Roy, en mesme rang, et le Roy menoit ses bestes à l'abrevoir et les ramenoit, (c'est à dire, faisoit toutes les affaires,) selon son conseil. Quand il le voyoit venir, il se levoit pour le recevoir, alloit au devant de luy et le faisoit asseoir. Puis les Prestres s'approchoient, et avec eux les Maistres des Arts, qui se tenoient debout au dessous du Cater. Chaque Prestre avoit un Astre à servir particulierement, sans qu'il luy fust permis d'en servir aucun autre, et on le nommoit le serviteur de tel astre, tout de mesme que les Arabes servoient chacun son dieu, et se nommoient Gabdosamse, Gabdiagoth, Gabdolgasi, c' est à dire, Serviteur de Samse ou du Soleil, Serviteur de Jagots, Serviteur du Gazi. Le Cater disoit donc au Prestre ; ' Ou est aujourd 'hui l'astre que tu sers !' et le

---

[*] "Les prestres estoient distinguez en sept ordres, dont le premier estoit celuy des Caters, qui estoient ceux qui servoient tous les sept astres, chaque astre sept ans. Avec le Cater estoit le Docteur Universel. Le second ordre appartenoit à ceux qui servoient six astres, et qui estoient ceux qui suivoient immediatement apres le premier degré. Apres cela ils nommoient celny qui en servoit cinq et audessous, le suivant et l' inferieur."—*Ibid.* p. 46.

Prestre respondit, ' il est en tel signe, tel degré, telle minute.'
Puis il demandoit la mesme chose à un autre, et quand il avoit eu
response de tous, et qu'il scavoit la position de tous les astres, il
s'adressoit au Roy, et luy parloit ainsi. ' Il est à propos que
vous fassiez aujourd'hui telle chose, que vous envoyez telle armée
en tel lieu, que vous vous vestiez de telle maniere, que vous
parliez en tel temps, que vous fassiez assemblée en tel temps ;' et
de mesme de tout ce qu'il trouvoit bon dans toutes les affaires
du Roy, et dans tout le gouvernement de son Royaume. Le Roy
escrivoit tout ce que disoit le Cater, et tout ce qu'il desapprou-
voit.

" Puis il se tournoit vers les artisans et leur parloit ainsi.
' Grave, toy, telle figure sur telle pierre', ' et toy, plante tel
arbre', ' et toy, fais le plan geometrique de tel ouvrage', et ainsi
de suite à tous, depuis le premier jusques au dernier. Incontinent
ils sortoient tous, et se rendoient promptement chacun à sa bouti-
que, où ils mettoient la main à l'œuvre, travaillant aux ouvrages
qui leur avoient été commandez, et suivant exactement le dessein qui leur avoit esté prescrit par le Cater, sans s'en éloigner
aucunement. Ils marquoient ce jour là dans le registre des ouvrages qui s'y faisoient, et le registre estoit plié, et mis en garde
dans les thrésors du Roy.

" Leurs affaires se faisoient selon cet ordre; puis le Roy,
quand il luy survenoit quelque affaire, faisoit assembler les
prestres hors la ville de Memphis, et le peuple s'assembloit dans
les grandes rues de la mesme ville. Alors ils entroient l'un après
l'autre chacun en son rang, le tambour battant devant eux pour
faire assembler le monde, et chacun faisoit voir quelque trait
merveilleux de sa magie et de sa sagesse. L'un faisoit paroitre
sur son visage, aux yeux de ceux qui le regardoient, une lumiére
pareille à celle du soleil; de sorte que personne ne pouvoit
arrester sa veue sur luy. L'autre paroissoit revestu d'une robe
chamarrée de pierreries de diverses couleurs, vertes ou rouges, ou
jaunes, ou tissue d'or. Un autre venoit monté sur un lyon,
environné de grands serpens entortillez autour de luy en forme de
cengles. Un autre s'avancoit couvert d'un dais ou pavillon com-
posé de lumiere. Un autre paroissoit environné d'un feu tourno-
yant autour de luy, en sorte que personne ne le pouvoit approcher.
Un autre se faisoit voir avec des oyseaux terribles, voltigeans
autour de sa teste, et tremoussans de leurs aisles, comme des
aigles noires et des vaultours. Un autre faisoit paroistre en l'air
devant luy des personnages effroyables et espouvantables, et des
serpens aislez. Enfin, chacun faisoit ce que luy enseignoit son
astre qu'il servoit: mais tout cela n'estoit que phantosme et illusion, sans aucune verité"—the *gramarye* of European superstition.—*Merveilles d' Egypte;* pp. 5-10.

NOTE 18, PAGE 95.—Spirits of the Pyramids.

" Tous ces esprits sont veus manifestement par ceux, qui

approchent d'eux et des lieux de leur retraite, et y hantent long-temps. Il y a pour tous certaines offrandes particulieres, par le moyen desquelles il se peut faire que les thresors des Birba et des Pyramides paroissent, et qu'il se forme amitié et familiarité entre les hommes et les esprits, suivant ce que les sages ont estably."—*Murtadi, Merveilles d' Egypte*, p. 66.

" Les fables que les Arabes nous racontent sur ces gardiens et ces esprits attachés aux Pyramides, ne seroient-elles pas fondées sur les figures monstrueuses disposées probablement à l'entour de ces monuments, et dont la sphinx est la seule qui subsiste?"—*Langlès, Notes on Norden*, t. 3, p. 272.

Note 19, Page 96.—The Sphinx.

" On dit que c'estoit anciennement un oracle, qui donnoit response à ceux qui luy parloient et demandoient son avis et conseil en beaucoup de choses."—*De Breves*, p. 279.

Abd'allatif speaks of the Sphinx with great admiration : " On voit sur la figure une teinte rougeâtre et un vernis rouge, qui a tout l'éclat de la fraicheur. Cette figure est tres belle, et sa bouche porte l'empreinte des grâces et de la beauté. On diroit qu'elle sourit gracieusement."—*Relation*, &c. p. 179.

The face was mutilated by a fanatic sheikh of the Sofy sect, in 1379, " et depuis cette époque, les sables inondent le territoire de Djizeh."—*Langlès, Notes on Norden*, t. 3, p. 339.

Note 20, Page 99.—Heliopolis.

The name Heliopolis or Beth-Shemesh, the dwelling—is still preserved in that of the adjacent spring *Ain-Shems*—the Fountain of the Sun.

Abd'allatif describes Ain-Shems as a small town, " qui étoit entourée d'un mur, qui l'on reconnoît encore aujourd'hui, quoique détruit. On voit facilement que ces ruines appartiennent à un temple ; on y trouve des figures effrayantes et colossales de pierre de taille, qui ont plus de trente coudées de long, et dont tous les membres sont dans des dimensions proportionnées. De ces figures, les unes étoient debout sur des piédestaux ; les autres assises dans différentes positions singulières, et avec une parfaite régularité. La porte de la ville subsiste encore adjourd'hui. La plupart de ces pierres sont couvertes de figures d'hommes et d'autres animaux, et d'un grand nombre d'inscriptions en caractère inconnu. Il est rare de rencontrer une pierre qui n'offre, ou une inscription, ou quelque objet gravé en creux, ou une figure en relief."

He proceeds to mention " les deux obélisques si renommés, que l'on appelle *les deux aiguilles de Pharaon*,"—one of them erect, " la tête recouverte d'un espéce de chapeau en cuivre, en forme d'entonnoir, qui descend jusqu'à trois coudées environ du sommet,"—the other lying on the ground broken in two, with its cap taken away. " Autour de ces obélisques il y en a une multitude d'autres qu'on ne sauroit compter: ceux-ci n'ont que la moitié ou le tiers de la hauteur des grands. Parmi ces petits obélisques, on n'en voit guère qui soient d'une seule pierre; la plupart sont de plusieurs pieces rapportées. Le plus grand nombre ont été renversés, mais leurs bases sont encore en place."—*Relation*, &c. pp. 180-1.

Both the obelisks were erect in 1118, and De Sacy's conjecture is probably correct, that we should read 556 for 656—the year of the Hegira in which the one mentioned by Abd'allatif as lying broken on the ground, fell—corresponding to our year of Christ, 1160. Inside of the fallen obelisk, (of which not a trace is now to be seen), was found, according to Makrisi, our authority for the above date, nearly two hundred quintals of copper, and from its summit copper was taken of the value of ten thousand dinars. These copper caps, (on which, according to a writer cited by Makrisi, the figure of a man, seated and looking towards the East, was engraved,) were seen by Denys de Telmayre, A. D. 775; and Ephraim Syrus mentions them in his commentary on Isaiah, in the fourth century.—*De Sacy.*

The surviving obelisk was supposed by the Arabs to have been erected by Hushenk the Just, father of the Pischdadian dynasty of Persia, and famous for his doughty deeds in Peri-land, warring against the Dives. The sculptured figures, which were to be seen at Ain Shems in Bakoui's time, were similarly attributed to the Genies.

Note 21, Page 107.—Abhir.

With the utmost deference to the learned Klaproth, might not the illustrious race of the *Avars* have derived their name, (written indifferently Abares, Auairas, Awares, and Aviri,) from this Sanscrit word? The Gaelic *aodhair*, contracted *aoir*, a shepherd, (from *aodh*, a sheep), appears to be the same word.

I cannot help remarking how singularly the hereditary title Topa, or Master of the Earth, borne by the Khans of the Geougen, afterwards called Avars,—and that of Tobbaa, assumed by the Hamyarite dynasty of Yemen, resemble each other. The arms of the Tobbaas were carried as far as China, and an inscription in the *Musnad*, or ancient Hamyarite character, was long shewn on one of the gates of Samarcand, attesting their presence and their victories, " a thousand parasangs from Senaa," at least 500 years B. C. See Ebn Haukul's Oriental Geography, translated by Sir W. Ouseley, 4to. 1800.

Note 22, Page 107.

I am aware that the Philistines and Cherethim are identified in Scripture, and that Calmet and many learned commentators consequently bring the Philistines from Crete. Major Wilford's and Mr. Taylor's opinion appears to me nearer the truth—that Crete was colonised by the Cherethim, a tribe of the Philistines or shepherd race, who preserved their distinct appellation, though an integral part of the nation, in the same manner as one of the principal branches of the Pali in India (to all appearance the same as the Cherethim) is distinguished to this day by the kindred name of Ciratas.—Crete, it is remarkable enough, is said by Anaximander, (ap. Plin.) to have been named from the Curetes under their king Philistides.

With all deference, however, to those learned men, I cannot subscribe to their opinion that the Philistines came all the way from India. Gausanitis, or Goshan, in Mesopotamia, and Palestine to the East of the Tigris, seem to be the two ventricles, as it were, of that mighty heart, from which the streams of Pali and Ciratas flowed towards the East, and those of Philistim and Cherethim towards the West.

The argument in the text refers to the great migration from Caphtor to Canaan ; some Philistines had certainly settled on the borders of Canaan at a much earlier period. Abimelech, king of Gerar, was king of the Philistines in Abraham's time. Gerar, however, no longer existed as a capital, nor the Abimelechs as a line of kings, in the time of Joshua.

NOTE 23, PAGE 126.

Peter Martyr draws a sad picture of the moral degradation and political oppression of the Egyptians, at the commencement of the sixteenth century:—

·' Gens autem ipsa incolarum est imbellis, effœminata, inermis, discincta, mollis, timida: mechanicis tantum artibus aut mercaturae intenta: vitam silentio præterit ingloriam. Nec aliis legibus à Mameluchis gubernata, quàm absoluto judicio. Est præterea Mameluchi cujusvis tanta in incolas universos potestas, ut clava lignea, quam manu gestat semper, quemcunque incolam obvium ferire pro libito, vel levissimâ occasione sumptâ, liceat: quod scilicet ipsum transeuntem tetigerit, aut venienti non assurrexerit, vel minus honorifice salutaverit, aut non citus loco cesserit. Interdum etiam nullam nactus causam, dum aut temulentus aut insanus vel aliâs iratus incedens per urbem Mameluchus occurrit incolae, ipsum quotquot ictibus libet percutit, nec mussitare miser audet, neque in ejus auxilium vel labium movere quisquam intentat: quamvis pater filium, aut filius patrem à Mamelucho cædi conspiciat, æquo tamen vultu patiatur, necesse est. ......Incolae cuiquam arma ulla, vel gladiolum quidem acuta cuspide vel recta, apud se habere, equo vel pedibus ambulanti, vetitum est. Redituum autem, præter ordinaria vectigalia, lex est—principum voluntas. Exigunt, expilant, extorquent, et ad ossa usque excoriant. Propterea etsi animus ad vindicandum se in libertatem à tam impiâ servitute adesset, vires tamen deficerent: cum pecuniae, quae sunt nervi belli, illis desint; exercitique minime sint armis. .....Voluptatibus omnifariam dediti, futurorum omni curâ posthabitâ, vivunt; suoque Mahometae se magis gratum facere tunc arbitrantur, quando ardentius delectationibus incumbunt.

" Judicate igitur, serenissimi reges, quàm infausto sydere regiones hae gubernentur, in quibus servi dominantur, liberi serviunt, graves opprimuntur, stulti extolluntur; ubi nulla fides, nullum jus, nulla pietas, misericordia rara, avaritia immensa; in domibus summa ob multas uxores discordia, foris ingens inter se odium."—*Legatio Babylonica*, lib. 3, fol. 84.*

Nor was the Egyptian policy of the Grand Signors less oppressive than that of the Caliphs and Sultans:—

" Now the Turk, to break the spirits of this people the more, oppresses them with a heavier poverty than any of his other Mahometan subjects; and, therefore, if there be one Vizier more ravenous than another, he sends him thither, and connives at all his extortions, though afterwards, according to the Turkish policy, he knows how to squeeze him into the treasury, so satisfying the people; the prince drains them, and they discern him no otherwise than as their revenger."—*Blount's Voyage into the Levant; Harl. Voyages*, vol. 1, p. 529.

The following passage from Vansleb I need only preface by reminding the reader that the Copts are the *sole* remnant of the ancient Egyptians:—

" I must needs confess that there is no nation in Egypt so much afflicted as are the Copties, because they have nobody amongst them who deserves to be honoured for his knowledge, or feared for his power and authority; for all that were rich or wealthy are destroyed by the cruelty of the Mahometans; therefore the rest are now looked upon as the scum of the world, and worse than the Jews. The Turks abuse them at their pleasure; they shut up their churches, and the doors of their houses when they please, upon light occasions, altogether unjust, to draw from them some sums of money."—*Present State of Egypt*, 1672, p. 174.

" It shall be the basest of kingdoms, neither shall it exalt itself any more among the nations, for I will diminish them, that they shall no more rule over the nations. Her power shall come down —I will sell the land into the hand of the wicked—I will make the land waste, and all that is therein, by the hand of strangers. I the Lord have spoken it."—*Ezekiel.*

Note 24, Page 127.—Manfalout.

Manfalout has been almost swept away by the Nile. Besides " certain huge and high pillars and porches, whereon are verses engraven in the Egyptian tongue," Leo Africanus mentions " the

* The writings of Peter Martyr " abound in interesting particulars not to be found in any cotemporary historian. They are rich in thought, but still richer in fact, and are full of urbanity, and of the liberal feeling of a scholar who has mingled in the world. He is a fountain from which others draw, and from which, with a little precaution, they may draw securely."—*Washington Irving, Life of Columbus.*

ruins of a stately building, which seemeth to have been a temple
in times past," as standing "neare unto Nilus"—It has long since
suffered the fate of those at Antaeopolis, and elsewhere—and
Ombos will follow.

Among the ruins, he adds, the citizens "find sometimes coin
of silver, sometimes of gold, and sometimes of lead, having on the
one side hielygraphic notes, and, on the other side, pictures of
ancient kings."—*Geographical History of Africa*, p. 325.

Note 25, Page 132.—Siout.

Leo Africanus, at the beginning of the sixteenth century, describes Siout as " most admirable in regard of the hugeness and
of the variety of old buildings, and of epitaphs engraven in
Egyptian letters ; although at this present the greatest part
thereof lyeth desolate. When the Mahometans were first lords of
this city, it was inhabited by honourable personages, and con-
tinueth as yet famous in regard of the nobility and great wealth of
the citizens."—*Geographical History*, &c. p. 325.

Siout was the birth-place of many celebrated Arab literati,
especially of Gelaleddin Aboul Fadh! Abdal-rahman Mohammed,
surnamed Assiouti,—a most voluminous writer, who flourished
under Saladin, and to whom we owe the story of the fair Bedouin
and the Garden of Roda.

Note 26, Page 132.

Mallem Athanasius, the last of the Copts that spoke his native
tongue, was living at Siout in 1673, when Vansleb ascended the
Nile. " I could not benefit myself much by him, because he was
deaf, and about four-score years of age ; nevertheless I had the
satisfaction to behold that man, with whom the Copties' language
will be utterly lost."—*Present State*, &c. p. 219.

Note 27, Page 133.

The Balsam, carried originally, says Arab tradition, from Yemen by the Queen of Sheba, as a present to Solomon, and planted
by him in the gardens of Jericho, was brought to Egypt by Cleopatra, and planted at Ain Shems, or Heliopolis, now Mataria, in
a garden which all the old travellers, Arab and Christian, mention
with deep interest. The Balsam of Jericho, or Balm of Gilead,
has long been lost ; it may not be uninteresting to trace the
gradual extinction of that of Mataria.

The Christians, we are informed by an Arab writer, cited by
D'Herbelot, attached a peculiar religious value to the Balm of
Mataria, using it " pour faire ce que les Grecs et les autres
Chrétiens Orientaux appellent *myron*, qui est la chrême de la
confirmation." " Les souverains Chrétiens," says Makrisi, " le
recherchent à l'envi les uns des autres, et tous les Chrétiens, en
général, l'ont en grande estime: il ne croient point qu'un Chrétien

soit devenu parfait Chrétien, si l'on ne met un peu d'huile de baume dans l'eau baptismale, quand on l'y plonge."*—*De Sacy, Notes on Abd'allatif*, p. 88.

The Balm of Mataria was also indispensable at the coronations of the European sovereigns:—

> " Not all the water in the rough rude sea
> Can wash the balm from an anointed king!"

The first writer, I believe, who mentions it, is the author of the Apocryphal Gospel of the infancy of Christ— a work supposed to have been translated from a Greek original of ancient date,— p. 69, *Sike's edition*, 1697.

Abd'allatif gives a minute account of the plant, and of the method of gathering the balm. " On le cultive," he says, " dans un lieu enclos, et soigneusement gardé, de l'étendue de sept feddans."—p. 20-1.

The garden, Ebn al Ouardi tells us in the thirteenth century, was a mile square—the only spot (and this assertion, as old as Ebn Haukul's time, is reiterated by every traveller,) where it was preserved. De Salignac, in 1522, describes this garden as two bow-shots long, by a stone's cast broad.

Sir John Mandeville, about 1330—(his authority is not to be contemned while he treats of the well-known regions of Egypt, Mount Sinai, and Palestine)—has dedicated a chapter of his marvellous narrative to the ' Field of Balsam,' which he asserts would no where else bear fruit, nor even there, unless under the culture of Christian gardeners. They call the tree, he says, *Enonchbalse*, the fruit *abebissam*, the liquor or gum, *guybalse*. The incisions were made with bones or stones, never with iron, or the gum would be corrupted. It was an infallible specific for fifty different diseases, but was very rarely to be obtained pure.—*Voiage*, &c. p. 60.

---

* The Greek word, which the French have softened into *crême*, is retained with greater purity in the *chrism* or *chrisome* of our old English writers. Till the revisal of the liturgy in 1551, the chrism or consecrated oil was applied immediately after baptismal immersion; the infant's head was then enveloped in the *chrisome-cloth*, a vesture of white linen, originally, in all probability, emblematical of those robes of righteousness provided for the redeemed soul by the Saviour. and wrapped in which, by an affecting image, its little body was consigned to rest, if the Almighty was pleased to recal the spirit he had given within a month after its birth. Such an infant was called a *chrisome-child*. " Every morning," says Jeremy Taylor, alluding probably to the beautiful idea that the smiles of infants are the medium of their converse with angels—" creeps out of a dark cloud, leaving behind it an ignorance and silence deep as midnight, and undiscerned as are the phantasms that make a *chrisom-child* to smile."—And perhaps to a thoughtful mind, Mrs. Quickly's comparison of Falstaff's death to the peaceful departure of a *chrisom-child* is, in the reflections it suggests, the most awful in the whole compass of literature.

In process of time the word *Chrisom* came to be used indifferently for the unction, the vesture, and the infant; it is in the last sense only that it now survives. as heading the most numerous column in the London bills of mortality.

One tree only existed in Bakoui's time, (1403,) which, he says, "en commençant à pousser, ressemble au grenadier et au hanna; on en tire la baume dans des vases de verre. Il s'en fait un grand commerce; on compte qu'on en recueille par un an 200 livres d'Egypte; il y a là un Chrétien, qui seul a le secret de la preparer et de la purifier."

But the fullest account of this garden is to be found in Breydenbach's curious folio, the "Peregrinatio in Montem Syon, ad venerandum Christi sepulchrum, atque in Montem Synai, ad divam Virginem et Martyrem Katherinam," performed in 1483, and printed at Mentz, in 1486. Arriving from Mount Sinai, weary and way-worn, and having for many days tasted only the foul water of the desert, one can well imagine his delight in welcoming the "sweet, clear, and cold" waters of Mataria, and reposing in a "spacious and delicious" edifice, built over the fountain of the Virgin, its windows opening on the garden, and completely perfumed by the fragrance of the balsam. This palace,' as a cotemporary of Breydenbach's calls it, was built by the Soldan, who paid it an annual visit at the season when the balm was gathered. The earliest and choicest balm was obtained in December, incisions being made thrice in that month, and the produce was reserved exclusively for the Soldan, who made presents of it to the Cham of Tartary, Prester John, Xanssa Lord of the Tartars, and the Grand Turk: the subsequent produce was sold, but much adulterated.

Dismissing their camels here, Breydenbach and his companions rested for the remainder of the day, after sending to Cairo for a dragoman, without whose escort no Christians were allowed to enter. Wine, they complain, was the only luxury they could not obtain here; every thing else was to be had in abundance, and on reasonable terms.

When the Holy family, on their flight from Egypt, arrived at Mataria, they went from house to house, asking, but in vain, for a cup of water: faint, thirsty, and sorrowful, the Virgin sat down to rest herself, when suddenly the sacred fountain sprung forth at her side. The balsam, adds Breydenbach, with fond and amiable superstition, refuses to yield her produce to any irrigation save that of the fountain of the Virgin.*

In Breydenbach's time, therefore, the garden appears to have been flourishing. Shortly afterwards, most unaccountably, the balsam plants—for the single shrub mentioned by Bakoui had been extensively propagated, it seems—all died out—whether through carelessness of the gardener, through fraud or envy of the Jews, or through religion and piety being offended, no one could tell; "however that may be," says Peter Martyr d'Anghiera, the Spanish Ambassador, who visited the spot in 1502, "all those

* Peter Martyr says that Iaches, king of Cyprus, with permission of Caytbeius (Qaetbai e' Zaheree) the Sultan, attempted to rear it in Cyprus, irrigating it with water brought from Mataria; but the plant would not live. *Legatio Babylonica, lib.* 3.

plants have perished from the very roots, nor does the slightest trace of them remain." This must have been some years before his visit, as the interior of the Sultan's palace, deserted ever since the balm failed, had already fallen to ruin.

Baumgarten, five years afterwards, tells the same tale, adding that " the balm failing, a neighbouring fountain was dried, which, as they told us, used to moisten the trees, and make them fruitful." The fountain, however, was still as sweet and plentiful as ever, when the plenipotentiary of Castille was there, who tells his sovereign, in the most elegant latinity, that, though water was forbidden him by his physicians, he could not, remembering who had bathed in that fountain, abstain from taking three such copious draughts of it, that his stomach swelled to such a degree that he was obliged to loosen his girdle.

One solitary plant, however, appears to have been recovered, and the fountain, (Baumgarten would have supposed by sympathy,) had sprung up again, when Leo Africanus, the protégé of Leo X., finished that 'golden volume,' his Description of Africa, in 1526. " At Amalthria," says he, " there is a garden containing the only balm-tree, (for in the whole world beside there is not any other tree that beareth true balm,) growing in the midst of a large fountain, and having a short stock or body, bearing leaves like vine-leaves, but not so long; and this tree, they say, would utterly wither and decay, if the water of the fountain should chance to be diminished. The garden is surrounded with a strong wall," (in Peter Martyr's time only by a mound of earth,) "whereinto no man may enter without the special favour and licence of the Governor."

" Ils sont dedans un grand jardin," says Belon, in 1548, " enfermez en un petit parquet de muraille, que l'on dit y avoir esté fait depuis que le Turc a osté l'Egypte des mains du Souldan; et dit on que ce fut un Bacha, qui estoit lieutenant pour le Turc, qui les estima dignes d'avoir closture à part eux. Lorsque les veismes, il n'y en avoit que neuf ou dix plantes, qui ne rendent aucune liqueur."—*Observations*, &c., p. 195.

Vincent le Blanc, who visited " the garden of true balm" in 1578, says "it is but small, and there is but little of it." He tells the same story, that it would flourish only under Christian culture, and dies in the hands of Infidels; and adds that about the end of May they slit the bark, not with iron, but with something else, and the liquor distils out, which they receive in a glass. Yet, he says, " in some parts of the West Indies, in Nova Hispania, and Carthagenia, there is some of no less esteem than this of Egypt."

De Breves, in 1605, speaks of the garden as " gardé avec grand soin; et avant que d'y entrer, le Bostandji ou jardinier pria un chacun de ne point toucher aux plantes. Là dedans nous vismes sept ou huit petits arbrisseaux de baume, ayant chacun son quarreau à part; ils sont fort petits, de la hauteur d'un pan et demy, ou deux, ayant la feuille petite comme de la marjolaine sauvage, ses branches fort desnuées de feuilles. Le Bostandji nous donna deux ou trois petites phioles de baume, et un petit du bois; il rend une fort bonne odeur. Nous en vismes un qui avoit esté incisé, qui distilloit sa liqueur dans une petite phiole. En nous promenant dans ledit jardin, quelqu'un des nostres, ayant marché sur une des dites plantes, en rompit une branche tout à fait; ce qu'ayant apperçu le pauvre jardinier, il en devint palle et transi de douleur et de frayeur, comme s'il eust esté condamné à la mort, et se desesperoit, disant qu'autre que sa vie ne pouvoit reparer ce dommage, le sçachant le Grand Seigneur ou le Bassa: car ceux qui sont à la garde de ces plantes en respondent sur leur teste. En fin on appaisa ce pauvre homme, avec un peu d'argent qu'on luy donna."—*Relation etc.*, p. 271.

Two plants only, and almost dead, existed in 1612, when Brenning visited Mataria; they had been drooping, according to Radziwil, ever since Hassan Pasha, the predecessor of Ibrahim who governed Egypt when he visited that country in 1583, had strangled the Ethiopian who had the care of the garden, and was the only one who understood their culture.*— *Hierosol. Peregrinatio*, p. 177.

Sandys mentions one—" the whole remnant of that store, which this orchard produced, destroyed by the Turks, or envy of the Jews, as by the others reported."

This last survivor perished in 1615, in consequence of an inundation of the Nile.

Thevenot's account of Mataria, in 1657, throws so much light on the preceding descriptions, and gives so accurate an idea of the present appearance of the garden and its facilities for pic-nics, that I cannot resist transcribing it:—" Vous y voyez une petite salle presque quarrée, qui autrefois etoit une simple grotte, maintenant elle est enclose avec un jardin, dont on a le soin : au commencement de cette salle, à main gauche, est un bassin qui est à rez-de-chaussée du pavé, un peu plus long que large. . . . . L'eau qui vient en ce bassin de cette salle, et partout le jardin, se tire par deux bœufs, qui font tourner une saki dans la cour, par le moyen de laquelle ils élevent cette eau. . . . . . Après avoir vu cette salle, on passe dans un grand jardin, enfermé aussi de murailles, où il y a plusieurs arbres, mais entr'autres il y a un gros sycomore, ou figuier de Pharaon, fort vieux, qui porte toutefois du fruit tous les ans; on dit que la Vierge passant par là auprès avec son fils Jesus, et voyant que des gens la poursuivoient, le figuier s'ouvrit, et la Vierge y étant entrée dedans, il se referma ; puis ces gens étant passez, il se rouvrit, et resta toujours ainsi ouvert jusqu'à l'année 1656, que le morceau qui s'étoit separé du tronc fut rompu.† . . . Ce

---

* As far back as 1575 or 6, the Pasha had attempted to introduce some fresh plants from Mecca, " mais au bout de quelque temps elles moururent." *Peregrinations du Sieur Jean Palerne*, p. 142.

† " The Copts say that when our Lord Jesus Christ and his most Holy

jardin est assez agréable pour se reposer, et on y dîne ordinaire-
ment dans quelque allée couverte d'orangers et de limoniers,
dont il y a si grande quantité, et qui font un tel ombrage, que le
soleil n'y passe point du tout, mais ils sont si bas, qu'il faut se
baisser extrêmement, pour passer en plusieurs de ces allées, au
milieu desquelles il y a des canaux faits pour conduire l'eau par
tout le jardin; on vous fait passer l'eau par l'allée ou vous êtes
et vous y faites rafraîchir votre vin; mais il faut porter là ce que
vous voulez manger, car on n'y trouve que des oranges belles et
bonnes en quantité, et des petits limons."—*Voyages au Levant*
tom. 2, p. 440.

Two prints of the ' house of Joseph and Mary,' as the hut
erected over the sacred fountain was then called, as it existed in
1681, may be found in the *Voyages de Lebrun*, tome 1: planches
76, 77.

The well is now open to the sun, and the balm survives only in
tradition.

———

Between Mataria and Cairo, a garden and pleasure-house of
the Mamaluke Sultans existed in Belon's time, 1548—of which
he gives the following description:—

" Quand nous l'eusmes veu, tournasmes bride vers le Caire,
nous destournants de nostre chemin, en declinant à main
dextre, pour aller voir un autre jardin, qui n'est qu' à une lieu du

mother hid themselves in this opening of the Sycomore, they saved themselves from the soldiers' violence by the favour of a spider's web that covered
them suddenly, and appeared very old, though it was made in an instant by
a miracle; so that they imagined not that any person could be hid within,
much less the persons whom they were seeking."—*Vansleb, Present State of
Egypt*, p. 141.

No mention of this tree or of its miraculous history is to be found in the
Gospel of the Infancy of Christ.

A large sycomore is still reverenced at Mataria as the Virgin's tree. But
the stump of another, which bore the same title, was shewn in the garden,
and the fragments of its trunk were preserved as relics by the Franciscans at
Cairo, in 1672.—*Vansleb.*

———

Another sacred tree was to be seen at Cairo in the days of Jacques de
Vitry, Bishop of Acre, who died in 1244. " At Cairo is a very ancient date-
tree, which spontaneously bent itself to the blessed Virgin when she wished
to eat of its fruit, and rose again when she had gathered it. The Saracens,
seeing this, cut the tree down, but the following night it sprung up again
as straight and entire as before, and consequently they now venerate and
adore it. The marks of the axe," adds the Bishop, " are visible to this day."
—*Jacobi de Vitriaco Hist. Orientalis; Liber 3, ap. Martenne, Thes.* v. 3, p. 375.

The Virgin is said, in the Koran, to have borne our Saviour leaning against
a withered date-tree, which miraculously let fall ripe fruit for her refreshment.—*Sale's Koran*, c. 19, p. 250.

The latter tree was said in the tenth century to be preserved in the " dome
or vault" of Bethlehem, and held in high repute.—*Ebn Haukul's Oriental Geography*, p. 40.

Caire, ou il y a une grande et spacieuse salle, qui fut faite par les Cercasses au temps que le Souldan étoit Seigneur d'Egypte. Cestuy edifice est une grande espace pavée de grandes pierres quarrées, et est couverte dessus en manière de terrasse pour defendre du soleil, dont la converture est soustenue à pilliers de pierre de taille à claires voyes. Le Nil y arrive tout joignant les murailles, non pas le courant, mais quand il inonde. Au costé de levant de ceste salle, il y a un beau petit jardin, dedans lequel sont plusieurs arbres de casse, des arbres de henne, des rosiers, et josuin jaune: mais aux costez de septentrion et de midy, il y a deux petits reservouers en maniere de viviers, qui servent à garder l'eau pour boire. Tout ce bastiment est peinct par le dessus. Les poutres et aix sont de palmiers. Depuis que l'Egypte est rendue tributaire au Turc, il a toujours continué tomber en decadence."—*Observations*, &c. p. 109.

Prince Radziwil, in 1583, describes another royal palace, the Gaurea—in which he dined, returning from Mataria. It was erected, he says, by Sultan Gaur, (or El Ghoree, the last of the Mamaluke Sultans,) who attached to it an elegant mosque with two lofty minarets, in which he was buried. The porticoes of this palace, supported by numerous and beautiful columns, may vie, he says, with any for elegance. In the centre is a tank, fifty cubits square and six deep, which the Sultan, whenever, as was his frequent custom, he held a solemn banquet for his court and people, filled with sherbet, that whoever would might drink as much as he liked. Four flights of marble steps descended from the brink of the pond, for the convenience of the people, who descended, step by step, as the sherbet diminished. Refreshments, meanwhile, were laid out for them under the porticoes, while the Sultan looked on from the upper story of the building. Ibraham Pacha, adds Radziwil, occasionally resided in this palace;—possibly the same described by Belon, repaired and enlarged.

The Gypsies wandered over Lower Egypt in great numbers, about the middle of the sixteenth century:—

"Il n' y a lieu en tout le monde qui soit exempt de telle pauvre gent ramassée que nous nommons de faux noms Egyptiens ou Baumiens—car mesme estants entre la Materée et le Caire, nous en trouvions de grandes compagnies, et aussi le long du Nil en plusieurs villages d'Egypte, campez dessous des palmiers, qui estoyent aussi bien estrangers en ce pays là comme ils sont aux nostres."—*Belon, Observations*, &c. livre 2, c. 41.

"Nous voyons en allant," (à Matarée) "plusieurs pauvres gens campez par les camps comme les Arabes, et nous estans enquis quels ils estoyent, on nous dit que c' estoyent de ceux que nous appellons en noz quartiers Sarrasins ou Boemiens, que les Italiens nomment Zingani." 1581.—*Peregrinations du S. Jean Palerne; du.* 1606, p. 138.

NOTE 28, PAGE 137.

Between Siout and Girgeh we visited Akhmim and Gebel Sheikh Heridy.

The legend of the serpent into which Sheikh Heridy's soul is said to have migrated, is well known, and perhaps of Indian origin; at least, the Hindoos appear to have been acquainted with it. See Major Wilford ' On Egypt and the Nile.'—*Asiatic Researches*, vol. 3, p. 344, edit. 4to.

At Akhmim—the ancient Chemmis or Panopolis, and the retreat and abode, according to the Arab writers, of the most powerful magicians—we found little of interest. Nonnus, author of the *Dionysiaca*—that " vast repertory of Bacchic fable—the Grecian Ramayuna," as Mr. Keightley calls it, was born there; and it has produced two great men among the Arabs—Dhou el Noun, surnamed El Akhmimi, the founder of the religious sect called Soufi, who died A. D. 859—and Zulmin ebn Ibrahim, a skilful chemist, not inferior, we are told, to Geber ben Haian, in that art, and who added the science of mysticism to his other acquirements; the temple of Akhmim was his constant resort and study " as a museum of antiquities, where wondrous images and statues of exquisite labour were to be seen."—*Casiri, Bibliotheca Arabico-Hispana*, vol. 1, p. 441.

Man, as usual, has whetted the scythe of Time: " the pillars and principal stones of Akhmim," were employed, according to Leo Africanus, in building Menshieh, on the opposite bank of the Nile; and of the zodiaks, sculptures, and other " arcana sapientiae," recorded by Edrisi*—the " restes admirables de palais, d' obelisques, et de statues colosses," mentioned by D'Herbelot— nothing now remains except an arch almost buried in the earth, and a few massive stones of the great Temple of Perseus, in a hollow, picturesquely surrounded by palm trees, the representatives of those mentioned by Herodotus.

Perseus, according to the report of the natives, frequently appeared in the temple and the neighbourhood of Panopolis; " a beardless and naked youth," such as he is represented in the works of Grecian art, is the description Murtadi gives of the guardian spirit of the Temple of Akhmim—well known, he adds, among the inhabitants of that place. The coincidence is curious —nor is it less interesting to find the name of the earliest hero of European romantic fiction attached to a spot, illustrious among the Arabs as a sort of Egyptian Domdaniel.

---

* Edrisi decidedly prefers the temple of Akhmim to those at Dendera and Esne. " In prædictâ urbe Echmim extat aedificium illud, quod appellatur Beraba; sunt autem plures Berabae, inter quas est Beraba Asnae, Beraba Dandarae, et Beraba Echmim: at haec et aedificio firmior et rebus memoria dignis ornatior est; nam in isto domicilio sunt nonnullae stellarum, et artium quarundarum, picturae, scripta diversa, variaeque scientiae. Istud domicilium, quod Beraba dicitur, est in media urbe Echmim, ut diximus."— *Geogr. Nubiensis*, p. 42.

s 2

NOTE 29, PAGE 144.

A talisman was supposed to be preserved at Bellini, to hinder crocodiles from descending lower.—*Bakoui.*

NOTE 30, PAGE 160.

Near this tomb is another containing paintings of animals beautifully executed, but almost destroyed, and apparently since Burckhardt's time, who mentions them as " the most elaborate and interesting work of the kind " that he had seen in Egypt. He adds the curious remark that, " among the innumerable paintings and sculptures in the tombs and temples of Egypt," he " never met with a single instance of the representation of a camel."

NOTE 31, PAGE 171.

" Mount Meru made also part of the cosmographical system of the Jews; for Isaiah, making use of such notions as were generally received in his time, introduces Lucifer, in Sanscrit Swarbhanu, or Light of Heaven, boasting that he would exalt his throne above the stars of God, and would sit on the Mount of the congregation, on the sides of the North. Meru has also the name of *sabha,* because the congregation or assembly of the gods, is held there on its Northern side."—*Wilford on the Sacred Islands of the West. Asiatic Researches,* vol. 8, p. 284.

NOTE 32, PAGE 193.—Thebes.

The reader will not be displeased to compare Father Protais' account of the ruins of Carnac with those given by modern travellers; they have suffered much, it seems, within the last hundred and seventy years.—I do not know how it may be with others, but to me the glimpses of the progress of ruin one meets with in the old travellers are as affecting as the varying shades of age deepening over a beauty's features in a succession of portraits taken at different stages of her life; this will plead my apology, I hope, for the present and similar notices of the changes wrought by the foot of Time, falling heavier and heavier every year he makes his rounds over the monuments of antiquity.

After a brief but accurate description of Luxor, Father Protais proceeds as follows:

" Le deuxième village est el Hamdie, ou Loxor el Cadim, ou Carnac. La tradition des gens du pays dit que c' estoit autrefois la demeure d'un Roy; il y a bien de l'apparence, car on y voit de grands et beaux restes d'un chasteau, aux avenues duquel il y a des sphinx de part et d'autre, la teste tournée vers l'allée dans la posture à peu près qu'on donne aux lions de throne de Salomon. Ils ont vingt-une semelle de longueur, distans de deux les uns des

autres. J'en ay veu quatre allées toutes garnies, avant que d'arriver au Palais ; je ne sçay pas s'il y en a d'autres, parce que je ne vis que la moitié du contour : j'en comptay soixante de chaque costé dans la premiere allée, et cinquante-un dans la seconde, le tout fort bien ordonné. Les portes sont grandes et exhaussées au delà de toute mesure et de la croyance, couvertes des plus belles pierres qu'il est possible de voir; j'en mesuray une de trente-cinq semelles. Je ne pus rien connoistre dans la cimetrie des bastimens, tant ils sont en desordre et ruinez, outre que le peu de temps que nous avions à y demeurer ne nous permit pas d'observer toutes ces choses ; pour les bien examiner piece à piece, il faudroit du moins un mois, et je n'y fus pas plus de trois heures et demie. Je croy qu'il y a plus de mille figures demy relief, et quelques-unes tout relief. Il y a un tres-grand nombre de colonnes; j'en comptay environ 120 dans une seule salle, qui estoient de cinq grandes brasses de grosseur. * Je remarquay sept aiguilles, deux desquelles sont assez regulieres, excepté que l'une a demy pied de face plus que les deux de Loxor, et que l'autre est beaucoup plus petite. Il y en a trois par terre, brisées, qui à moitié, qui tout à fait, et deux autres de jaspe rompues par le haut, sur lesquelles il y a de grands personnages gravez avec quantité d'ornemens fort particuliers. Il y a un grand bassin d'eau dans la cour du chasteau avec un tour de belles pierres : on me dit que cette eau seule blanchissoit fort bien le linge ; pour l'eprouver, j'y trempay un mouchoir, qui conserva l'odeur du savon durant quatre ou cinq jours. A l'un des portaux du palais il y a deux grandes statues d'une pierre blanche comme albastre, mais le visage en est tout ruiné : elles ont l'epée à la ceinture. †
Une autre paroist encore vers le milieu du chasteau, de mesme taille, c'est à dire, de la hauteur de trois hommes bien proportionnez."

He supplies some further particulars in a letter dated Cairo, 6 Jan. 1670:—"Je croy qu'il y a plus d'un million de statues et de figures de bas relief. Dans les bas relief des murailles et des piliers toutes les figures sont de bas relief, et il n'y en a aucune qui soit veue de front: il m'eust fallu un mois tout entier dans un semblable lieu pour en observer toutes les particularitez : je me contentai de tirer seulement les postures d'une douzaine de diables les plus extravagans avec leurs troupes d'hommes et de femmes qui les adorent, et quelques frontispices de temples, lesquels ne sont pas fort riches en architecture, mais ils sont bastis de tres belles pierres;

* Some of the French writers have certainly exaggerated the dimensions of the Theban pillars, measuring them by *brassées*. Perry, finding them much shrunk in his time, hesitates between the possibility of "oversight and error," on their part, and the likelihood "that these pillars, being planted in a rich fruitful soil, and having taken deep root in the earth, have a sort of vegetable growth, and so increase and lessen in their dimensions as times and seasons vary !"—And yet there is much information, and good sense in his ' View of the Levant,' fol. 1743, p. 345.

† These are the statues, now decapitated, which Mr. Ramsay was so much pleased with.

ce qui me plaisoit le plus, c'estoit le plat-fond et l'azur, et les autres couleurs qui sont liées comme de l'èmail, paroissant aussi fraiches que si elles avoient été appliquées depuis un mois."

" Ce que je viens de dire n'est que bagatelle au regard de ce qui se trouve vis à vis, à une lieue de là, du costé du Ponant, selon le rapport de plus de cinquante personnes, de qui je me suis informè; c'est un lieu qui s'appelle l'ancienne ville de Habou, pleine d' antiques et de curiositez incomparablement plus belles que celles de Hamdie; outre qu' il y a quantité de momies que les Arabes brulent tous les jours, aussi bien que leurs divinitez de bois. Le lieu où sont les momies se nomme Biout (beit) el Melouc: on découvre de loin avec des lunettes d'approche deux épouvantables Idoles, masle et femelle, assises dans des chaises, tournées au Levant, lesquelles doivent avoir la teste à peu près comme celle des Pyramides du Caire appellé Aboul et Saoul. * Elles sont bien proportionnez; on discerne aisément l'homme d'avec la femme ; leurs noms sont Tama et Cama. †

" Tout proche de là est un lieu nommé Legourné, ou el Abouab, où les temples et les statues se sont conservées si fraisches, et les couleurs si vives, qu' il semble, (disent les habitans,) que le maistre n' a pas encore lavé ses mains depuis son travail, —ce sont leurs propres termes. On en decouvre quelque chose du bord du Nil. Les chréstiens de Loxor, voyant que j'avois grande envie d' aller sur les lieux pour en considerer les beautez, s'offrirent de me mener à Habou, mais pour plusieurs raisons je ne le jugeay pas à propos, dont je me suis repenti; mon dessein est d'y retourner non seulement par curiosité, mais à cause des Chrestiens qui sont comme de pauvres brebis sans pasteur . . . . . il y en a qui ont passé cinquante années sans confession et sans communion, n'ayant ni eglise ni prestre."

He closes his letter from Cairo — " J'espere y retourner bientost, et n'en pas revenir avec tant de precipitation; mais il me faut faire un petit voyage sur la Mer Rouge, où je vais tous les ans pour visiter les pauvres esclaves dans les galeres du Turc, et leur administrer les sacremens."—*Relation du Voyage du Said, ou de la Thebayde, fait en* 1668, *par les P. P. Protais et C. F. d'Orleans, Capucins Missionaires. In Thevenot's Collection of Voyages*, &c. tom. 2, part 2.)‡

The good father never revisited Thebes, falling a victim to the plague the year following, 1671. (*Vansleb.*)—His companion, Father Carlo Francisco d'Orleans, was afterwards superior of the

* He means the sphinx, called by the Arabs Abou-el-hol, the Father of terrors, or Abou-el-haoun, the Father of the column.

† They are still called so—Shama and Tama.

‡ Father Protais evidently mistook Memphis for Thebes, as Breydenbach did in the fifteenth, and Burcardus de Monte Sion in the thirteenth century. —" From Babylon," (old Cairo,) says the latter, ".Thebes is two leagues distant, and the desert of Thebais, once densely peopled with monks, lies adjacent to it."—*Descriptio, &c., apud Canisii Lectiones Antiquae*, tom. 4, p. 26. The more enlightened pilgrims never fell into this mistake.

Capucins at Cairo.—*Letter of Dr. Huntingdon—Ray's Collection*, &c., vol. 2, p. 463.

Pére Siccard's exaggerated account of more than one thousand columns to be seen at Carnac, and of many hundreds at Luxor— to say nothing of his mistake of the statues in front of the propyla there for sphinxes— contrast unfavourably with the simple and accurate statement of his humble predecessor, who had but three hours and a half to examine them in! Among the precise facts, however, mentioned by Siccard, is the existence of six obelisks—two of which, small ones but the most interesting, were of porphyry — at the time of his visit to Thebes about 1714. (See his interesting plan of a work on Egypt: *Lettres edifiantes et curieuses*, tom. 5, p. 255). *

These small obelisks, evidently the same as those mentioned by Protais, are described by Norden as follows :—" On voit au devant d'un petit temple deux autres obélisques, mais beaucoup plus petits que les precedents. Ils peuvent avoir à peu près onze à douze pieds de hauteur, et leurs faces n'ont qu'un pied et demi de largeur. Quant à la matiere, elle est de granit, et d'un grain si fin qu'elle approche beaucoup du porphyre. Ils ont servi, selon toutes les apparences, de piédestaux à deux idoles, et ils sont ornés d'hieroglyphes peints de divers couleurs ; et ces hieroglyphes représentent, pour la plus grande partie, des figures qui s'embrassent." *Norden, Remarques sur les obelisques.*—vol. 1, p. 171 *of his Travels —Langlè's edition.*

They probably stood behind the sanctuary, where two pedestals of red granite are still to be seen. When they were destroyed I know not, but it must have been before Pococke's visit in 1737. He only found four obelisks, all of red granite —three standing, and one, the last towards the S. E. fallen. Perry, a year or two afterwards, found two only erect, and in his time *two* pillars of the great colonnade of the first court were standing — the other six lying on the ground, " like a pile of mill-stones thrown down" — there could not be a juster simile.

I need not dwell longer on the tale of ruin.

Siccard appears to have been the first traveller who recognised Thebes in the ruins of Carnac and Luxor. Lucas supposed it to have been situated much more to the South†—near a little Turkish fortress called Naassa, where he describes the ruins of what appeared to him, he says, the greatest city that ever existed in the world—ruins which, like the gardens of Irem, have been rendered invisible to all subsequent travellers.

* In his list of "restes de l'ancienne Egypte paienne," he reckons "dix-huit obélisques, deux à Alexandrie, dix à Thebes, quatre à Phile, une à Arsinoe, et une à Heliopolis.—*Lettres edif.* tom. v. p. 495.

Father Siccard fell a victim to his humanity in attending the sick and dying while the plague raged at Cairo, in 1726. See a sketch of his life and character, *Lettres edif.*, &c., p. 354.

† Lucas had visited Luxor and Carnac some years before Siccard ; he speaks of " plusieurs obelisques," but his account is strangely confused and inaccurate.

" Je demeurai comme interdit à l'aspect d'un ouvrage le plus grand et le plus magnifique. C'est un palais grand comme une petite ville; quatre avenues de colonnes conduisent à quatre portiques. On voyoit à chaque porte entre deux grandes colonnes de porphyre deux figures d'un beau marbre noir, de geans, qui ont chacun une masse à la main. L'avenue de colonnes qui conduit à chaque porte, est de trois colonnes en triangle de chaque côté composée de plus de 1500 colonnes. Sur ce chapiteau de chaque triangle il y a un sphynx, et sur l'ordre des trois colonnes qui suivent, un tombeau, et ainsi successivement de chaque côte dans toutes les quatre allées. On en voit beaucoup de tombées. Chaque colonne a soixante et dix pieds de haut, toutes d'une seule pierre, de manière que dans les quatre avenues il faut qu'il y ait plus de cinq à six mille colonnes.

" Je trouvai la premiere salle de ce palais toute peinte de trés-beaux sujets d'histoires, et il ne paroissoit pas qu'il y eût long-temps que cette peinture fût achevée. On y voyoit des chasses de gazelles; en d'autres endroits des festins; et quantité de petits enfans qui jouoient avec toutes sortes d'animaux. Je passai de là à d'autres appartemens tout revêtus de marbre, dont les voutes étoient soutenues par des colonnes de porphyre et de marbre noir. Quoique les denombremens ne permettent pas d'aller partout, nous trouvâmes le moyen cependant d'aller en haut, d'ou j'eus le plaisir et en même tems le chagrin de promener ma vue sur les ruines de la plus grande ville qui ait été, ce me semble, au monde. Je me figurais dans çe tems là que ce pouvoit être Diospolis, l'ancienne Thebes à cent portes, et ceux de mes amis qui ont fait un cours d'antiquitez, semblent en convenir. Ils trouvent même dans çe que je rapporte une exactitude et une precision que n'est pas venue dans les auteurs jusqu'à nous. Je me flatte ainsi que cela donnera quelque merite à ma relation, et qu'on me sçaura gré de ma diligence.

" On découvroit, du côté du desert qui est au Levant, environ douze Pyramides, qui ne cedent rien à celles du Grand Caire. Outre quantité de bustes, de plus de trente pieds de haut, de figures d'hommes, j'y remarquai un fort grand nombre de palais qui paroissent encore tous entiers, mais si ensevelis dans les ruines, que l'on n'en voit plus les portes, et même j'entrai dans quelques uns par les fenetres. Je partis de ce lieu le cœur tout contrit de voir que tant de beaux édifices fussent deserts et abandonnez à l'injure du tems; que la demeure de tant de rois soit devenue la retraite des serpens et des autres animaux semblables! En revenant à Naasse nous passâmes par un endroit qui est sur le penchant de la montagne, tout plein de puits quarrez, qui servoient à enterrer les gens du pays; tous ces lieux sont tout à fait deserts."

This extraordinary tissue of lies circumstantial is illustrated by a bird's eye view of the chateau, and by prints of a pyramid, fourteen hundred feet high, and of a female bust, seventy-two, without the pedestal!!!

Note 33, Page 203.

Edrisi, in the twelfth century, describes Essouan as a small but densely populated town, abundant in all sorts of vegetables, and noted for its excellent breed of camels, goats, &c.—all very fat and well flavoured.—*Geogr. Nubiensis*, p. 18.

Ebn al Ouardi, in the following century, speaks of it as " très peuplée, mais on ne peut y parvenir que par la montagne Alaki ou Allaki, située dans un lieu bas et couvert de sables, sous lesquels, en creusant, on trouve l'eau. Il y a dans cette montagne des mines d'or et d'argent; et au midi du Nil est une autre montagne dans un desert, où est une mine d'émeraudes, la seule de cette espèce qu'on trouve dans le monde."—*Notices des MSS. etc.*, vol. 2, p. 31. In this singular account the Gebel Ollaki, or Golden Mountain of the present day—the Hemacuta, I conceive, of the Hindoos, East of Dakke, is misplaced to the North of Essouan. The emerald mine is in the desert, East of Edfou.

Syene still deserved the name of "the great, ancient, and populous city of Assuan," in Leo's time. " The citizens are exceedingly addicted unto the trade of merchandise, because they dwell so near unto the kingdom of Nubia, upon the confines whereof standeth their city; beyond which city Nilus dispersing himself over the plains through many small lakes becometh innavigable. Also the said city standeth near unto that desert over which they travel unto the port of Suachen upon the Red Sea, and it adjoineth likewise upon the frontiers of Ethiopia. . . . . . Here are to be seen also many buildings of the ancient Egyptians, and most high towers, which they call in the language of that country *Birba*. Beyond this place there is neither city nor habitation of any account, besides a few villages of black people, whose speech is compounded of the Arabian, Egyptian, and Ethiopian languages. These being subject unto the people called Bugiha, (Beeja,) live in the fields after the Arabian manner, being free from the Soldan's jurisdiction, for there his dominions are limited."—*Description of Africa*, p. 238.

Note 34, Page 223.

" And it was about the sixth hour, and there was darkness over all the earth until the ninth hour. And the sun was darkened." — " This obscuration of the sun was observed at Heliopolis, in Egypt, by Dionysius the Areopagite, afterwards the illustrious convert of St. Paul at Athens; who, in a letter to the martyr Polycarp, describes his own and his companion the sophist Apollophanes' astonishment at the phenomenon. Apollophanes exclaimed, as if divining the cause, ' These, O Dionysius, are the vicissitudes of divine events.' Dionysius answered, ' Either the Deity suffers, or he sympathises with the sufferer.' And that sufferer, according to tradition, recorded by Michael Syncellus of Jerusalem, he declared to be the unknown God, for whose sufferings all nature was darkened and convulsed."—*Hales' Analysis of Ancient Chronology.*

NOTE 35, PAGE 227.

While Elephantine was the boundary city, Philae seems to have been the extreme out-post of the Roman Empire, to the South.* Diocletian, after settling the Nubians, originally inhabitants of the great Oasis, along the banks of the Nile, built a strong fortress on the island, and, in the view of cementing a friendly alliance with them and the Blemmyes, who inhabited the interior country, erected "temples and altars," common to the Romans and Barbarians, under the care of priests chosen from both nations. Narses, the Pers-Armenian refugee,† while stationed there as lieutenant of Justinian, received the Imperial mandate to destroy the temple; he did so, says Procopius, and, throwing the priests into prison, sent the images of the Gods to Byzantium.—*Procopius, De Bello Persico*, lib. 1, cap. 19.

NOTE 36, PAGE 227.

"Agatharcides, et Diodore après lui, ont parlé des mines d'or abondantes que renfermoient des montagnes situées dans ces cantons et sur les bords de la mer. Agatharcides rapporte même un fait intéressant à saisir, et qui prouve que ces mines etoient exploitées dès la plus haute antiquité. 'On y trouve encore aujourd'hui,' dit cet auteur, 'une immense quantité d' ossemens humains, des outils, et des marteaux de bronze, dont on se servait autrefois, parce que, dans les anciens temps le fer étoit tres rare.' Ces mines n'ont point cessé d'être connues des Arabes. L' Edrisi, et Abulfeda en parlent: le premier dit qu' elles produsoient de l'or et de l' argent. On les fouilloit encore de leur temps, mais elles commençoient à être moins abondantes, et il est probable qu' elles ont éte negligées depuis. Ils nomment les montagnes où elles se trouvent, Ollaki ou Alalaki, et les placent à quinze journées d'Asuan, et à huit journées d'Aidab."—*Gossellin; Recherches sur la Geographie des anciens;* t. 2, p. 144.

See also Note 33.

NOTE 37, PAGE 238.

The Franks found the Ethiopian scourge a most formidable

---

* Procopius makes a marked distinction between Elephantine and Philae: "νησον τινα εν ποταμω Νειλω αγχιστα πη της Ελεφαντινης πολεως ευρων ὁ βασιλευς ὁντος, φρουριον τε ταυτῃ δειμαμενος εχυρωτατον. . . . διο δη και Φιλας επωνομασε το χωριον."

† Not the illustrious conqueror of Italy, but "the brother of Isaac and Armatius, who, after a successful action against Belisarius, deserted from his Persian sovereign, and afterwards served in the Italian war." —*v. Gibbon*, c. 46, n. 17.

weapon at the battle of Ascalon:—" D'abord les Ethiopiens ou Azoparts qui, selon leur usage, combattent un genou en terre, s'avançérent sur la premiere ligne, et attaquérent vivement les Français . . . . . . Ces mêmes Azoparts, hommes horribles et très-noirs, portaient en outre des fléaux en fer, instrument terrible avec lequel ils battaient violemment les cuirasses et les casques, frappaient les chevaux à la tête, et dont les coups redoutables retentissaient d'une manière épouvantable dans les rangs des fidèles."—*Albert d' Aix, Hist. des Croisades, livre* 6, p. 366, *ed. Guizot;* or p. 287 of the *Gesta Dei per Francos.*

Note 38, Page 275.

Is not the word Re, ' the Sun'—which with the demonstrative article prefixed, became Ph're or Pharaoh, the hereditary title of the kings of Egypt — recognisable in most of the primitive dialects of mankind as implying a *king* or *prince?* We find *righ,* or *ri,* in the Celtic —*reich,* or *recks,* in the Teutonic languages; *rec* in Hebrew, *reis* in Arabic and Turkish, *rajah* in the East Indies, *eree* and *rhio* in Otaheite and the Sandwich Islands; see Armstrong's Gaelic Dictionary, sub voce *righ.*

Note 39, Page 280.

" Armand," or Herment, is described by Father Protais as almost entirely abandoned, " les gens du pays ne m'en purent dire la raison; ils l'appellent *Balab* (bellad) *Mouse ;* il y a encore un temple d'idoles, ou l' on va par un chemin couvert et souterrain." " They call it in Arabic *Beled Muse,* or the country of Moses, because the Egyptians believe that Moses was born there."— *Vansleb, Present State* &c. p. 243.

Bakoui speaks of Ghouft, the ancient Coptos, as follows:— " On y voit un bâtiment extraordinaire qui a 360 colonnes, chacune d'une seule piece. Sur le sommet de ces colonnes est une figure d'homme, ayant sur la tête un espèce de bonnet ou mitre (calansara). Le toit de ce batiment est de pierres, dont les extremités posent sur des colonnes, et on n'y aperçoit aucunes jointures." The 360 columns are probably according to the usual Arab façon de parler, but there must have been some monument of uncommon grandeur at Ghouft even to account for such an exaggeration.

Note 40, Page 282.—Dendera.

" Les gens du pays disent que ce palais a été bati par les demons, et que l'on voit la nuit plusieurs fantômes se promener dans ses ruines."—*P. Lucas, Voyage au Levant*, tom. I, p. 109. Bakoui notices the *birbe* of Dendera " et autres bàtimens, qui sont autant de talismans," and De Guignes, in a note on the passagè, suggests the probability that the dread of the natives, lest the talismans should be discovered and injured, may contribute aᶜ much as the belief in concealed treasures to their aversion to the excavating propensities of the Franks.—*Notices des MSS. &c.*, tom. 2, p. 436.

Note 41, Page 288.—Memphis.

Rapid must have been the work of decay and destruction since the time of Abd'allatif:—" Malgré l'immense étendue de cette ville et la haute antiquité à laquelle elle remonte, nonobstant toutes les vicissitudes des divers gouvernements dont elle a successivement subi le joug, quelques efforts que différens peuples aient faits pour l'anéantir, en en faisant disparoître jusqu'aux moindres vestiges, effaçant jusqu à ses plus légères traces, transportant ailleurs les pierres et les matériaux dont elle etoit construite, dévastant ses édifices, mutilant les figures qui en faisoient l'ornement: enfin, en dépit de ce que quatre mille ans et plus ont dû ajouter a tant de causes de destruction, ses ruines offrent encore aux yeux des spectateurs une réunion de merveilles qui confond l'intelligence, et que l'homme le plus éloquent entreprendroit inutilement de décrire. Plus on la considère, plus on sent augmenter l'admiration qu'elle inspire ; et chaque nouveau coup-d'œil que l'on donne à ses ruines est une nouvelle cause de ravissement. A peine a-t-elle fait naître une idée dans l'ame du spectateur, qu'elle lui suggère une idée encore plus admirable ; et quand on croit en avoir acquis une connoissance parfaite, elle vous convainc au même instant que ce que vous aviez concu est encore bien au-dessous de la vérité."—*Relation*, &c., p. 185.

Besides a beautiful monolithic shrine, called the Green Chapel, (destroyed in 1449,) he specifies idols that, whether their number or size he considered, surpass description; "mais ce qui est encore plus digne d'exciter l'admiration, c'est l'exactitude dans leurs formes, la justesse de leurs proportions, et leur ressemblance avec la nature. Nous en avons mesuré une qui, sans son piédestal, avoit plus de trente coudées: sa largeur, du côté droit au côté gauche, portoit environ dix coudées ; et du devant au derrière, elle étoit épaisse en proportion. Cette statue étoit d'une seule pierre de granit rouge ; elle étoit recouverte d'un vernis rouge, auquel son antiquité sembloit ne faire qu' ajouter une nouvelle fraicheur." —*Relation.* &c., pp. 185-7.

This, probably, was the statue of Sesostris discovered by Caviglia, or one of its brethren that stood before the temple of Vulcan.

Abulfeda, who flourished a century later, speaks of the antiquities of Memphis as considerable, but neglected and perishing ; the green and other colours, he says, remain as vivid as ever.

" On voit encore les ruines de cette ville," is all the notice

Bakoui bestows on them at the commencement of the fifteenth century.

Furer, in 1565, asserts that two giants or colossi of porphyry, originally elevated on lofty bases and sculptured with hieroglyphics, were then lying prostrate in Memphis—the name he gives to Old Cairo; " one of them," he says, " measures twenty feet from the head to the extremity of the torso,—the other wants the head. The Arabs will have it they are the images of the son and daughter of Pharaoh. Very many other statues, a camel especially, of stupendous size, a lion, a sphinx, besides other animals, are seen there—all of red marble, but all broken and destroyed." *Itinerarium*, p. 19. I am inclined to think he never saw them, and has misunderstood and misstated information similar to that which Radziwil obtained in 1583—that two colossi, twenty cubits high, each of one stone, most beautifully sculptured, both fallen, but entire—one of them representing a Pharaoh, the other a Queen, perhaps his wife—were lying on the ground five miles to the south of the Pyramids: he did not see them himself, he tells us, but received this account from persons at Cairo, who assured him they had.—*Hierosolymitana Peregrinatio*, p. 164.

" A city, great and populous, adorned with a world of antiquities! But why spend I time about that that is not, the very ruins now almost ruinated? Yet some few impressions are left, and divers thrown-down statues of monstrous resemblances; a scarce sufficient testimony to shew unto the curious seeker that there it hath been. Why then deplore our human frailty?

Mors etiam saxis nominibusque venit.

When stones as well as breath
And names do suffer death."

Sandys, p. 132.

NOTES.

EDOM AND THE HOLY LAND.

Note 1, Page 294.

" Camels are the ships of Arabia, their seas are the deserts."—*Sandys.*

Note 2, Page 303.

" As this was the first time that I rid upon a camel, I could hardly endure the shakings, which the manner of walking of this fantastic beast caused me to suffer. I confess, when I saw myself upon this colossus, without any stay, lifted up in the air, seated upon an ugly beast; my feet in two ropes instead of stirrups, holding in my hand a cord made with the strings of a palm-tree, which cut my hands, it seemed to me very strange; I resolved, nevertheless, to overcome all these difficulties; and, instead of vexing myself, I made a sport of that which would have troubled other persons." — *Vansleb's present state of Egypt*, p. 196.

Note 3, Page 306.

" The tracks of the chariot-wheels are not only to be seen on the shore, but as far into the sea also as one's sight can reach; and, if they should at any time be defaced, either by chance or through curiosity, the divine power immediately orders the winds and floods to restore them to their former condition." —*Orosius, quoted by Baumgarten, who confirms the tale, lib.* 1. c. 21.

NOTE 4, PAGE 307.

The El Tih, Ard El Tia, or Tiah beni Israel, lies, according to the best Arab geographers, between Aila and the mountains As Schorah, or Mount Seir, to the East, the Sea of Kolsum or Gulph of Suez, to the West, Palestine, to the North, and the Sinaite promontory, to the South. " Major autem pars terrae hujus At Tiah arenis constat, alia loca salebrosa sunt: reperiuntur quoque palmae et fontes late dimanantes pauci." — *Abulfedae Tabula Syriae.*

This, in Ptolomy's time, was the country of the Saraceni, whose name, (derived, Mr. Farren thinks, from the word *Sarakeen,* robbers,—the epithet bestowed on them by their enemies,) was afterwards popularly extended to the whole Arab race. Ptolomy distinguishes them from the Pharanitae, who then inhabited the country south of Gebel Tiah; but Procopius, four centuries later, extends their power over the whole peninsula, describing them as the ancient inhabitants of the Phaenicon, or palm-forest, extending to a great distance along the coast, and which their prince, Abocharubus, who dwelt there, had nominally given to Justinian.*

The monks of Sinai, in the day of their power, appear to have made good their claims as representatives of the Emperor; they are still in possession of extensive palm-groves, near Tor, but those of Wady Feiran—all, indeed, in the peninsula, are said to have once belonged to them.

Procopius, I may add, as well as Bakoui and others of the Arabian geographers, consider Aila as the eastern boundary of Egypt.

Sir John Mandeville gives a graphic description of the Bedouins, who inhabit the desert between Sinai and Jerusalem.

---

* " Sur les bords de ce golfe est un canton où se trouvent plusieurs sources, et que sa fertilité a rendu celebre : on l'appelle Phænicon, à cause des palmiers qu' il produit. Ces arbres forment un bois pour lequel on a le plus grand respect, parce que les environs, exposés à toute l'ardeur du soleil, sont brulans, sans eau et sans ombrage. . . . . .
" On y voit un ancien autel construit en pierres dures, et dont l'inscription est en caractères inconnus.
" Vers ces lieux on remarque des montagnes élevées de différentes couleurs : elles se prolongent pour former un cap, et s' étendent ensuite jusqu'à Petra, dans le pays des Arabes Nabathéens, et jusqu' à la Palestine."— *Periples combinés d'Agatharcides et d'Artemidore. Gosselin, Geographie des Anciens,* t. 2, p. 232.
M. Gosselin conceives that the palm-groves near Tor represent the ancient Phaenicon.

" Thei ben folke fulle of alle evylle condiciouns. And thei have none houses but tentes, that thei maken of skynnes of bestes, as of camaylles and of other bestes, that thei eten; and there-benethe thei couchen hem, and dwellen in place where thei may fynden watre, as on the Rede See, or elleswhere. For in that desert is fulle gret defaute of watre; and oftentime it fallethe that where men fynde watre at o tyme in a place, it faylethe another tyme. And for that skylle they make none habitations there. Theise folk that I speke of, thei tylen not the lond, ne thei laboure noughte; for thei eten no bred, but zif if be ony that dwellen nyghe a gode toun, that gon thidre and eten bred som tyme. And thei rosten here flesche and here fische upon the hote stones azenst the sonne. And thei ben stronge men and wel fyghtynge. And there is so meche multitude of that folk that thei ben,withouten nombre. And thei ne recchen of nothing, ne don not but chacen aftre bestes, to eten hem. And thei recchen nothing of here lif; and therfore thei dowten not the Sowdon, ne non other prince; but thei dar well werre with hem, zif thei don ony thing that is grevance to hem. And thei han oftentyme werre with the Soudan; and namely that tyme that I was with him. And thei beren but o scheld and o spere, with-outen other armes. And thei wrappen here hedes and here necke with a gret quantytee of white lynnen clothe. And thei ben ryghte felonouse and foule, and of cursed kynde."—*Voiage and Travaile*, &c. pp. 77, sqq.

" They are of mean statures, raw-bone, tawny, having feminine voices, of a swift and noiseless pace—behind you, ere aware of them."—*Sandys.*

" Sono huomini molto piccoli, e di color leonato scuro, e hanno la voce feminile e li capelli lunghi, stesi, e neri. Sono veramente questi Arabi una grandissima quantità, e combattono continual-mente fra loro."—*Barthema, Itinerario*, 1503.

" And they had hair as the hair of women," is expressly stated in the prophetical description of the Arab locusts (Rev. ix. 8.) a metaphor, by the way, which the Arabs apply to themselves, to express their numbers; See Antar, vol. 1, p. 6.—" I must assail you without further preparation, and I shall command these armies, numerous as the locusts, to assault you, and to grind you like grain, and to ride you like lions;"—and again, vol. 2, p. 267; " they call on Antar, and their spears are like a descent of locusts on a towering sand-hill."

Every reader of ' Antar,' that most vivid picture of the desert-life of the Arabs, must have been struck by the constant refer-ence to their dwelling " in the presence of all their brethren," as a motive of action.

NOTE 5, PAGE 312.

" Alvah—bois qui adoucit les eaux de Marah dans le desert.

Moyse en avoit un morceau qui lui avoit venu par succession des patriarches depuis Noe, qui l'avoit conservé dans l'Arche." — *D'Herbelot.*

Note 6, Page 313.

" The twelve fountains, and the seventy palm-trees of Elim, are emblems of the twelve apostles of our Saviour, and the seventy disciples, sent forth to scatter the sweet waters of the Gospel over the world."—*Michael Syncellus, Chronographia. Script. Byz.* v. 6, p. 102.

Note 7, Page 318.—Sea of Edom.

" It is now an opinion generally received, that the Red Sea is the Idumean Sea, taking its name from Edom, or Esau, the Arabian patriarch ; and Edom signifies red. The Arabians were, doubtless, the first navigators of the Indian Ocean, and, as they entered that sea by passing the straights of Babelmandel, they carried the name of the Red Sea, from whence they commenced their course, to the utmost extent of their discoveries. Hence the Indian Ocean received the title of Red ; and the Greeks, who translated every thing rather than introduce a foreign word, made it the Erythraean Sea." — *Vincent's Periplus,* vol. 1, p. 350.

Note 8, Page 323.

The early pilgrims, who travelled in immense caravans, were often in great distress from want of water; Baumgarten describes their sufferings most affectingly :—

" Travelling all that day and night, without eating, resting, or sleeping, we could not avoid falling off our camels, while we were half-sleeping, half-waking. A thousand strange dreams and fan-cies came into our heads, whilst hungry and weary, and we sat nodding on our camels. We thought we saw somebody reaching us victuals and drink, and putting out our hands to take it, and stretching ourselves to overtake it when it seemed to draw back, we tumbled off our camels, and by a severe fall found it a dream and illusion. We underwent the same hardship all the twenty-second, and twenty-third days, mutually pitying one another's leanness and misery, and exhorting each other to patience and resignation."—*Travels,* lib. 1. c. 27.

Conf. Isaiah, c. 29. v. 8.

" As when a hungry man dreameth, and lo ! he seemeth to eat,
But he awaketh, and his appetite is still unsatisfied ;

And as a thirsty man dreameth, and lo! he seemeth to drink,
  But he awaketh, and he is still faint, and his appetite still
    craving;
So shall it be with the multitude of all the nations,
Who have set themselves in array against Mount Zion."

NOTE 9, PAGE 330.

Baumgarten and his friends found a very different reception :—

" There was running by us a bitch with whelps, that belonged to one of the Arabians, who happening to bring forth her litter there, and seeing us leave her, was horribly afraid to be left there alone with her whelps. For a long time she seemed to be deliberating, at last fell a howling most mournfully, and chose rather to save herself by following us, than stay behind and perish with her puppies.*

" That day, about noon, we came to a certain garden, where we were most barbarously used by the people who lived there. For, understanding that we were Christians, they came flocking out of their holes with a design to rob us; and, raising a hideous cry, threatened us with their dreadful bows and spears; some of them knocking us down off our camels, others taking us up, and protecting us from the fury of the rest. Our interpreter neglected us for some time, but did his part at last. However, we were five times knocked down, and had part of our provisions, that were not well enough hid, taken from us, and with a great deal of difficulty, after much noise and severe drubbing, we were let go, upon payment of eight pieces of silver a man."—*Lib.* 1, c. 22.

Belon, one of the best of the early travellers, gives a pleasing account of Wady Feiran, in 1548. After entering the valley by a " grande ouverture entre moult hautes montagnes"—and praising the " beau ruisseau d'eau douce de claire fontaine," " la premiere eau droictement douce courante que nous eussions trouvé sur le chemin depuis le Caire," he proceeds as follows :—" Nous trouvasmes, un grand village à l'entrée de ceste bouche, habité d'Arabes, nommé Pharagou, ou il n'y avoit que trois ou quatre maisons basties; car les villages de ces pays là ne consistent pas en maisons élevées, mais au nombre d'hommes qui habitent dessous les palmiers au descouvert ou dessous les rochers. . . . . Le village de Pharagou nous sembla plaisant, au regard des pays que nous avions cheminé; car il y a bel ombrage de grenadiers,

---

* George, the Carthusian Prior, the companion of Baumgarten, relates that, on their return from Sinai, the poor famished animal, after one bitter howl of recognition, made a meal on the remains of her offspring.—*Georgii Prioris Ephemeris,*—*ap. Pezii Thesaurus,* tom. 2, pt. 3, p. 493.
The " Ephemeris" seems to be the same work with Baumgarten's, under a different name.

palmiers, oliviers, figuiers, poiriers, et autres arbres fruictiers.
. . . . Les hommes de ce pays sont contents d'habiter dessous
les palmiers au descouvert, qui est la cause qu'ils sont de couleur
d'olive. Et pour ce qu'il ne pleut gueres sur eux, il leur suffit
d'avoir leurs maisons faites de rameaux de palmiers, appuyées là
en contre les troncs pour les defendre quelque peu de la vehe-
mence du soleil."—*Observations, etc. c.* 61, fol. 222 *verso.*

Note 10, Page 338.

Poor Baumgarten found it otherwise. After delivering our
letters from the Patriarch at Cairo, " and having a room assigned
us, and eat something, when we would have gone to rest, we
were surrounded by a crowd of Arabians, who put all sorts of sleep
out of our mind. They broke into our room, seized our things as
if they had been their own, and in a barbárous manner repeated
a certain sort of word *tlus, (feloosh?)* which with them signifies
money; with which having stopped their hellish mouths and
greased their ugly fists, we shut our doors again, and composed
ourselves to our much desired rest."—*Lib.* 1, *c.* 23.

Note 11, Page 341.

"There is the Chirche of Seynte Kateryne, in the whiche ben
manye Lampes brennynge. For thei han of Oyle of Olyves
ynow, bothe for to brenne in here Lampes and to ete also. And
that plentee have thei be the myracle of God. For the Ravenes,
and the Crowes, and the Choughes, and other Fowles of the
Contree assemblen hem there every zeer ones, and fleen thider
as in pilgrymage : and everyche of hem bringethe a Braunche of
the Bayes or of Olyve, in here Beekes, in stede of offryng, and
leve hem there; of the whiche the Monkes maken gret plentee of
Oyle : and this is a gret marvaylle. And sithe that Foules, that
han no kyndely wytt ne resoun, gon thidre to seche that gloriouse
Virgyne; wel more oughten men than to seche hire and to
worschipen hire. Also, behynde the awtier of that Chirche, is
the place where Moyses saughe oure Lord God in a brennynge
Bussche. And whanne the Monkes entren in to that place, thei
don of both Hosen and Schoon or Botes alweys ; because that oure
Lord seyde to Moyses, Do of thin Hosen and thi Schon ; for the
place that thou stondest on is Lond holy and blessed. And the
Monkes clepen that place Bezeleel, that is to seyne, the Schadow
of God. And besyde the highe Awtiere three degrees of heighte
is the Fertre of Alabastre, where the bones of Seynte Kateryne
lyzn. And the prelate of the Monkes schewethe the relykes to
the Pilgrymes. And with an instrument of sylver, he frotethe
the bones; and thanne ther gothe out a lytylle oyle, as thoughe it
were a maner swetynge, that is nouther lyche to Oyle ne to
Baume ; but it is full swete of smelle: And of that thei zeven a
lityl le to the Pilgrymes; for there gothe out but lytlle quantitee

of the likour. And after that, thei schewen the Heed of Seynte Kateryne, and the Clothe that sche was wrapped inne, that is zit alle blody. And in that same clothe so y-wrapped, the Aungeles beren hire body to the Mount Synay, and there thei buryed hire with it. And thanne thei schewen the Bussche that brenned and wasted nought, in the whiche our Lord spak to Moyses, and othere relykes ynowe. Also whan the Prelate of the Abbeye is ded, I have undirstonden be informacion that his Lampe quenchethe. And whan thei chesen another Prelate, zif he be a gode man and worthi to be Prelate, his lampe schal lighte, with the grace of God, withouten touching of any man. For everyche of hem hath a lampe be himself. And be here lampes thei knowen well whan ony of hem schalle dye. For whan ony schalle dye, the Lyghte begynnethe to chaunge and to wexe dym. And zif he be chosen to ben Prelate, and is not worthi, his Lampe quenchethe anon."—*Mandeville*, p. 71. sqq.

Note 12, Page 343.

There were a hundred, when Rudolph the knight of Frameynsperg was their guest, in 1346. All strangers, he tells us, were entertained three days, and on their departure each was presented with ten loaves, sufficient for ten days' subsistence.

They had then, as now, two small bells only,—hanging, at that time, in the principal church.

" Item, in prædicto monasterio, et capella Moysis, versus plagam Aquilonis, situm est templum Idolorum rotundum, ad quod nullus Christianorum ingredi permittitur."—*Itinerarium*, &c. *ap. Canisii Lectiones Antiquæ*, t. 4, p. 359.

Note 13, Page 345.

Mandeville, in 1325—Baldensel, in 1336—Anshelmus, (author of a Descriptio Terræ Sanctæ,) in 1509—Furer, 1565—and all subsequent writers identify Sinai with Gebel Mousa.

Frameynsperg, 1341—Breydenbach, 1483—Baumgarten, 1507 —and Belon, 1548 . . . with St. Catherine's.

Mandeville tries to solve the mystery : " Either mountain," he says, " may be called Mount Sanai, since the whole surrounding country is called the Desert of Sin."

The Arab geographers appear to comprehend the whole nucleus of the Sinaite mountains under the name Tor Sina. The dual number, Sinein, is also used by them, " comme qui diroit les deux Sinai," being " deux croupes separées—Horeb et Sinai." —*D'Herbelot*.

Note 14, Page 346.

Belon's good sense—a rare quality in the middle of the sixteenth century, refused credit to the legend. " Cestuy est le rocher dont sortit l'eau pour abbreuver les enfans d'Israel. Toute fois il est joignant un ruisseau courant qui vient de la sommité du Sinai. Cela nous fait penser ou que ce n'est pas celuy que frappa Moyse, ou qu'il n'y eust encor point d'eau en ce ruisseau là: mais, sauf meilleur jugement, nous penserions que les Caloires devroyent monstrer le roc à la source de la fontaine, dont sort l'eau le haut de dessous la montagne."—*Observations*, &c. p. 227.

Baldensel, in 1336, says that the water produced by the rod of Moses " is in the monastery." Mandeville, a few years earlier, tells us, that " before the zett is the well where Moses smote the stone, of the which the water came out plenteously." The legend, therefore, cannot have been attached to the stone in the El Ledja before the 14th century.

Note 15, Page 348.

The Cypress was regarded with peculiar veneration by the Greek Christians in the middle ages, as the tree of which the shaft of our Saviour's cross was made:—

" The Cristene men, that dwellen bezond the See, in Grece, seyn that the tree of the Cross, that we callen Cypresse, was of that tree that Adam ete the Appülle of: and that fynde thei written. And thei seyn also, that here Scripture seythe, that Adam was seek, and seyde to his sone Sethe, that he scholde go to the Aungelle, that kepte Paradys, that he wolde senden hym Oyle of Mercy, for to anoynte his Membres with, that he myghte have hele. And Sethe wente. But the Aungelle wolde not late him come in ; but seyd to him, that he myghte not have of the Oyle of Mercy. But he toke him three Greynes of the same Tree, that his Fadre eet the Appelle offe; and bad him, als sone as his Fadre was ded, that he scholde putte theise three Greynes undre his Tonge, and grave him so: and he dide. And of theise three Greynes sprong a tree, as the Aungelle seyde that it scholde, and bere a fruyt, thorghe the whiche fruyt Adam scholde be saved. And whan Sethe cam azen, he fonde his Fadre nere ded. And whan he was ded, he did with the Greynes as the Aungelle bad him ; of the whiche sprongen three Trees, of the whiche the Cross was made, that bare gode fruyt and blessed, oure Lord Jesu Crist ; thorghe whom Adam and alle that comen of him scholde be saved and delyvered from drede of Dethe withouten ende, but it be here own defaute."—*Voiage and Travaile*, &c., p. 13, 14.

But the European superstition, by which the tremulous shiver of the aspen-leaf is accounted for, is still more beautiful:

" The blessed cross, whereon
The meek Redeemer bowed his head to death,
Was framed of aspen wood, and since that hour
Through all its race the pale tree hath sent down
A thrilling consciousness, a secret awe,

Making them tremulous, when not a breeze
Disturbs the airy thistle-down, or shakes
The light lines of the shining gossamer.
   Child, (*after a pause.*) Dost thou believe it, father?
   Father.   Nay, my child,
We walk in clearer light. But yet, even now,
With something of a lingering love, I read
The characters, by that mysterious hour
Stamp'd on the reverential soul of man
In visionary days, and thence thrown back
On the fair forms of nature. Many a sign
Of the great sacrifice which won us heaven,
The woodman and the mountaineer can trace
On rock, on herb, and flower. And be it so!
They do not wisely that, with hurried hand,
Would pluck these salutary fancies forth
From their strong soil within the peasant's breast,
And scatter them—far, far, too fast! away
As worthless weeds:—oh! little do we know
When they have soothed, when saved!*"

FELICIA HEMANS.

NOTE 16, PAGE 352.

Justinian, says the historian Procopius, did not build the monastery on the summit of Mount Sinai—for no one can pass the night on it, on account of the continual clashing noises and other supernatural sounds heard there*—but far below it; and at the foot of the mountain he built a very strong fortress, and stationed in it a guard of soldiers to bridle the Saracens.—*De Aedificiis Dn. Justiniani*, lib. 5.

Would it not appear from this passage that the original monastery stood on the small plain, nearly on the site of the deserted Convent of St. Elias, and that, when the garrison was withdrawn and the monks were left defenceless in the midst of enemies, daily drawing the circle closer round them, they descended to, and occupied, the fortress? The existence of the church and the Mosaic portrait of Justinian certainly militate against this supposition; but what proof is there of their being contemporary with him?

* Marvellous sounds, of supernatural repute, still haunt the neighbourhood of Mount Sinai. One of the most romantic of these legends is that of the disappearance of a convent, situated to the west of the peninsula, between the Sinaite mountains and the Gulf of Suez, which no one in these modern times, says Breydenbach, has ever been able to discover, though the music of its bells may be heard daily on the breeze at the canonical hours. Some Arabs declared they had been within it, but that the moment they recrossed the threshold they lost sight of it.

This idea probably arose from the natural phenomenon at Gebel Narkous, or the Mountain of the Bell, on the coast north of Tor; a legend of "a bodiless hand ringing a bell" is attached to it by Sir Frederick Henniker. Burckhardt says that the Bedouins believe the sounds to proceed from a convent buried in the sand.

Note 17, Page 353.

" On the eighteenth day, about sun rising, we came down the west side of Mount Horeb by a very steep and dangerous way, and came into a valley betwixt Mount Horeb and Sinai, in which there was a monastery dedicated to forty saints," and hence " we began to ascend Mount Sinai." .... " At last the ascent grew so difficult that all our former toil and labour seemed but sport to this. However, we did not give over, but imploring the Divine assistance, we used our utmost endeavour. At last, through untrodden ways, through sharp and hanging rocks, through clefts and horrible deserts, pulling and drawing one another, sometimes with our staves, sometimes with our belts, and sometimes with our hands, by the assistance of Almighty God, we all arrived at the top of the mountain. The top of Mount Sinai is scarce thirty paces in compass; there we took a large prospect of the countries round about us, and began to consider how much we had travelled by sea and land, and how much we had to travel, what hazards and dangers, and what various changes of fortune, might probably befal us: while we were thus divided between fear and hope, and possessed with a longing for our native country, it is hard to imagine how much we were troubled."—*Baumgarten.*

Note 18, Page 356.

" Le Mont Sinai est la plus petite des montagnes ; mais elle est en tres-grande consideration aupres de Dieu par sa dignité, et par le rang qu'elle tient par dessus les autres montagnes."—*Saadi, Gulistan, ap. D'Herbelot.*

END OF VOL. I.

LONDON:

F. SHOBERL, JUN. 51, RUPERT STREET, HAYMARKET.

Printed in Great Britain
by Amazon

58835108R00235